D0560168

SHAKESPEARE
Meaning & Metaphor

SHAKESPEARE
Meaning & Metaphor

Ann Thompson
and John O. Thompson

University of Iowa Press Iowa City

HOUSTON PUBLIC LIBRARY

R0159527318
HUM

International Standard Book Number 0-87745-166-4
Library of Congress Catalog Card Number 86-51085
University of Iowa Press, Iowa City 52242
Copyright © 1987 by the University of Iowa
All rights reserved
First edition, 1987

No part of this book may be reproduced or utilized in any form or by any means, electronic or mechanical, including photocopying and recording, without permission in writing from the publisher.

Printed in Great Britain

This book is dedicated to the memory of our grandmothers,
Frances Ellen Harris and Winifred Ross

Contents

Acknowledgements

None of this material has been published previously. We have however given related papers to groups of scholars at the Universities of Leeds, Liverpool and Manchester and at Birmingham Polytechnic. We have also addressed the Renaissance Society of America in Southern California and the International Shakespeare Association in West Berlin. We would like to thank those who invited us to speak and those who contributed to the discussions on these occasions.

We have also subjected our students at Liverpool to more discussions on metaphor than they might have anticipated, and we are particularly grateful to those who took the Renaissance Literature MA course in the English Department and those who took the Symbolism course in Communication Studies in recent years for helping us to develop our ideas.

A number of individuals have read and commented on chapters, answered queries and generally contributed criticisms and suggestions. Specifically, we would like to acknowledge the assistance of Tony Barley, Philip Edwards, Lynette Hunter, Arthur Kinney, Kenneth Muir and Richard Proudfoot. Philip Edwards kindly allowed us to make use of his edition of *Hamlet* in proof stage and Richard Proudfoot directed us towards an investigation of printing metaphors.

We have worked on this book in a number of places and have enjoyed the library facilities at the Henry E. Huntington Library in California, the University of California at Los Angeles and the University of Hawaii, in addition to our regular use of the University Libraries in Liverpool and London and the British Library, whose Inter-Library Loan service is becoming increasingly important as the funding of University libraries declines. We are also grateful to the following individuals for providing us with very pleasant houses in which to work: Michael and Alessandra Griffiths of Lucignano in Tuscany, David and Helen Laird of San Gabriel, California, David Callies and Valerie Wayne of Honolulu.

The transition from manuscript to print has been made possible by the considerable and much appreciated labours of the Liverpool English Department secretaries, Catherine Rees and Tina Benson.

Shakespeare Editions

Shakespeare quotations and line references are from G. Blakemore Evans (ed.), *The Riverside Shakespeare* (Houghton Mifflin, Boston, 1974). Variants in early editions are discussed when relevant, as are editorial emendations. The Riverside, which is a modern (American) spelling edition, preserves what seems to us to be an arbitrary sprinkling of archaic spellings. Consequently we have modernized as follows: in Chapter 1, 'vile' for Riverside's 'vild' on p. 30 (*Troilus and Cressida*, 1.3.340); in Chapter 2, 'mongrel' for Riverside's 'mungrel', 'mungril' and 'mongril' on pp. 56 and 70 (*King Lear* 1.4.49, 2.2.22 and 3.6.68), 'vile' for 'vild' again on p. 76 (*King Lear*, 4.2.45) and 'flay' for 'flea' on p. 79 (*King Lear*, 1.4.308); in Chapter 3, 'split' for 'spleet' on p. 103 (*Hamlet*, 3.2.10) and 'ribbon' for 'riband' on p. 124 (*Hamlet*, 4.7.77); in Chapter 5, 'quote' for 'cote' on p. 168 and p. 169 (*The Rape of Lucrece*, 812 and *Love's Labour's Lost*, 2.1.246), 'margin' for 'margent' on p. 168, and p. 169 (*The Rape of Lucrece*, 102, *Love's Labour's Lost*, 2.1.246 and *Romeo and Juliet*, 1.3.86), 'sixth' for 'sixt' on p. 189 (*Cymbeline*, 5.4.20) and 'agate' for 'agot' on p. 191 (*Love's Labour's Lost*, 2.1.236). We have retained modern American spellings.

Introduction

The recent explosion of interest in metaphor within the fields of linguistics, psychology, anthropology and philosophy has as yet made little impact on English literary studies, where a confused and impressionistic notion of 'imagery' still reigns, despite frequent expressions of dissatisfaction with its lack of methodology and its inappropriateness to some sorts of texts. Our intention in this book is to effect a meeting, or rather a series of meetings, between a powerfully metaphorical text, the Shakespearean canon, and a number of the most notable 'extra-literary' theories of metaphor, and to report on the results.

We believe that these meetings can be productive: the theoretical approaches can illuminate Shakespearean usage and the Shakespearean examples can in their turn illuminate the theories. Since most of the extra-literary discussions of metaphor have concentrated on everyday metaphors expressed in comparatively simple sentences ('Man is a wolf', 'The chairman ploughed through the discussion'), it can be salutary to test them against the linguistic and syntactic complexity of Shakespeare. At the same time, considerable new knowledge about the micro-level of the language of the plays and poems can result from examining them in the light of the theoretical work.

We had better say at the outset that we do not claim to have found any theory of metaphor sufficiently comprehensive to account fully for Shakespearean usage. Indeed we would be extremely sceptical about any such claim. Rather, we proceed by way of a series of relatively self-contained and free-standing studies, taking, in most cases, a single example of a theoretical approach and matching it with an appropriate body of Shakespearean metaphor. The five studies that make up this book, then, are attempts to bring some current work originating mainly in linguistics and philosophy to bear on the Shakespearean text, considered at a certain level. We shall try to make clear at this point what that level is, and what sort of use of our theoretical sources the reader can expect.

Shakespeare is no doubt sufficiently 'valued' in our time; the quotation marks we have just put around 'valued' reflect our appreciation of the oddity of his position as cultural talisman and saleable commodity, but our potential cynicism about his commercial status has to be set against our sense of good fortune in living in an era in which encountering exciting productions of the plays is not a rare experience. Perhaps a revered Great Dramatist whom no one ever really performed or read might conceivably have been sustained by the Anglo-Saxon world culture industry if it had been necessary. In fact, though, these texts, nearly four hundred years on, still work for non-specialist audiences and readers.

If you were asked what sort of language, in general, would have that sort of capacity for communicating over time, across cultural and linguistic changes of some magnitude, you might very well predict that it would need to be relatively clear, simple, unadorned. Taking, by today's standards, an unusually optimistic view of the cognitive abilities of the average audience, you might relax the plainness requirement, but the sort of decoration or heightening which would be likely to retain an ability to get across would surely itself be characterized by clarity. Your notion of an author apt to survive as stageable would perhaps be someone rather like Racine.

The facts about Shakespearean language are, however, quite otherwise. These texts, which work in the theatre and on the cinema or television screen for wide audiences, are so intricate in detail that it is not at all easy for final-year specialist university students to produce an accurate paraphrase of a short passage in an examination. Our interest in investigating the micro-level of the Shakespearean text has been fuelled by our increasing awareness of this as a puzzle: the point is not to insist that such a rich and complex text should be valued (such an insistence would be superfluous), but to account for how it can be that such a strange, fluid, peculiar text *is* so valued, is still capable of giving pleasure so widely.

Traditionally, literary criticism has felt obliged to argue for the unity, within the 'organic whole' of a play or an authorial canon, of the linguistic micro-level of the text and the macro-level(s) on which character and narrative unfold. Now it may very well be the case that Shakespeare's continuing communicability is largely a functions of macro-level skills, of what would not be lost in translation. (This is strongly suggested by the viability and success not only of foreign-language stage and screen productions of Shakespeare but even silent screen versions.) We would not hesitate to contemplate a Shakespeare who was theatrically 'alive' despite rather than because of the detailed wording of the text. Indeed, thinking about this possibility is good practice for liberating oneself from the circularity and mysticism of the 'organic unity' picture. However, we have what is in our view strong experiential evidence of the contribution of the linguistic micro-level to the current life of the plays. This consists in the invariable awfulness of productions in which the actors try to get through the play without themselves quite understanding the lines. By contrast, intelligence of delivery at the verbal level seems capable of sustaining productions which in other respects may be very modest or even actively ill-conceived.

So far we have been writing as if the puzzle of the power of the text at the micro-level is fundamentally authorial: how is it that Shakespeare survives while others don't? But it is our experience that, when actually given a serious chance on the stage, the drama of the period as a whole shares this capacity to communicate to a surprising (and unfortunately not yet widely recognized) extent. So an interest in how Shakespearean modes of textual elaboration work has wider implications for figurative language in Renaissance drama generally—and perhaps even for drama in other periods too.

Many people who write about Shakespeare's works do so without paying very much explicit attention to the micro-level of language. There is a widespread if tacit assumption that language as a focus of interest comes rather low in the pecking order in which it is preceded by such topics as character, theme and plot. Of course this hierarchy has been shuffled from time to time and language has sometimes seemed nearer to the top of the pack—one could see the popularity of imagery studies in the 1930s and 1940s as a reaction to an overemphasis on character in the previous generation—but by and large it has maintained a low profile. Anyone who has taught Shakespeare will be aware of the reluctance of students to write about questions of language, and the undergraduate essay which inserts a dutiful paragraph or two on 'the language of the play' after everything else has been 'covered' is not without its parallels at the professional level.

We presume that a major reason for the unpopularity of language studies is that they often run the risk of seeming overly narrow and specialist. This is particularly true of what one might describe as the rhetorical tradition in Shakespeare criticism, meaning studies which are primarily historical and theoretical in their approach, applying the terminology and structures of Renaissance rhetorical theory to Shakespeare's practice. Obviously it is important to establish that Shakespeare acquired, probably at Stratford grammar school, a much more comprehensive grounding in rhetorical theory than most of us have today,[1] and that the plays contain abundant evidence of his competence to deploy all the tropes and schemes identified by contemporary rhetoricians;[2] but it is hard to convince a modern reader or playgoer that these pedantic not to say mechanical skills contribute very largely to the effect of the play as a whole. At worst, the rhetorical tradition comes down to a mere listing and labelling of linguistic 'tricks' which, if anything, get between us and the 'real meaning' of the play.

Recent critics who draw on this tradition have attempted to revivify it in a number of ways. Jane Donawerth, for example, in *Shakespeare and the Sixteenth-Century Study of Language,*[3] broadens her canvas by considering not just individual examples of language use but 'ideas *about* language' in the plays in relation to the commonplaces and controversies of the time. This enables her to move into more congenial areas of theme and character as she discusses questions such as the reliability of language and the relative virtues of self-expression and restraint. In a very different (and more ambitious) way, Marion Trousdale escapes the limitations of traditional rhetorical analysis in *Shakespeare and the Rhetoricians*[4] by arguing that the particular views of language and language-learning held in Shakespeare's time entailed a view of literary composition, not just at the level of individual sentences and speeches, but at the higher level of the dramatic structure as a whole.

Both Donawerth and Trousdale draw heavily on the work of Renaissance rhetoricians and make almost no use of twentieth-century theoretical approaches, though Trousdale has some interesting remarks at the very beginning and again at the very end of her book on the differences between modern structuralism and what she calls 'Elizabethan methodism'—meaning a belief in the importance of theory and the efficacy of rules. More relevant to our own project is the work of Keir Elam in *Shakespeare's Universe of Discourse*[5] which consistently makes use of modern authorities (mainly linguists and semioticians) alongside Renaissance ones. His application of speech-act theory to the dialogue of Shakespearean comedy raises interesting questions about the extent to which the highly stylized exchanges of the stage are governed by the same rules and conventions as everyday conversation. He does not however have very much to say about metaphor, mainly because he feels it has already received more than its share of attention for obvious reasons:

> Metaphor, metonymy, synecdoche and irony have achieved a general academic respectability that one can scarcely imagine being accorded to epistrophe or chiasmus or hendiadys. Nowhere is this more apparent than in Shakespearean stylistic criticism: 'imagery'—i.e. tropical language, and especially metaphor—has been the staple of a critical industry that has given only token acknowledgement to 'sound patterns' as potential objects of analysis. And the poetic or dramaturgic principle behind this choice is not so far to seek: the trope is deemed capable of participating fully in the thematic development of the drama . . . while the scheme remains a more or less inert mode of verbal *appliqué,* able at best to provide an attractive formal framework to the drama proper. (243-4)

Elam's discussion of anaphora, chiasmus, hyperbole and other schemes is anything but inert. His point about the attractions of metaphor for literary critics seems an important one and we have ourselves felt the pressure of its assumptions. Many readers become impatient with rhetorical or stylistic analysis and will not accept that it has any validity or interest for its own sake: they demand to know how one's findings affect 'the meaning of the play'—how, in Elam's words, the tropes 'participate fully in the thematic development of the drama'. An extreme form of this approach can be seen in a book such as Ralph Berry's *The Shakespearean Metaphor*[6] where metaphor is treated as something which can control or organize an entire play: notions of acting are seen to dominate *Richard II,* for example, and 'the idea of the Chorus' governs both *Romeo and Juliet* and *Henry V.* This inflation of the significance of metaphor can lead, paradoxically, to a situation in which the actual verbal detail of individual examples is under-discussed. At the same time, a recent approach which does explore the verbal detail, George T. Wright's 'He ldiadys and *Hamlet*'[7] (an article Elam might well see as a rare and gallant attempt to confer academic respectability on an unfashionable scheme) feels obliged to make the move into thematic analysis by finding in the very structure of the scheme ('They drank from cups and gold' is a classic example) a reflection of the play's obsession with doubleness and disjunction, misleading parallels and false relationships.

The insistence on the thematic implications of figurative language has however, as Elam says, been most influential in studies of 'imagery', which we would take to be the main alternative to studies of rhetoric, and an approach which has proved far more popular for this reason as well as because of its greater accessibility to those (such as most undergraduate students) who do not have a background in Renaissance rhetoric. From the very beginning, in the pioneering work of Caroline Spurgeon and Wolfgang Clemen,[8] there has been a drive from particular images to 'running' or 'dominating' images and an assumption that the most interesting and important images are those which 'add up' in some sense, contributing either to the overall meaning of an individual play or, if added up across several plays, to a biographical impression of the author. Either way, we are back with the notion of 'organic unity'. It seems to us, as to other critics of the imagery approach,[9] that while images *may* be studied in these ways it is arbitrary to limit our interest in them to their possible thematic or biographical implications. It is far too easy to neglect images which do not fit in with our preconceptions of 'what the play is about' and to impose overly narrow definitions on what is acceptable as an image in the first place. We shall take up this question again in Chapter 5, but we should stress here the importance for us of the analysis of images being a two-stage process in which due care and attention can be paid to the first stage—the examination of the immediate linguistic detail in its own right—without the obligation to hurry on and subordinate them into a larger (and usually more predictable) thematic or biographical pattern. Our emphasis in this book will be less on ultimate meanings and more on immediate ones: we shall be asking not so much 'What does this metaphor mean'? but 'How does it come to mean what it means'?

We cannot here attempt a comprehensive sketch of the range of non-literary approaches to metaphor analysis that have been developed over the last few years. Fortunately, the interested reader can acquire a good sense of recent activity in the field by turning to several excellent collections of articles,[10] as well as to Paul Ricoeur's extensive review of the tradition in *The Rule of Metaphor*.[11] One broad tendency in the field must be described, however, if our selection and use of specific theoretical initiatives in the following pages is to be understood.

Encountering a metaphor, a listener or reader has to do two things: he or she must recognize that the utterance in question *is* metaphorical, and he or she must understand it or grasp its point. These may not in practice be successive, discrete operations,[12] but their conceptual distinctness from one another is plain. While it is the mechanisms of the second of these operations that primarily interest us, the recognition question has bulked large in linguistic and philosophical treatments of the phenomenon, and this has had its effect on the orientation of much of the work on the comprehension question.

When metaphor came onto the agenda of linguists working in a generative grammar framework (where the aim of the exercise is the formulation of a set of rules capable of generating all, and only, the grammatical sentences of a language), the easiest conclusion to draw was that a metaphor is recognized as such because it is grammatically deviant in some particular way: 'The stone died' is a classic example. The listener's task was seen as the translation of the metaphorical expression into another, non-deviant expression ('The stone-like individual died') which is presumably—since listeners agree on the interpretation of metaphors—related to the original expression in a rule-governed way.[13] However, it was soon noticed that whole sentences which are in no way grammatically deviant can be used metaphorically: consider, for example, 'The rock is becoming brittle with age' in the context of (1) a group of people on a geology expedition, and (2) a group of students discussing a senior professor.[14]

A similar sort of problem for a simple deviance model for metaphor-recognition arose in the philosophical literature. There, the temptation was to make not ungrammaticality but literal falsity the trigger mechanism for detecting metaphor: consider 'Juliet is the sun'. But counter-examples were quickly found here as well: consider any metaphor expressed negatively, such as 'No man is an island'. Such examples were christened 'twice-true metaphors'.[15] Furthermore, to insist on literal falsity as the hallmark of metaphor opens up an intuitively unacceptable chasm between metaphors and similes, since the latter are usually literally true: 'Juliet is *like* the sun' is perfectly acceptable.[16]

It is now widely felt that deviance accounts of metaphor can be saved, and the linguistic-philosophical split on the nature of deviance resolved, by situating the problem within the wider field of 'conversational implicature' as proposed in an influential article by H.P. Grice.[17] The basic idea is that, faced with any sort of intentional, and intended-to-be-noticed, violation of one or more of the broad maxims that govern normal conversation (Be as informative as possible; Be truthful; Be relevant; Be clear), the listener takes the speaker to be implying something more, or other, than has actually been uttered. Falsity, tautology, semantic deviance within the sentence, and discontinuities over large units of discourse are all capable of triggering inferential processes whereby the listener tries to see the violation as having a point. Metaphorical interpretation is one of these inferential routes.

The approach to metaphor *via* notions of deviance (whether from grammar or from truth) seems to us to have both positive and negative aspects when we turn to an elaborated literary text. The advantages, to the literary critic, of such a reorientation seem at least twofold. First, as in a 'What's-wrong-with-this-picture'? children's game, the search for exactly which elements in an expression operate to distinguish it from the semantically unanomalous and the literally true develops one's eye for detail in a way which ultimately enriches the reading experience considerably. Secondly, although 'with the term ''deviant'' purified of derogatory connotations in the theoretical vocabulary of generative grammar'[18] there ought not to be any implication that deviant expressions are to be deplored, none the less the approach seems to carry with it a demythologizing aura which is liberating when so revered a figure as Shakespeare is concerned: to approach a passage asking not 'Why is this so wonderful'? but 'How is this peculiar'? can unblock reflection on the actual verbal arrangement of the text in a helpful fashion.

However, at a certain point any surreptitious privileging of plain sense-making over deviance does raise problems when the question of consistently heightened literary language must be addressed. It is hard to escape a picture of language in which the smooth unrolling of non-deviant sentences is suddenly broken by the appearance of an anomalous expression triggering metaphoric interpretation. But what if a high level of rhetorical elaboration is normal rather than exceptional, whether in the literature of a particular period or even more broadly in educated writing and speech? What if, as Stern points out, in dealing with 'metaphors whose setting is poetry or literature', we are 'independently cued by their context to interpret them metaphorically'?[19]

Various as the approaches we discuss in the following chapters are, they share in our view a potential for moving beyond the unrealistic aspects of the metaphor-as-deviation picture.

Our strategy in the five chapters which follow is strictly selective, both in terms of the theoretical frameworks and the Shakespearean examples. In Chapter 1 we apply a seminal work on everyday metaphor, *Metaphors We Live By* by George Lakoff and Mark Johnson (a linguist and a philosopher respectively) to a consideration of some of the time metaphors in *Troilus and Cressida*. In Chapter 2 we take an article by Eva Kittay and Adrienne Lehrer, 'Semantic Fields in the Structure of Metaphor', as representative of how I.A. Richards' tenor-vehicle distinction can be elaborated in the light of a particular linguistic approach, and study some of the animal metaphors in *King Lear* in terms suggested by their account of semantic field analysis. Chapter 3 continues the exploration of linguistic/rhetorical theories of metaphor by examining the startling claim of Group μ in their *Rhétorique générale* that 'metaphor is the product of two synecdoches, as in a different way is metonymy'. We discuss the relationships between metaphor, metonymy and synecdoche, selecting our Shakespearean examples from the many references to the human body and its parts in *Hamlet*. In Chapter 4 we move away from linguistic approaches to one based disciplinarily in philosophy, though linguistically knowledgeable—J.F. Ross's *Portraying Analogy*. Here we restrict our exemplification to a

single short text, Sonnet 63. Chapter 5 continues in the
philosophical arena as we test the argument advanced by Donald
Davidson in his influential article 'What Metaphors Mean' that
there is no such thing as metaphorical meaning. At this point we
consider metaphors drawn from books and printing, allowing
ourselves to range across the entire Shakespearean canon.

How do these approaches progress beyond the deviance
paradigm? In different ways, both Ross and Lakoff and Johnson
present a picture of how ordinary, unheightened language works
which stands at odds with the standard view of literal meaning.
While Davidson is determined to keep a sharp literal/metaphorical
distinction in place, he provides good reasons for doubting whether
the whole enterprise of giving a rule-bound 'translation' from
metaphorese to literalese, as it were, can actually be carried
through. The cognitive seriousness of metaphor—that is, the
degree to which a donor semantic field (vehicle) is capable of
restructuring a recipient field (tenor) is stressed by Kittay and
Lehrer—perhaps overstressed for some metaphors, but certainly
not for all. Their sense of metaphor's utility is shared with,
particularly, Lakoff and Johnson. The semantic relationships
which allow metaphor to function cognitively in this way (class
membership and the part–whole relation) are explored by Group
μ—as it happens in a fashion which descends directly from the
accounts in rhetorical handbooks of Shakespeare's time. The
ordinary, inescapable nature of these relationships makes metaphor
look like a much less surprising figure than the deviance paradigm
would suggest, a result also derivable from Lakoff and Johnson,
who alert us to how metaphorical everyday language is, and Ross,
who stresses how mobile and context-sensitive word-meanings are
in general.

We should emphasize again that we see our book as a series of
meetings. We do not pretend to offer a thoroughgoing critique of
any of the theoretical approaches to metaphor that we make use of
any more than we pretend to offer a complete reading of any of our
Shakespearean texts (even Sonnet 63!). We do however hope to
provide a productive and provocative set of encounters between the
linguistic and philosophical theories and the Shakespearean
examples.

We address ourselves primarily to students and critics of
literature without a grounding in linguistics or philosophy. We

10

hope that linguists, philosophers and other non-literary specialists with an interest in metaphor will read our book and we would be delighted to think they could learn something from it, but we are not trying to tell them that they *must* study literary metaphor or that their theories are invalid if they do not take account of it. We are however trying to tell literary scholars that a great deal of interesting work is being done on metaphor outside their own field and that some of it at least has much to offer them. It *is* possible to 'borrow' non-literary approaches and thereby avoid the vagueness and theme-centredness of imagery studies as well as discover new levels of complexity and detail in familiar lines. Finally, we believe our work raises questions about the great divide that has traditionally been assumed to exist between everyday and literary metaphor. Modes of analysis primarily developed for application to everyday metaphor are surprisingly successful when applied to Shakespeare; conversely the at times impossibly heightened and complex language of the plays turns out to have its roots very firmly in the ground.

Notes

1. Shakespeare's likely education has been explored in some detail in this respect by T.W. Baldwin in *William Shakespere's Petty School* and *William Shakespere's Small Latine and Lesse Greek* (both University of Illinois Press, Urbana, Illinois; 1943 and 1944 respectively).
2. The standard work in this field is still Sister Miriam Joseph's *Shakespeare's Use of the Arts of Language* (Columbia University Press, New York, 1947).
3. University of Illinois Press, Urbana, Illinois, 1984.
4. Scolar Press, London, 1982.
5. Cambridge University Press, Cambridge, 1984.
6. Macmillan, London, 1978.
7. *PMLA* 96 (1981), 168-93. We refer to this article in Chapter 3 below, p.101 and n.19, p.128.
8. Caroline Spurgeon, *Shakespeare's Imagery and What It Tells Us* (Cambridge University Press, Cambridge, 1935); Wolfgang Clemen, *The Development of Shakespeare's Imagery* (Methuen, London, 1951).
9. Useful summaries of objections to the imagery approach can be found in R.A. Foakes, 'Suggestions for a New Approach to Shakespeare's Imagery', *Shakespeare Survey* 5 (1952), 81-92; Kenneth Muir, 'Shakespeare's Imagery—Then and Now', *Shakespeare Survey* 18 (1965), 46-57; and Robert Weimann, 'Shakespeare and the Study of Metaphor', *New Literary*

History 6 (1974), 149-67. (This entire issue of *New Literary History* is, incidentally, devoted to metaphor.)

10. These collections are: Marvin K.L. Ching, Michael C. Haley and Ronald F. Lunsford (eds.), *Linguistic Perspectives on Literature* (Routledge and Kegan Paul, London, 1980); Richard P. Honeck and Robert R. Hoffman (eds.), *Cognition and Figurative Language* (Erlbaum, Hillsdale, New Jersey, 1980); Mark Johnson (ed.), *Philosophical Perspectives on Metaphor* (University of Minnesota Press, Minneapolis, 1981); David S. Miall (ed.), *Metaphor: Problems and Perspectives* (Harvester, Brighton, 1982); Andrew Ortony (ed.), *Metaphor and Thought* (Cambridge University Press, Cambridge, 1979); and Sheldon Sacks (ed.), *On Metaphor* (University of Chicago Press, Chicago and London, 1979).

11. Routledge and Kegan Paul, London, 1978; translated by Robert Czerny from *La métaphore vive* (Editions du Seuil, Paris, 1975).

12. For a recent experimental–psychological demonstration that metaphoric comprehension does not necessarily involve longer reaction–times than literal comprehension, see Howard R. Pollio *et al.*, 'Need Metaphoric Comprehension Take Longer Than Literal Comprehension?', *Journal of Psycholinguistic Research* 13 (1984), 195-214.

13. This example is discussed at length in Samuel R. Levin's *The Semantics of Metaphor* (Johns Hopkins University Press, Baltimore, 1977). This book is one of the most detailed attempts to work out what sort of rules would account for metaphorical construal within a generative grammar framework, specifically that proposed by Jerrold J. Katz in *Semantic Theory* (Harper and Row, New York, 1972). Unfortunately, while the book is full of good things, the Katzian formulations look seriously dated today.

14. This example is given by Michael J. Reddy in 'A Semantic Approach to Metaphor', collected in Ching *et al.*, (see above, n.10), pp. 63-75. For a recent discussion of the problems involved in taking ungrammaticality as a signal for metaphorical interpretation, see Josef Stern, 'Metaphor and Grammatical Deviance', *Nous* 17 (1983), 577-99.

15. The phrase was coined by Ted Cohen; see 'Figurative Speech and Figurative Acts', *Journal of Philosophy* 72 (1975), 669-84.

16. We say more about the simile–metaphor relationship in Chapter 5 below, pp. 171, 182 and n.13, p. 203. Our own feeling is that the relationship is a very close one but that, as philosophers in particular have been fond of pointing out, simile is actually as mysterious as metaphor, rather than it being the case that metaphor can be *explained* as a hyperbolic variant of the corresponding simile. On this subject, see Andrew Ortony, 'The Role of Similarity in Similes and Metaphors' in the Ortony collection (see above, n.10), pp. 186-201.

17. H.P. Grice, 'Logic and Conversation', in Peter Cole and Jerry L. Morgan (eds.), *Syntax and Semantics 3: Speech Acts* (Academic Press, New York, 1975), pp. 41-58.

18. Stern (as cited in n.14 above), p. 577.

19. Ibid., p. 581.

1

Time Metaphors in
Troilus and Cressida

Literal or Referential Time

Troilus and Cressida has, for Shakespeare, a surprisingly tight time-scheme. The specific location in time of the first two scenes is difficult to pinpoint precisely[1] but from 1.3 onwards it can be confidently asserted that the action of the play covers a period of just three days. In the war plot these can be differentiated as follows:

1. The day on which Hector's challenge for a single combat 'tomorrow' is issued to the Greeks. This day covers 1.3, 2.1, 2.2, 2.3 and 3.3, while 4.1 is a night-time scene which concludes the first day and takes us through to the morning of the second.
2. The day on which the challenge fight between Hector and Ajax takes place. This day begins in 4.1 and covers 4.3, 4.4, 4.5 and 5.1, while 5.2 is another night-time scene which concludes the second day and takes us through to the morning of the third.
3. The day after the challenge fight, on which Hector dies. This day begins in 5.2 and continues through the battle scenes to the end of the play when another night is imminent.

The events of the love plot follow the same pattern:

1. The day which leads us to the lovers' first night together. This day covers 3.1 and 3.2, by which time it is evening.
2. The day after, on which Cressida moves from Troy to the Greek camp in the morning and accepts Diomedes as a lover in the evening. This day begins in 4.2 and covers 4.4 and 4.5, with 5.2 again taking us through from the end of the second day to the morning of the third.

13

3. The day after that, on which Troilus seeks Diomedes in the battle but fails to kill him, and receives Cressida's letter. This day begins in 5.2 and continues to the end of the play.

It is clear that the temporal integration of the two plots is carefully managed; both come to a climax in 4.5 when, in the same scene, Cressida arrives in the Greek camp and Hector fights with Ajax. The two separate night-to-dawn sequences are coordinated, with 4.1 and 5.2 serving both to mingle characters and events from the two plots and to take us through from one day to the next.[2] In a sense Shakespeare has given Hector's challenge a specious significance in order to bring the events of the war plot artificially and neatly into temporal parallel with those of the love plot.

It is possible to be so exact about the time-scheme because the play contains a remarkable number of specific references to the literal timing of its events. Characters refer frequently and precisely to events as taking place 'yesterday', 'this morning', 'today', 'tonight', 'tomorrow', and so on. They tell us if it is early or late in the day and they often reflect on the passage of time, as when Troilus laments that 'Night hath been too brief' (4.2.11) or Aeneas deplores 'How have we spent [ie. wasted] this morning' (4.4.140). From 1.3 onwards there is a striking, indeed diagrammatic consistency about the time references apart from the following discrepancies:

1. In the war plot there is a general contradiction between references to 'this dull and long-continued truce' during which Hector has become 'resty' from inaction (1.3) and other references to episodes in the fighting 'today', the greeting of returning warriors, and so on.
2. In the love plot there is a comparable discrepancy in the later stages when Thersites knows about Diomedes' 'Trojan drab' in 5.1 strictly before the first tryst can have taken place. This and the letter to Troilus (delivered the next day in 5.3) imply a longer time-scheme for the development of Cressida's relationship with Diomedes than is literally possible.
3. Hector's challenging trumpet (supposedly blown midway between the walls of Troy and the Greek camp) is heard in Troy at the end of 4.4 but is not heard by the Greeks who sound *their* trumpet at the beginning of 4.5 (the relevant stage directions are separated by 20 lines of dialogue) and remark on the lack of a

response. They finally hear Hector's trumpet some 50 lines later.

These discrepancies can all be justified on dramatic grounds. The discrepancy in the love plot creates an effect very similar to the famous 'double time' scheme in *Othello* whereby we are encouraged to believe in the possibility of Desdemona's adultery with Cassio even though we know there has been no opportunity for it. Equally, in the war plot, Shakespeare again needs two effects which strictly speaking are mutually contradictory: he wants the impression of ongoing warfare but he also needs the truce to give greater impact to Hector's challenge and to the subsequent resumption of general hostilities. The discrepancy of the trumpets is more problematic from the point of view of staging (unless an interval occurs between 4.4 and 4.5) but it contributes notably to the integration of the two plots since the exchange of Cressida can take place between the two trumpet calls, thus effectively suspending both plots at their simultaneous moment of climax. The net effect of the discrepancies in performance is probably to heighten rather than to dissipate the audience's sense of temporal precision and density.[3]

In addition to the short-term time references to 'yesterday', 'tomorrow' and so on, *Troilus* contains many references to a longer time scheme extending before and after the compressed events of the actual play. In the love plot, both Troilus and Cressida claim, albeit hyperbolically, to have been in love for a long time, and Cressida's father Calchas refers to the many previous occasions on which the Greeks have asked for Cressida to be included in an exchange of prisoners. In the war plot we are frequently reminded of the abduction of Helen which began the conflict seven years ago, and there are numerous references to previous events, such as Achilles' past achievements. The lovers also look to the future, swearing eternal fidelity, while the warriors threaten future violence and the whole narrative is cast in an ironic atmosphere of prophecy and prediction. The audience has total foreknowledge of both plots: we know that Cressida will betray Troilus and that Troy will fall, though only one of these stories can be concluded in stage time.

All this attention to the facts of time, to the referential time of the characters' literal experience, represents a base from which the play can move into heightened time language and intricate time semantics when it wants to. As soon as time *as a concept* is thematized in the play's language, matters get more complicated. But this complication in turn, we shall argue, can be seen as an elaboration on quite everyday time language, which is itself already and inevitably metaphorical.

Lakoff and Johnson: Everyday Metaphor

George Lakoff and Mark Johnson's *Metaphor We Live By*[4] is a discussion of everyday, inescapable metaphoricity. Much of it consists of demonstrations of how, underlying what seems to be ordinary literal language, concepts are in fact being related and developed metaphorically. One kind of thing gets regularly, perhaps automatically, understood and experienced in terms of another. Lakoff and Johnson present these conceptual metaphors simply by putting into capital letters the most direct expression of the underlying equivalence that they can think of, almost always in the form X IS Y.

One aspect of concept X is comprehended in terms of another concept, concept Y. But:

> It is important to see that the metaphorical structuring involved here is partial, not total. If it were total, one concept would actually *be* the other, nor merely be understood in terms of it. (12-13)

For instance, Lakoff and Johnson can adduce a great many ordinary expressions underlying which is the conceptual metaphor ARGUMENT IS WAR ('Your claims are indefensible', 'He attacked every weak point in my argument', 'His criticisms were right on target'(4)). And this is more than merely a way of speaking: arguments in our culture frequently do get conducted in war-like terms. But the ARGUMENT IS WAR metaphor in revealing some aspects of argument conceals others, notably its cooperative aspects. Or—to move on to the time question—Lakoff and Johnson are able to take over a proverb directly as one of their formulae, TIME IS MONEY, and list a number of expressions beneath which this equivalence is operating ('This gadget will save you hours', 'He's living on borrowed time', 'You don't use your time profitably'(7-8)). But:

16

Time isn't really money. If you *spend your time* trying to do something and it doesn't work, you can't get your time back. There are no time banks. I can *give you a lot of time,* but you can't give me back the same time, though you can *give me back the same amount of time.* And so on. Thus, part of a metaphorical concept does not and cannot fit. (13)

The implications of this partial fit will obviously vary from case to case. Lakoff and Johnson's work opens onto ideological critique at times: here, seeing X as Y can be actively oppressive, as when LABOUR IS A RESOURCE turns out to underlie phrases such as ' "a virtually inexhaustible supply of cheap labour"'— a neutral-sounding economic statement, that hides the reality of human degradation' (237; cf.65). Or it may be argued that more would be revealed of X if instead of accepting the standard X IS Y we experimented with a novel X IS Z, as when Lakoff and Johnson suggest that LOVE IS A COLLABORATIVE WORK OF ART might serve us better than such everyday metaphors as LOVE IS A JOURNEY, LOVE IS MADNESS or LOVE IS HEALTH (139-43). But in other cases the demonstration that we are thinking metaphorically does not lead to the conclusion that we should, or could, think otherwise—though the partiality of the fit can always cause us to trip.

Lakoff and Johnson distinguish three broad categories of conceptual metaphors: structural, ontological and orientational. In *structural metaphors,* one concept is metaphorically structured in terms of another. All the examples we have so far considered would be classed as structural metaphors. *Ontological metaphors* are those whereby that which is not inherently an entity or substance is treated as such, and *orientational metaphors* are those whereby that which is not inherently spatial or bounded is referred to as if it were (by using such terms as up–down, in–out, front–back, on–off, deep–shallow and central–peripheral (14)). The latter two types of metaphor are not immune from ideological critique: to treat inflation as an entity ('Inflation is lowering our standard of living'), or to treat more as better because our commonest orientational metaphors claim that MORE IS UP and BETTER IS UP, are potentially misleading tricks of thought. But often the chief interest of Lakoff and Johnson's analysis of ontological and orientational metaphors lies in simply making them visible. Who would have thought that there was a metaphor underlying 'The ball is in front of the rock'? Yet,

Some things, like people and cars, have inherent fronts and backs, but others, like trees, do not . . . The rock has received a front–back orientation, as if it had a front that faced you. This is not universal. There are languages—Hausa for instance—where the rock would receive the reverse orientation and you would say that the ball was behind the rock if it was between you and the rock.(42)

Since Lakoff and Johnson's interest is in everyday metaphor, it does not go without saying that the analysis of elaborated or heightened uses of language is advanced by their work. In looking at time metaphors in *Troilus and Cressida* it does seem to us that *Metaphors We Live By* is an enlightening text, as we hope our readers will agree, but perhaps this is so because time enters into the play on so many levels, from the literal as already discussed to full-fledged set-pieces such as Ulysses' 'Time hath, my lord, a wallet at his back . . .', passing through metaphorical passages in which time is a conceptual component but not the focus of attention. A virtue of Lakoff and Johnson's approach is the way in which it links literal and metaphorical surface forms by allowing both to be seen as sharing a conceptual base that is metaphorically structured. Time-talk is *ordinarily* metaphorical: we shall want to examine how far elaborated Shakespearean time-metaphors build on that and how far they depart from that.

Time's elusive nature makes it a prime candidate for everyday ontological metaphor. By conceptualizing the intangible as though it were a physical object, we feel we can grasp it better (as it were!). Time is even more strikingly a candidate for orientational metaphor, since it seems impossible not to think of time as directional, and the idea of direction inescapably brings with it front–back orientation. Lakoff and Johnson encapsulate one result of combining the ontological and orientational moves in the formula TIME IS A MOVING OBJECT.

However, might it be the case that we metaphorize time in these respects inconsistently? An apparent inconsistency arises where the in-frontness or behindness of past and future is concerned. We speak of 'the weeks ahead of us' (future in front) and of 'the following weeks' (future behind), meaning the same thing.

Moreover, the apparently contradictory metaphors can mix with no ill effect, as in 'We're looking *ahead* to the *following* weeks'. Here it appears that *ahead* organizes the future in front, while *following* organizes it behind. (41)

Lakoff and Johnson show that here the inconsistency is only apparent: if TIME IS A MOVING OBJECT, it is one which moves towards us: its 'front' is in front of us and its back, time further in the future, is still further in front of *us* although it is at the same time behind time's front. (The tail of a dog running towards us is further in front of us than the dog's nose is.) Thus all future weeks are thought of as following behind the week ahead as that week comes towards us.

A real inconsistency can still be spotted between expressions which are governed by the TIME IS A MOVING OBJECT metaphor ('I can't face the future', 'Christmas is coming') and others in which TIME IS STATIONARY AND WE MOVE THROUGH IT ('As we move further into the 1980s', 'We're approaching Christmas'). Lakoff and Johnson distinguish two levels of metaphorical compatibility among expressions, *consistency* and *coherence.* Expressions governed by the same conceptual metaphor are mutually consistent. Expressions governed by wholly unrelated metaphors would be mutually inconsistent and incoherent. But expressions governed by different metaphors are coherent, even though not consistent, if the different metaphors can be shown to be sub-cases of a single broader metaphor. In the time case, this broader metaphor can be expressed as TIME PASSES US: both TIME IS A MOVING OBJECT and TIME IS STATIONARY AND WE MOVE THROUGH IT entail that, from our point of view, time goes past us from front to back (44).

The two sub-cases of time passing lead to different sorts of ontologizing. Lakoff and Johnson see everyday personification ('Our biggest enemy right now is inflation', 'Life has cheated me') as a key variety of ontological metaphor which 'allows us to comprehend a wide variety of experiences with nonhuman entities in terms of human motivations, characteristics, and activities' (33): the non-object is treated not only as an object but as that variety of object to which we ourselves belong. (Usually the process of specification is taken still further: not only is the non-object a person, but it is a particular kind of person. Not stopping at INFLATION IS A PERSON, we move to INFLATION IS AN ADVERSARY.) Now if time is to be personified, this will most easily come about as the result of a further specification of TIME IS A MOVING OBJECT. But the appropriate ontologization for the time of TIME IS STATIONARY AND WE MOVE THROUGH IT would have to be as a space—perhaps a landscape or a territory—rather than as a person.

Let us now turn to some of the *Troilus and Cressida* time personifications with these considerations in mind.

Time is a Person

In the Renaissance period, as now, there were many everyday ways of talking about time which involved a greater or lesser degree of personification. We still use expressions like 'Time flies', 'Time waits for no man' and 'Time brings the truth to light', and Tilley's collection of sixteenth and seventeenth-century proverbs indicates that a wide range of these expressions was current then. In the Renaissance, moreover, these proverbs were vividly reinforced by the visual representations of Time in the emblem books, the most common images being those of Time the Reaper (an old man carrying a scythe and an hourglass), and Time as Occasion (a man or woman with a large forelock of hair but bald behind, illustrating the proverb 'Take time (occasion) by the forelock for she is bald behind' (Tilley, T311)).[5] Shakespeare's personifications of Time in *Troilus* draw heavily on the colloquial and traditional background represented by the proverbs and the emblem books but they can also be analysed in accordance with Lakoff and Johnson's discussion of ontological and orientational metaphors.

Time is conventionally though briefly personified at an early stage in the play in Pandarus' vague denial of responsibility for the outcome of Troilus' love affair: 'Well, the gods are above; time must friend or end' (1.2.77-8),[6] a commonplace expressed more solemnly later by Hector in relation to the outcome of the war itself:

> The end crowns all,
> And that old common arbitrator, Time,
> Will one day end it.
>
> 4.5.224-6

Here the personification is slightly more specific since Time is alluded to as 'old' and as being the ultimate and universal judge (both commonplace attributes). These references are however untypical of the play since Time seems neutral in them rather than hostile, even potentially friendly if we can read a sort of familiarity into 'old'. The impression is not completely remote in tone from Viola's remark when the confusions and misunderstandings are escalating in *Twelfth Night:*

> O time, thou must untangle this, not I,
> It is too hard a knot for me t'untie.
>   2.2.40-1

In all these cases, the reference to Time seems the equivalent of a shrug—a gesture disclaiming personal responsibility.

The association of Time with Nestor[7] is the principal location of 'friendly' Time references in *Troilus* and perhaps helps to explain the unusual tone of 'that old common arbitrator' which follows quickly on from Hector's courteous greeting of Nestor:

> Let me embrace thee, good old chronicle,
> That hast so long walk'd hand in hand with time.
>   4.5.202-3

This example illustrates (though again, as we shall see, untypically) three of the most significant attributes or specifications of the TIME IS A PERSON ontological metaphor in this play:

1. Time is moving.
2. Time is facing in a specific direction in relation to the person in question.
3. Time is doing something with his hands (a more surprising characteristic but one which we shall argue carries particular resonance in this play).

In this instance all three of these attributes contribute to the unusually friendly conception of Time: his motion is that of 'walking', implying a convenient pace for his elderly human companion Nestor, he is presumably facing in the same direction as Nestor, and he is holding his hand in a gesture of friendship or even mutual assistance. We are reminded of the amiable characters with whom Time is said to 'amble' in *As You Like It:*

> a priest that lacks Latin, and a rich man that hath not the gout; for the
> one sleeps easily because he cannot study, and the other lives merrily
> because he feels no pain . . . .
>   3.2.319-22

Rosalind's examples of 'who Time trots withal' and 'who Time gallops withal' are closer to the majority of *Troilus* instances in that in them the speed and movement of Time are *not* convenient or friendly to his human companion(s): he is out of step if not going in the opposite direction.

This view of time as contrary or hostile to human beings is most forcefully present in *Troilus* in Ulysses' second elaboration on the figure in his long speech to Achilles in which he stresses the importance of continuing to perform heroic deeds and the dangers of resting on one's laurels:

> For Time is like a fashionable host
> That slightly shakes his parting guest by th' hand,
> And with his arms outstretch'd as he would fly,
> Grasps in the comer. The welcome ever smiles,
> And farewell goes out sighing.
>
> 3.3.165-9

Here Time is not actually in flight but is on the very verge of flying *towards* those who are arriving but *away* from those (including Achilles) who are leaving. His arms and hands are 'outstretch'd' as if to assist his flight but also in a gesture of welcoming embrace to Achilles' rivals, while he presumably turns his back on 'farewell', the 'parting guest', after a casual or slighting handshake. Thus all three attributes—movement, orientation or direction, and hand-gestures—are in this instance hostile (from Achilles' point of view) rather than friendly.

Clearly, traditional notions from the proverbial and emblematic stock of commonplaces underlie this passage, especially

> Times flees away without delay ⎫
> Time has wings   ⎬   (Tilley, T327)
> Take time (occasion) by the forelock for she is bald behind.
>   (Tilley, T311)

These underlying commonplaces help to explain the significance of the hands and arms of Time since hands are needed to grasp things and arms can become substitutes for wings. Elsewhere we might expect the notion of Time's movement to be expressed through specific reference to his feet, as indeed happens in the passage from

As You Like It quoted above which takes off from a reference to 'the
lazy foot of Time'.

   Time, or rather Night viewed as specific interval of time, has a
similar combination of attributes in a later passage in *Troilus* in
4.1, the scene where Troilus and Cressida are parting after their
first night together (not yet knowing that it will also be their last).
Troilus, adopting the traditional style of the *aubade,* upbraids the
Night:

> Beshrew the witch! with venomous wights she stays
> As tediously as hell, but flies the grasps of love
> With wings more momentary-swift than thought.
>   4.2.12-14

Night, like Time-as-host, is seen as a person capable of having
human companions and choosing to avoid some and linger with
others. Again the notion of outstretched arms carries the double
meaning of flying and embracing: Night is flying away from the
lovers who are attempting to grasp her—and each other
presumably—in an embrace.

   Further embraces are interrupted by Time when the lovers
experience their final parting in 4.4. Troilus responds to Cressida's
'Is't possible'? with a complex and passionate speech:

> And suddenly, where injury of chance
> Puts back leave-taking, justles roughly by
> All time of pause, rudely beguiles our lips
> Of all rejoindure, forcibly prevents
> Our lock'd embrasures, strangles our dear vows
> Even in the birth of our own laboring breath.
> We two, that with so many thousand sighs
> Did buy each other, must poorly sell ourselves
> With the rude brevity and discharge of one.
> Injurious time now with a robber's haste
> Crams his rich thiev'ry up, he knows not how.
> As many farewells as be stars in heaven,
> With distinct breath and consign'd kisses to them,
> He fumbles up into a loose adieu;
> And scants us with a single famish'd kiss,
> Distasted with the salt of broken tears.
>   4.4.33-48

In this passage the vague entity which is metaphorically getting between the lovers ('injury of chance' = injurious Chance?) becomes Time performing an act of robbery with violence. There is a sense of a physical adversary and hand-to-hand fighting ('justles', 'forcibly prevents', even 'strangles') with perhaps a submerged sense that Time is Troilus' rival ('beguiles'), but the main accusation is of robbery performed hastily: Time, having no time, is stealing time. Grabbing and grasping hand-movements are implied as Time 'crams up' and 'fumbles up' his booty. Although he is envisaged as bodily intervening between the lovers he is again engaged in rapid motion, on the point of flight.

Time is not given a specific front–back orientation here, though he is in the related passage which is perhaps the most famous of this play's time metaphors:

> Time hath, my lord, a wallet at his back,
> Wherein he puts alms for oblivion,
> A great-siz'd monster of ingratitudes.
> Those scraps are good deeds past, which are devour'd
> As fast as they are made, forgot as soon
> As done.

3.3.145-50

We are of course back with Ulysses warning Achilles of the dangers of inaction. The wallet hung behind the back was a common figure in this sort of allegorical context but it is elsewhere associated with ordinary people rather than with personified Time, and the things placed inside it usually symbolize what the bearers would prefer to forget, their evil deeds rather than their good ones.[8] Hands are again important though: Time needs hands to put the alms in his wallet and there is perhaps also a suggestion of the traditional gesture of the outstretched hand requesting alms.

It is worth noting here that *Troilus* is a play particularly concerned with handling and grasping on the literal as well as the figurative level. Literally, the plot has to do with the physical abduction of Helen which leads to other references to the handling of stolen goods. There are many references to hand-to-hand fighting between the warriors and to the 'beating' of a less heroic character like Thersites, as well as references to the handling of food and to love-making as an activity performed partly with the hands and arms. Many of the symbolic gestures we can perform with our hands and arms are also significant in the play: characters frequently shake hands or embrace on greeting or parting, they shake hands on a bargain or pact, clap their hands in token of admiration, give their hands in marriage (or its equivalent) and 'hand over' a person in agreed exchange. As with the play's literal time references, this means that to some extent the verbal elaborations can be grounded in what the characters are actually doing.

Oblivion

Returning to Ulysses' speech, we should explore further the idea of devouring and the problematic concept of 'oblivion'. Time is of course traditionally defined as *edax rerum:* 'Time devours (consumes, wears out) all things' (Tilley, T326), but the 'alms' in becoming 'scraps' in this passage are twice devoured: as the leftovers of one meal they become the substitute for another. Critics have frequently commented on the prevalence of metaphors from food and cooking in *Troilus* and their obvious association with Time as the ultimate consumer,[9] but who or what exactly is the 'monster' which seems to be involved in the process in this passage? The play's two most recent editors are in complete disagreement on this point: Kenneth Palmer in the New Arden edition (1982, pp.212-13) argues that the monster is Oblivion, while Kenneth Muir in the Oxford Shakespeare (1982, p.129) says the monster is Time. The syntax allows for some ambiguity so interpretation depends on a reading of the passage as a whole which must in turn be supported by reference to comparable metaphorical passages in this and other plays.

Essentially, one is choosing between a more and a less fully personified (or 'animalified') reading of the phrase 'alms for oblivion'. Muir, who does not comment on his reading, presumably follows Alice Walker (the New Shakespeare, Cambridge, 1957, pp.190-1) in taking this to mean simply 'good deeds to be forgotten', while Palmer argues that it is 'part of the allegory', hence meaning something like 'offerings [of food] to [the entity called] Oblivion'. Now a textual variant intervenes: Palmer reads the next line as 'A great-siz'd monster of ingratitudes', following both the Quarto and Folio original texts, whereas Muir and Walker accept Hanmer's emendation to 'ingratitude'. This affects the interpretation since 'monster of ingratitude' could mean simply 'ungrateful monster' (i.e. monstrous because ungrateful),[10] while 'monster of ingratitudes' could carry the more vivid, animated sense of 'monster composed of (many instances of) ingratitude'.

But is Time or Oblivion more likely to be characterized in this way? Alice Walker says that 'Time is monstrously ungrateful because his interest is in the newcomer. To take "oblivion" as the monster makes nonsense of the symbolism of the wallet on the back of *Time*'. But Ulysses does not mention Time's behaviour as a host until twenty lines after this; moreover, it does not seem to follow that if Oblivion is the monster the wallet must be his or its. If anything it is more nonsensical to think of Time giving alms to himself, which is what this reading implies. And although Time is many things in this play, he is not specifically associated with ingratitude whereas oblivion is, both here and elsewhere. Palmer cites examples of Shakespeare linking oblivion or forgetfulness with ingratitude in *Twelfth Night, Lear,* and *As You Like It.* In the latter two plays the notion of monstrosity is also present: ingratitude has teeth and a sting or is seen as a 'marble-hearted fiend'.[11] The parallels with *The Rape of Lucrece* and *Measure for Measure* are even more telling: in the former the heroine rails at Time 'whose glory is . . . To feed oblivion with decay of things' (947) while in *Measure for Measure* the Duke remarks to Angelo (with some irony by this stage in the play):

> O, your desert speaks loud, and I should wrong it
> To lock it in the wards of covert bosom,
> When it deserves with characters of brass
> A forted residence 'gainst the tooth of time
> And razure of oblivion.
>
> 5.1.9-13

In both these examples, as in the one from *Troilus,* Time and Oblivion are seen as a sort of hostile partnership who destroy by devouring. In *Lucrece* Time actually feeds Oblivion (as in *Troilus* on the Palmer reading), while in *Measure for Measure* we have the closely comparable context of a discussion of 'desert' and reputation.

Time and Oblivion have previously appeared together in

Troilus, in the scene immediately before this one when Cressida makes her vow of fidelity:

> If I be false, or swerve a hair from truth,
> When time is old and hath forgot itself,
> When water-drops have worn the stones of Troy,
> And blind oblivion swallow'd cities up,
> And mighty states characterless are grated
> To dusty nothing, yet let memory,
> From false to false among false maids in love,
> Upbraid my falsehood!
>
> 3.2.184-91

The degree of personification or animalification is complex here: the use of 'itself' in relation to Time implies less than full personification but Time is seen as being like human beings in losing his faculties as he gets old whereas Oblivion is perhaps just blind by nature or by definition. Oblivion is in fact regularly less person-like and more vaguely monster-like than Time; in this case Oblivion is in syntactic parallel with the water-drops as an *agent* of the destruction which is ultimately caused by Time, yet in itself Oblivion combines the important notion of forgetfulness with that of destruction.

We would feel then that Palmer is probably right: the monster is Oblivion, but Time and Oblivion are closely associated in these passages and in a third passage from *Troilus* which we shall discuss below under 'Time as Space'.

Implicit Time: Creation is Birth

The personifications of Time are an obvious and explicit group of time metaphors in *Troilus* but it is also frequently the case that time is an important factor in a metaphor without being explicitly referred to. In the first scene of the play for example, Pandarus responds to Troilus' impatience with the remark 'He that will have a cake out of the wheat must tarry the grinding' and goes on to make an extended metaphorical comparison between the baking of a cake and Troilus' courtship of Cressida. There is no specific mention of time as such but time is nevertheless the essential medium which provides the link between the two activities: courting a woman is like baking a cake because of the time factor involved in both. Time can likewise be seen as a suppressed presence in Ulysses' advice to Achilles:

> Perseverance, dear my lord,
> Keeps honor bright; to have done is to hang
> Quite out of fashion, like a rusty mail
> In monumental mock'ry.
>
> 3.3.150-3

Time here, without being named, enters the metaphor as the medium in which fashions change, armour rusts and men die. It is equally the medium in which all living things grow to maturity—if they are permitted to do so. Ulysses has previously used a suppressed time metaphor from horticulture to express his view of Achilles:

> the seeded pride
> That hath to this maturity blown up,
> In rank Achilles must or now be cropp'd,
> Or shedding, breed a nursery of like evil,
> To overbulk us all.
>
> 1.3.316-20

This metaphor has a persuasive function: by representing Achilles' pride as a weed Ulysses makes the natural organic cycle seem threatening so that it becomes a virtue to interrupt or 'crop' it.[12]

'Vegetative' metaphors are comparatively rare in *Troilus,* but there is an interesting group of suppressed time metaphors taken from the human life-cycle and centring particularly around the notions of conception and birth. Such metaphors are common in everyday language, as Lakoff and Johnson demonstrate. In discussing our most frequently used causation metaphors they see the fundamental human experience of birth as providing a grounding for the general concept of 'creation' which has at its core the concept of 'making' a physical object but which extends to abstract entities as well. Examples of the CREATION IS BIRTH metaphor in everyday language include the following:

Our nation was born out of a desire for freedom.
His writings are products of his fertile imagination.

28

His experiment spawned a host of new theories.
Your actions will only breed violence.
He hatched a clever scheme.
He conceived a brilliant theory of molecular motion.
Universities are incubators for new ideas.
The theory of relativity first saw the light of day in 1905.
The University of Chicago was the birthplace of the nuclear age.
Edward Teller is the father of the hydrogen bomb.

(74-5)

Several of these examples show that an important sub-group of the CREATION IS BIRTH metaphor might be labelled the IDEAS ARE BABIES group, in which we conceptualize a whole range of abstract entitites—thoughts, plans, theories, predictions—in terms of the human baby or foetus. In this group time enters as the medium (or midwife) and there is often some kind of reference to the proverb-group represented by such sayings as 'Time brings the truth to light' and 'Truth is the daughter of Time' (Tilley T324, T580).

These metaphors are so familiar and natural to us that it is sometimes difficult to distinguish between what is literal and what is metaphorical. When Ulysses says to Nestor:

> I have a young conception in my brain;
> Be you my time to bring it to some shape
> 1.3.312-13

we immediately recognize the IDEAS ARE BABIES group, but the 'time is a midwife' component is more puzzling (even without the 'time is Nestor' complication) because one might argue that it is nearer to *literal* truth to say that time shapes conceptions than it is to say that midwives shape babies or foetuses.

There are several examples of this metaphor in the play, especially in 1.3, the Greek council scene which ends with Ulysses describing his 'young conception' to Nestor. The scene as a whole is concerned with planning and military strategy as the Greek leaders discuss why their previous policies have not brought them victory, how they can develop better ones and how they can put their policies into practice.

29

Agamemnon uses the IDEAS ARE BABIES metaphor to help explain why the Greeks have not taken Troy after seven years' siege:

> Sith every action that hath gone before,
> Whereof we have record, trial did draw
> Bias and thwart, not answering the aim
> And that unbodied figure of the thought
> That gav't surmised shape.
>
> 1.3.13-17

Strictly speaking there seems to be some conflict here between the metaphor from archery or bowls (military 'actions' are like projectiles which can go crooked or aside from the intended path) and that which sees the same actions as embryos which fail to achieve their proper 'shape', but the metaphors both provide a representation of the gap between the 'aim' or intention and the 'trial' or actual result. Agamemnon has indeed begun his speech with the rather vague notion that

> The ample proposition that hope makes
> In all designs begun on earth below
> Fails in the promis'd largeness.
>
> 1.3.3-5

If there is a specific metaphor underlying these words it must be that of a pregnancy which for some reason fails to fulfil the promise of its 'largeness'. Nestor picks up the same metaphor later in the scene when he is discussing with Ulysses the significance of the forthcoming single combat between Hector and a representative of the Greek forces:

> Our imputation shall be oddly pois'd
> In this vile action, for the success,
> Although particular, shall give a scantling
> Of good or bad unto the general,
> And in such indexes (although small pricks
> To their subsequent volumes) there is seen
> The baby figure of the giant mass
> Of things to come at large.
>
> 1.3.339-46

Here the notion of prediction is paramount: as the index of a book (if placed before the rest of the contents) predicts the whole volume, and as a 'baby figure' predicts a 'giant mass', so this single combat will predict (or be seen to predict) the outcome of the entire war.[13]

Once discovered or known, a baby or embryo can become vulnerable. There is a definite threat in Ulysses' statement to Achilles that

> The providence that's in a watchful state . . .
> Keeps place with thought and almost, like the gods,
> Do thoughts unveil in their dumb cradles.
> 3.3.196-200

He seems to mean that the state intelligence network not only knows what people are thinking but can 'unveil' (discover and destroy?) those thoughts even before they are uttered. This notion of a baby killed at birth has already occurred in two of our examples of personifications of Time, implicitly in the possible submerged reference to Chronos in 'devour'd/ As fast as they are made' (3.3.147-8) and more explicitly in Troilus' railing against a Time who

> forcibly prevents
> Our lock'd embrasures, strangles our dear vows
> Even in the birth of our own laboring breath.
> 4.4.36-8

In this second example the lovers' vows are 'babies' both because they are ideas or intentions and because they are recently undertaken and therefore 'young'. Yet Time, deviating shockingly from his role as midwife, strangles these babies at the very moment that their 'laboring' parents are giving birth to them.

As with the notion of handling or grasping, the ideas of birth and infancy are present in the play in a wider figurative and indeed literal sense. All the characters are 'infants' in comparison with Nestor who 'was a man/ When Hector's grandsire suck'd' (1.3.291-2) and 'whose wit was mouldy ere your grandsires had nails on their toes' (2.1.104-6). Troilus is particularly associated with infancy: he expresses his inexperience as a lover by saying he is 'skilless as unpractic'd infancy' (1.1.12) and he tells Cressida that

31

he is 'as true as truth's simplicity/ And simpler than the infancy of truth' (3.2.169-70), Calchas sees himself as newly born in the unfamiliar society of the Greeks (3.3.11-12) and Cressida herself jokes about the literal possiblity of pregnancy in 1.2 and 3.2. The play as a whole is concerned with questions of prediction and prophecy, anxieties about whether certain 'conceptions' will mature or not: Truth is the daughter of Time but what Time 'brings to light' for Troilus is that Cressida is as Ulysses puts it 'a daughter of the game' (4.5.63).[14]

Time as Space

In the implicitly temporal metaphors we have just been looking at, time enters into the figure as a medium of growth, that in which growing takes place. To spatialize time is, similarly, to think of time as that in which events take place, but with the 'that in which' now more firmly ontologized *as* place, as an area or a landscape. Recalling Lakoff and Johnson's discussion of the inconsistency that obtains between TIME PASSES US and TIME IS STATIONARY AND WE MOVE THROUGH IT, let us see what complications ensue when time is spatialized in *Troilus and Cressida,* given that an active, moving time is such an important element in the play's metaphorical repertoire.

The concept of 'passing' itself is more intricate than one might think. Literally, passing is a matter of change of spatial alignment, but time enters into the concept intrinsically in that the change, like any change, must take (place in) time. A and B can pass each other either by moving in opposite directions or by moving in the same direction; in the latter case passing can only take place if B overtakes A, by moving more quickly than A, i.e. by covering more space in less time. In passing A in this way, if A has been in competition with B for foremost place, B excels over A, *sur*passes A; this is passing as an event in a race. Thus the race as a metaphor of how human worth is validated involves a necessarily temporal spatialization, unlike the atemporal metaphor of worth as a pile or heap of goods.

Ulysses' strategy in his Time speech is to reintroduce temporality into Achilles' atemporal metaphors for his own worth.

So between Time the wallet-owner and Time the fashionable host we get two metaphors into which time enters implicitly but vitally. In the first, as we have already mentioned, the entity or mass of one's honour (like armour) is not immune from the ravages of time (rust). The second is the race metaphor. The paradox comes when Ulysses, having developed the race metaphor for eleven lines, boldly confronts an atemporal spatialization with the implications of what he has just said:

> Then what they do in present,
> Though less than yours in past, must o'ertop yours . . .
> 3.3.163-4

To which Achilles might reply, if he chose to stick to the metaphor of worth as a heap, 'How can the smaller pile ever exceed the larger pile? What has the past/present distinction to do with size of merit?' But what gives Ulysses' remark its persuasive force is the coherence, despite the inconsistency, between two MORE IS UP orientation metaphors (cf. Lakoff and Johnson, 14-17). 'O'ertop' expresses a relationship that larger piles literally bear to smaller piles. But it can also be used metaphorically to express the way in which the space covered in a given time by the winner of a race exceeds the space covered in the same time by the loser. Since the race is at least as good a metaphor for the measurement of worth as the pile is, the fact that 'o'ertop' can be used in both contexts allows Ulysses to conflate them. He has as it happens prepared for this by offering in the immediately preceding lines an image of a race—in its turn metaphorized as a battle—in which the victors do literally 'o'ertop' the loser:

> Or like a gallant horse fall'n in first rank,
> Lie there for pavement to the abject rear,
> O'errun and trampled on.[15]
> 3.3.161-3

This is an example of how time can enter into a spatial metaphor. To see time itself spatialized—though very straightforwardly—in a similar context, we can turn back to an early exchange between Pandarus and Cressida. Pandarus concludes his account of Troilus' witticism about the hairs on his own chin by saying

> But there was such laughing! and Helen so blush'd, and Paris so chaf'd, and all the rest so laugh'd, that it pass'd.
> 1.2.165-7

33

Cressida replies, 'So let it now, for it has been a great while going by'. 'Pass'd', though generally spoken on stage as a lame anticlimactic conclusion to Pandarus' story (as though he has lost confidence in it under Cressida's deflating scrutiny) is glossed by editors as 'outwent or surpassed description'. That is, Pandarus uses 'pass'd' as a superlative and one which has the competitive racing metaphor faintly underlying it (*OED* gives 'beats everything' as a colloquial equivalent to this usage, *v.*A.vii.19.). Cressida then retorts by spatializing time: the story has moved through time too slowly; it has passed by her (and us, the audience) too sluggishly. The witticism turns on reversing the direction of 'passing': for Pandarus, passing as excelling involves competitive same-direction motion; for Cressida, passing means we are stationary as the story passes us by (facing in the opposite direction to us) only slowly.

Even in the analysis of such an uncomplicated sentence as Cressida's retort, it is possible to feel confused about what is moving through what. Is time (the time of the story) passing Cressida by slowly, or is Cressida watching the story pass slowly through time? This sort of puzzle is bound to arise in an exacerbated form whenever time or a temporal concept is personified as acting in (spatial) time. We have already mentioned Nestor's walking hand in hand with Time. This graceful image becomes stranger once we consider—as we are probably not meant to do—the question of directionality. Walking is an activity which takes time: time must pass as Nestor and his companion walk. But how can the time that passes them or in which they move (time moving in the opposite direction to the walkers) be the same Time who moves in the same direction as Nestor?

Another case of paradoxical movement arises later in the same scene, as Hector turns from Nestor to Ulysses and recalls their previous meeting when the Greeks sent Ulysses and Diomedes as ambassadors to demand the return to Helen. Ulysses replies now to Hector:

> Sir, I foretold you then what would ensue.
> My prophecy is but half his journey yet,
> For yonder walls that pertly front your town,
> Yon towers, whose wanton tops do buss the clouds,
> Must kiss their own feet.

> 4.5.217-21

Broadly, Ulysses' meaning is obvious: he prophesied before the war commenced that (i) it would be long and bloody, and (ii) it would end in the destruction of Troy. Already (i) has come to pass, and (ii) is yet to follow. But how does this work out in detail once we personify the temporal term 'prophecy' and spatialize his movements? The 'journey' between the time of the embassy and the time of the fall of Troy can be thought of either in terms of the later time approaching Hector and Ulysses (TIME IS A MOVING OBJECT) or in terms of their approaching the later time (TIME IS STATIONARY AND WE MOVE THROUGH IT). But where is the *prophecy's* journey in all this? Is the prophecy moving with the characters towards a future time so that they are all now half-way there? This would be compatible with the fact that it is the time already experienced by Hector and Ulysses which confirms the prophecy so far, so the half-way that the prophecy has already come is the same half-way that the characters have come. On the other hand, the prophecy is a prophecy because it involves 'seeing' ahead (a notion which itself involves spatialized, stationary time) to the furthest-away time. So personified prophecy, having leapt ahead to that furthest time, can only be travelling *back,* at the same speed and in the same direction as moving-object time moves, that is, in the opposite direction to Hector and Ulysses. In the one reading, the prophecy's journey will be completed when all three of them (Hector, Ulysses and the prophecy), having travelled together through time, arrive at a fixed point in the future. In the other reading, the journey will be completed when the prophecy, returning as it were from that point in the future, collides with Hector and Ulysses travelling towards it.

Despite the paradoxes that can be teased out of both Nestor's walk with Time and the prophecy's journey through time in analysis, neither of these examples would be likely to confuse an audience. Perhaps we are all so accustomed to the inconsistency between the moving-time and stationary-time 'pictures' in everyday speech that accentuations of this inconsistency in more heightened language can pass virtually unnoticed. But earlier in this same scene Agamemnon, greeting Hector, develops the time-as-landscape spatial metaphor in a way which should give an alert audience more trouble:

> Worthy all arms! as welcome as to one
> That would be rid of such an enemy.

But that's no welcome. Understand more clear,
What's past and what's to come is strew'd with husks
And formless ruin of oblivion;
But in this extant moment, faith and troth,
Strain'd purely from all hollow bias-drawing,
Bids thee, with most divine integrity,
From heart of very heart, great Hector, welcome.
                                        4.5.163-71[16]

Hector's present welcome is being insisted upon despite whatever
has happened and whatever may be about to happen. The moment,
the here-and-now, is being contrasted with a landscape
surrounding it homogeneously on both sides, the landscape of past
and future. What is strange—and also somehow very
impressive—is the way in which the asymmetry between past and
future is ignored. In the other 'oblivion' passages we have already
looked at, time's effect on buildings and hence on memory (how
can that which is now formless be remembered?) has appeared in
Cressida's vow of fidelity, and oblivion's appetite (as implied here
by 'husks') has appeared in the devouring of the scraps from
Time's wallet. But while it is clear enough how the past could be
spatialized as a landscape strewn with the gnawed-at and the ruined,
it is much harder to see how 'what's to come', the future, can
already be similarly 'strewn'. One might say that the effect of
events receding into the past is that they become increasingly more
forgotten and unknown until finally they recede into oblivion and
are unknown totally; the future is unknown in a different way
because one cannot know what has not yet happened; so past and
future are both sites of the unknown in comparison to the present.
But the difference between these two unknowns is surely enough to
make the use of unknown-past vocabulary disconcerting when
transferred to unknown-future. Also, if this is the chief oddity of the
speech at close-reading level, there is a matching, symmetrical
oddity at the level of the pragmatics of the whole speech. What
Agamemnon is saying is, 'Although we can't tell what horrors lie
ahead in this war, still at this present moment we can behave well to
one another'. The forgotten past doesn't come into it; in fact, the
relevant past (of Helen's abduction and the long war) has notably
not been forgotten at all. Agamemnon has evoked past and future
as a single landscape, but has spoken of the future in terms
appropriate only for speaking of the past, while he should have

nothing to say (along these lines) about the past at all. Perhaps what he intends to say—and what we should understand him to say—about the past is that, at least for the moment, it *should* be forgotten, but this is not a meaning that can be construed from his actual words.[17]

Temporal Ironies

If Agamemnon's speech in greeting Hector nevertheless seems powerful, this is because the spatialized time it invokes corresponds rather well to a temporal experience other than that of Agamemnon in his own 'extant moment', namely that of Shakespeare and his audience. From the perspective of 1600 or 1987, it is perfectly true that what for the Greeks and Trojans of the play is past and what's to come is all homogeneously past, all laid out in the same 'landscape'—including, of course, the 'formless ruin' of Troy itself. The play's Prologue assumes this perspective: having set up the 'story so far', for 22 lines, the Prologue explains to his 'fair beholders'

> that our play
> Leaps o'er the vaunt and firstlings of those broils,
> Beginning in the middle; starting thence away
> To what may be digested in a play.
>
> Prologue, 26-9

The events of the Trojan War (including medieval accretions to the story) exist in a fixed order, laid out ('for all time') in a spatialized time in which we—or the play, athletically personified—can move about.[18]

This sort of time is available to the play's characters only in the reduced and uncertain forms of prophecy, calculation and promise. A true prophet like Cassandra can propose that the Trojans

> pay betimes
> A moi'ty of that mass of moan to come.[19]
>
> 2.2.106-7

But her temporal leap, being supernatural, is impotent: Troilus can dismiss her as mad. Calculators like Ulysses and Nestor can anticipate events and even anticipate how others will anticipate events, as in their anticipation that the outcome of the single combat between a Greek champion and Hector will be read as predicting the outcome of the whole war, like

> The baby figure of the giant mass
> Of things to come at large.
>
> 1.3.345-6

But their attempts to manipulate the 'mass' of the future fail miserably: the single combat is inconclusive, the selection of Ajax as a champion exacerbates the problem instead of solving it (Thersites comments that their 'policy . . . is not prov'd worth a blackberry . . . now is the cur Ajax prouder than the cur Achilles and will not arm to-day'; 5.4.9-15). and the reactivation of Achilles which is the goal of all their schemes is actually brought about by the unlooked-for death of Patroclus. As for those who commit themselves for the future by promises, let us return to the exchange of vows between Troilus and Cressida in 3.2.

We have already discussed Cressida's 'If I be false' speech (p.27 above). She makes it in response to Troilus' vision of a future in which 'As true as Troilus' will have become proverbial: 'Prophet may you be'! she exclaims. Troilus has shifted the issue, hyberbolically, from whether he will be true to whether he will be remembered for being true, whether his fidelity will be sufficiently outstanding to compel remembrance. This works as hyberbole only against a background sense of how much does get forgotten, of how powerful oblivion is. So apparently only for variation, Cressida in answering Troilus reverses the sign of the thing that is to be remembered: so great is her love that what could never be forgotten is the falsehood a betrayal would represent. The irony of this moment is elaborate. Not only are both characters (not to mention Pandarus who joins in with his own prediction) true prophets, but the vehicle for the 'memory' involved will be literature, as Troilus' speech suggests: he speaks of 'rhymes,/ Full of protest, of oath and big compare', of how 'As true as Troilus' will 'crown up the verse,/ And sanctify the numbers' and of how references to himself in this connection will have the full force of scholarly citation—'As truth's authentic author to be cited' (3.2.174-83). The truth of

Troilus, the falsehood of Cressida and the 'broker-between' role of Pandarus, thanks to writers like Chaucer and Henryson, did indeed become proverbial (even lexicalised) long after the stones of Troy had vanished.[20]

But there is a more local irony to Cressida's evocation of oblivion. Forgetting (for the lovers) or being forgotten (for Achilles) loom as dangers for the characters even within the play's own brief time, and at this very moment Cressida is herself, though far from finding herself at the end of time, about to forget. It seems appropriate then for the characters to spatialize time as a landscape of ruins and husks in a way that expresses their own finitude and their lack of mastery over that space. Moreover, instead of taking up a godlike position of omniscience and power in relation to his own narrative, Shakespeare himself seems anxious to remind us that his role too is finite, demiurgical at best. Another of 'Time's glories' according to Lucrece is 'To blot old books and alter their contents' (948): Shakespeare seems keenly aware both that it is wholly contingent that the Trojan War, unlike other temporally distant events, is not 'characterless' or blotted out, and that he is engaged in a revisionist 'alteration' of the Homeric and Chaucerian accounts. These considerations converge on a further dimension of the play's irony: perhaps it is better to be forgotten than to be remembered as Cressida and Achilles will now be.[21]

The Heightened and the Everyday

Having spent some time looking closely at *Troilus* time passages, let us step back and consider what Lakoff and Johnson have helped us to see in them.

What Lakoff and Johnson are saying is in some respects no different from what one can find in the Elizabethan rhetoricians. Here is Henry Peacham, in *The Garden of Eloquence* (1577):

> Necessity was the cause that Tropes were first invented, for when there wanted words to express the nature of diverse things, wise men, remembering that many things were very like one to another, thought it good to borrow the name of one thing to express another that did in something much resemble it . . .[22]

Peacham's 'wise men' are products of a fantasy about language origins; they are dummy human agents invoked to account for what we now see as the always-already-given social fact of language. Leaving them aside, Peacham's view is very Lakoff–Johnsonian, down to the delicacy of his 'in something' (non-complete equivalence) 'much' (inescapability of the likeness). Moving on to metaphor in particular, Peacham writes

> Metaphor [is] when a word is translated from the proper natural signification to another not proper but yet nigh and likely, and that either for necessity or else for pleasantness. This translation is taken from many places . . .[23]

Two of the 'places' he specifies are 'from the senses of the body', which is where Lakoff and Johnson ground their orientational metaphors (14-21), and 'from substantives', which seems to be his equivalent for Lakoff and Johnson's ontological metaphors.

Peacham's distinction between 'necessity' and 'pleasantness' can be interestingly aligned with the Lakoff and Johnson discussion of everyday and novel metaphor. Lakoff and Johnson see underlying conceptual metaphors as being realizable in three sorts of expressions. Taking the structural metaphor THEORIES ARE BUILDINGS as an example, we can realize this in the following ways:

1. A literal or virtually literal expression: 'We will show that theory to be without foundation' (46).
2. An expression extending the regularly used part of a metaphor: 'These facts are the bricks and mortar of my theory' (53). While the everyday metaphor sees theory-building as having outer shells, it 'stops short of mentioning the materials used'.
3. An expression activating unused parts of the metaphor: 'His theory has thousands of little rooms and long, winding corridors' (53). It is not part of the everyday THEORIES ARE BUILDINGS metaphor to specify how the interior of the building is laid out.

Expressions of varieties (2) and (3) 'fall outside the domain of normal literal language and are part of what is usually called "figurative" or "imaginative" language' (53). The other sort of expression that belongs in this category is:

4. An expression involving a 'novel metaphor, that is, a metaphor

not used to structure part of our normal conceptual system but as a new way of thinking about something, for example ''Classical theories are patriarchs who father many children, most of whom fight incessantly'' ' (53).

So (2), (3) and (4) can be classed as 'imaginative' language, *versus* (1) as relatively 'unimaginative'; while (1), (2) and (3) can be classed as 'everyday metaphor', less or more imaginative, *versus* (4) as 'novel metaphor'. Where then would Peacham's distinction between 'necessary' and 'pleasant' metaphors fall, in these terms? Novel metaphors can hardly be necessary (if they become so over time, they must cease being novel); 'unimaginative' language can hardly be 'pleasant' in Peacham's sense, because it slides past us unobserved. But expressions of varieties (2) and (3) participate both in 'necessity' (in their dependence on an underlying everyday metaphor) and in 'pleasantness' (because of their visibility, their relative if not absolute novelty). One of our favourite Lakoff and Johnson examples is 'Complex theories usually have problems with the plumbing' (53); it seems to us no less 'pleasant' than the 'theories-as-patriarchs' example, even though an everyday rather than a novel conceptual metaphor underlies it.

In the *Troilus* time metaphors we have looked at, we have been able to see the elaborate Shakespearean text as elaborat*ing* everyday conceptual metaphors for time, ontologizations and spatializations which, for whatever reasons, seem to be imposed on us by our habitual conceptual scheme whenever we try to talk about time. The *Troilus* time metaphors are not (4)-type novelties; they are (2)-or (3)-type extensions of the ordinarily used parts of an everyday conceptual metaphor or developments of its normally unused parts.

How does examining the *Troilus* time metaphors in this way differ from other close-reading approaches to the same material? We, like other scholars, have been looking for non-obvious connections among some passages in the play. But we have not emerged with a 'thematic' reading of the play in terms of the interconnectedness of our chosen passages. That is, we have not ascribed to Shakespeare a set of Ideas About Time, either novel or supremely-rendered-commonplace ('What oft was thought but ne'er so well expressed'), which, because he is writing drama and not an essay or a long poem, he has had to distribute amongst his characters, but which are gatherable-together as *his*. Rather, the connections we have found are rooted in the fact that various elaborations are elaborations *of* the same, or related, or complementary, everyday underlying conceptual time metaphors. We have also been able to avoid ascribing to the characters any particular, idiosyncratic views about time; Shakespearean characters are almost never characterized in terms of their unusual thoughts (unlike some of Jonson's 'humours' characters), and if a link can be found between Ulysses' and Troilus' time-personifications, it can hardly be because their characters are similar. Where they are alike is in their equal access to (i) the everyday time ontologizations and spatializations; (ii) procedures for elaborating these 'pleasantly' (strikingly, demandingly) in a way which can be integrated with their broader existences as agents engaged in such activities as persuading (Ulysses) and apologizing/promising (Troilus).

This is not to say that common patterns of elaboration which are ascribable not to the language but to Shakespeare cannot legitimately be identified. The Time–Oblivion complex, identifiable across works but not, so far as we know, an Elizabethan commonplace, is probably an example of a trick of Shakespearean thought. But it is as if the characters, again so diverse, who draw upon this complex do so as upon a generally-shared resource. Or, to attempt to express this in terms which recognize that the characters are constructions: Shakespeare elaborates, as characters' speech, everyday time metaphors; the everydayness of the underlying metaphors contributes to the text's cohesion; a certain authorial style in the elaboration also contributes to the text's cohesion; but these cohesions do not undermine the characters' individualities (do not turn the play into a long poem) because, in real life, our own individualities are not felt to be inconsistent with our sharing common conceptual schemes and common conceptual metaphors.

If, in this perspective, Shakespeare recedes as someone who is expressing his own thoughts about time through the mouths of his puppet characters, he undoubtedly returns in two capacities. First, the integrated organization of large-scale time ironies, literal time specifications and time metaphors emerges as impressively authorial. Of course, the medium in which this integration is achieved is in part itself that of everyday time metaphor. Irony, for instance, is achieved by Shakespeare lending characters his (and our) everyday-metaphorical time orientation, despite its difference from the orientation which they should naturalistically have. But also there is an integration between time metaphors and literal-time references which parallels the integration between the metaphorical hands of Time and the literal handlings and graspings so prominent in the play. Something which is part of the most basic, 'what happened' narrative level of the play is put into relationship with the elaborated, heightened language of the characters; the relationship may be ambiguous, but it does serve to link fact with talk. Second, it is remarkable how difficult, when closely examined, the language is. A drive towards difficulty must be ascribed to the authorial Shakespeare. What may have given him the confidence to pose such difficulty—such elaboration in the 'pleasantness' direction as to risk audience displeasure—was a sense of the groundedness of the elaborations in Lakoff-and-Johnson everyday metaphor. In the theatre, the audience hears something it can translate into the already-known, into what these characters might say, even if what they actually say is heightened to the point of paradox.

Notes

1. 1.1 and 1.2 take place on the same day: Pandarus tells Troilus in 1.1 that he saw Cressida 'yesternight' and he reminds Cressida herself in 1.2 of the 'thing' he told her 'yesterday'. Moreover, Aeneas reports in 1.1 that Paris is 'returned home and hurt' in today's fighting, but we see him return with the other warriors in 1.2 and Pandarus comments. 'Who said he came hurt home to-day? He's not hurt'; thus confirming the time scheme while contradicting Aeneas. But is this day the same as that specified in 1.3 and 3.1, the first day of the three-day sequence? It could be as far as Troilus and Cressida are concerned, but discrepancies arise over references to the warriors: Paris says he has not been fighting in 3.1: 'I would fain have arm'd to-day, but my Nell would not have it so'. And Hector is reportedly complaining of inaction in 1.3 although we have seen him return from the field in 1.2 and have also been told that Ajax 'cop'd' him in the battle 'yesterday'. These discrepancies are, as we shall argue, part of a wider pattern of contradictions about the war and whether or not there is a truce going on, so perhaps we should ignore them. Alternatively we could choose to assume that there is an unspecified but presumably short gap in time between 1.2 and 1.3. For further analyses of the time-scheme of *Troilus and Cressida,* see P.A. Daniel, 'Time Analysis of the Plots of Shakespeare's Plays', *New Shakespeare Society Transactions* 1877-9, 177-346 (for *Troilus,* 180-3) and Zdeněk Stříbrný, 'Time in *Troilus and Cressida',* *Shakespeare Jahrbuch* 112 (Weimar, 1976), 105-21.

2. The close integration of the two plots is argued succinctly by Richard Levin, *The Multiple Plot in English Renaissance Drama* (University of Chicago Press, Chicago, 1971), pp.160-8. Night-to-dawn sequences, though not the ones in *Troilus,* are discussed by Emrys Jones, 'The Sense of Occasion: Some Shakespearean Night Sequences', in Kenneth Muir, Jay L. Halio and D.J. Palmer (eds.), *Shakespeare, Man of the Theater* (Associated University Presses, London and Toronto, 1983), pp.98-104.

3. This sense of temporal precision and density can be found in other plays in which the plot centres on a night-time erotic encounter such as *Romeo and Juliet* and *Measure for Measure.* John Bayley however has argued that the sense of time in *Troilus* is unique in the canon in so far as events take place only in 'play time' without any sense of a more extended 'novel time'; see *The Uses of Division* (Chatto and Windus, London, 1976), pp.185-210. For a general discussion of attitudes to time in this period, see Ricardo J. Quinones, *The Renaissance Discovery of Time* (Harvard University Press, Cambridge, Mass., 1972). He discusses Shakespeare at some length (pp.290-443) and has a short section on *Troilus* (pp.372-9).

4. University of Chicago Press, Chicago and London, 1980. For a usefully critical review from an anthropological perspective, see Brenda Beck, 'Root Metaphor Patterns', *Récherches Sémiotiques/Semiotic Inquiry* 2 (1982), 86-97. One of us (J.O.T.) has reviewed the book in *Prose Studies* 6 (1983), 184-7.

5. M.P. Tilley, *A Dictionary of the Proverbs in England in the Sixteenth and Seventeenth Centuries* (University of Michigan Press, Ann Arbor, Michigan, 1950). (References are to numbered proverbs.) On the question of visual representations, see Chapter 3 on 'Father Time', in Erwin Panofsky, *Studies in Iconology* (Oxford University Press, New York, 1939), pp.69-93.

6. *Troilus and Cressida* was first published in a Quarto text in 1609 and then in the First Folio in 1623; significant differences between these two texts will be noted where relevant. Neither the early texts nor the Riverside have a consistent policy of giving Time a capital 'T' when personification is clearly intended.

7. Nestor's extreme old age is frequently stressed, e.g. at 1.3.291-301, 2.1.104-7, 2.3.250-6 and 4.5.24 as well as in the present passage.

8. But in Spenser's *Faerie Queene,* 6.8.23-4, Mirabella is depicted with a wallet at her back in which she puts 'repentance for things past and gone' though the wallet is torn and her repentance 'falls out anon'.

9. See, for example, Caroline Spurgeon, *Shakespeare's Imagery* (Cambridge University Press, Cambridge, 1935), pp.320-4; R.J. Kauffman, 'Ceremonies for Chaos: the Status of *Troilus and Cressida'*, *English Literary History,* 32 (1965), 139-57; Ralph Berry, *The Shakespearean Metaphor* (Macmillan, London, 1978), pp.74-87; and Kenneth Muir's edition of the play (Clarendon Press, Oxford, 1982), pp.29-31.

10. This is clearly the meaning of 'monster of ingratitude' in Jonson's *Every Man in His Humour,* 3.3.57, since in revising the play he altered it from 'an ingratitude wretch'.

11. See, for example, *Lear* 1.4.259 and 281-9, 1.5.40 and *As You Like It* 2.7.174-90. Murray Abend finds ten instances of the monster-ingratitude

association in ' "Ingratitude" and the "Monster" Image', *Notes and Queries* 194 (1949), 535-6.

12. Similar use is made of an organic metaphor in *Julius Caesar* 2.1.32-4 where Brutus persuades himself that it is right to kill Caesar partly by employing the metaphor of Caesar as a 'serpent's egg'.

13. Kenneth Muir notes in the Oxford *Troilus and Cressida*, p. 82 that 'prick' (line 343) can mean 'penis' and he takes this innuendo as the starting point of the 'baby' figure. We shall discuss the 'index' metaphor again in Chapter 5 below; see pp.166.

14. Ralph Berry discusses the connections between Time the consumer and Time the revealer of truth in his chapter on *Troilus* in *The Shakespearean Metaphor*. On metaphors of conception and birth, see also Jay L. Halio, 'The Metaphor of Conception and Elizabethan Theories of the Imagination', *Neophilologus* 50 (1966), 454-61; and Elizabeth Sacks, *Shakespeare's Images of Pregnancy* (Macmillan, London, 1980). See also our further discussion of these metaphors in Chapter 5 below (pp.177-201 and n. 37, p.206).

15. Hugh Maclean finds associations between time and horses or horsemanship in *Richard II, Richard III* and *Henry IV:* 'Time and Horsemanship in Shakespeare's Histories', *University of Toronto Quarterly* 35 (1965-66), 229-45.

16. Lines 165-70 are found in the 1623 Folio text only and not in the 1609 Quarto which has many similar omissions. It is possible that some of the strangeness here is attributable to Shakespeare's characterization of Agamemnon whose language in 1.3 is equally tortuous and difficult.

17. A valuable study of Agamemnon's language in relation to Renaissance notions of rhetoric and decorum is to be found in T. McAlindon, 'Language, Style and Meaning in *Troilus and Cressida*', *PMLA* 84 (1969), 29-43.

18. This sort of time is clearly a version of one of the 'two fundamentally different ways in which we conceive of and talk about time' (Richard M. Gale, *The Language of Time* (Routledge and Kegan Paul, London, 1968), p.7: not time viewed as 'the very quintessence of flux and transiency . . . [with] events . . . represented as being past, present and future, and as continually changing in respect to these tensed determinations', but rather 'the static or tenseless way of conceiving time, in which the totality of history is viewed in a God-like manner, all events being given at once in a *nunc stans*'. Gale remarks of this latter time, 'Here is no gnawing tooth of time—no temporal becoming—but only a democratic equality of all times'. This is true from the position of God, or the demiurgical position of the dramatist, as the Prologue expresses it, but we shall see that Shakespeare is more interested when spatializing time in imagining a space strewn with objects which time and oblivion *have* gnawed.

Perhaps this is a good place to signal that the recent philosophical literature on time, written by people trying to purify time discourse of the metaphoricity so basic to it, might be interesting to explore with the more paradoxical of Shakespearean Time-acting-in-time passages in mind. We have not done so systematically, but for a robust expression of the view that 'the passage of time or pure becoming is an illusion', and an attempt to 'give a plausible diagnosis of the cause of the illusion', see J.J.C. Smart, 'Time and Becoming' in Peter van Inwagen (ed.), *Time and Cause* (Reidel, Dordrecht, 1980); for a book-length argument to similar effect with a fullish bibliography, see D.H. Mellor, *Real Time* (Cambridge University Press, Cambridge, 1981); for the view that 'the pure becoming of the world and of time is no myth or illusion, however obscure it may be to our reason', see Richard Taylor, *Metaphysics* (Prentice-Hall, Englewood Cliffs, New Jersey, 1963), Chapter 6; 2nd edn, Chapter 8, to which Smart is replying; and for a challenging attempt to push the space–time analogy further than usual, see Richard Taylor, 'Moving about in Time', *Philosophical Quarterly* 9 (1959), 289-301.

19. This is, as it happens, an example of the TIME IS MONEY structural metaphor which also underlies Priam's opening speech in this scene (2.2.1-7) but is not otherwise of very great importance in the play except in the indirect sense that Time 'devalues' human achievements. On Cassandra's language, see Richard D. Fly, 'Cassandra and the Language of Prophecy in *Troilus and Cressida*', *Shakespeare Quarterly* 26 (1975), 157-71.

20. For a discussion of Shakespeare's use of Chaucer and Henryson, see Ann Thompson, *Shakespeare's Chaucer* (Liverpool University Press, Liverpool, 1978); and E. Talbot Donaldson, *The Swan at the Well: Shakespeare Reading Chaucer* (Yale University Press, New Haven and London, 1985).

21. A similar irony can be noted in Shakespeare's sonnets to the young man promising him immortality: it is notorious that his name has in fact been forgotten but in any case he is being immortalized as a person of appalling selfishness and superficiality.

22. Scolar Press Facsimile, Menston, Yorkshire, 1971, Blv.

23. Ibid., B2r-B2v.

2

Animal Metaphors in *King Lear*

King Lear's Animal Kingdom

Animals feature prominently on many levels in *King Lear*. Man himself[1] is seen as an animal existing both literally and metaphorically in a series of relationships with other creatures. Some of his contacts with them are, for a Jacobean audience, quite mundane: he eats animals and uses their skins for clothing; he uses horses and asses for purposes of transportation; he keeps dogs and cage-birds as pets; he is troubled by vermin; he entertains himself with sports like hunting and bear-baiting. Even on this mundane or literal level there are social or cultural layers of signification going beyond the functional; a man who can send for his horses is likely to be a man with more wealth and status than one who is troubled with lice, and a man who professes to eat no fish is likely to be making a statement about his religious allegiance rather than his dietary preference.

Moreover, when men think and talk about animals, or, perhaps more importantly, when they refer to animals in the course of thinking and talking about something else, they have at their disposal a whole range of meanings and associations over and above literal ones. Some of these meanings and associations are still available to us as they were to audiences and readers in the seventeenth century, but some of them have become obsolete. Despite the accumulation of knowledge in the natural sciences, we are like our Jacobean ancestors in so far as we still base many of our assumptions about animals not on scientific observation or on individual experience but rather on a set of inherited commonplaces which tend to privilege and isolate certain traits

47

regardless of objective fact. In our common talk we still assume, for example, that lions are brave, wolves are vicious and asses are stupid, but on the other hand we need an editor or commentator to explain to us the now unfamiliar connotations of the civet cat or the pelican.[2]

Commonplace assumptions about animals are rife in *King Lear:* tigers are cruel, goats, wrens and flies are lecherous, wagtails are frivolous. Edgar, when he is pretending to be mad Tom, describes himself as a 'hog in sloth, fox in stealth, wolf in greediness, dog in madness, lion in prey' (3.4.93-4). Then as now the most important thing about these attributes is that they are essentially human ones, illustrating our tendency to anthropomorphize the rest of creation. We select or even invent a trait or habit in an animal which interests us because we can interpret it in human terms and then reapply it to our own kind. Having made the commonplace assumption that lions are brave or that asses are stupid, we can praise a man by calling him lion-hearted or insult him by calling him an ass; the objective truth about the animals in question hardly comes into it. Similarly, we can select a single feature of an animal's existence, or life-cycle, such as the fact that the snail has a 'house' consisting of its shell or that the cuckoo lays its eggs in other birds' nests, and exploit the coincidental parallels with human experience. Many of these commonplaces about animals become codified into proverbial form.

Men are even prepared to extend this kind of anthropomorphism to the animal patterns they find in, or impose upon, the stars. Edmund in *King Lear* derides his father's belief in astrological influences:

> An admirable evasion of whoremaster man, to lay his goatish disposition on the charge of a star! My father compounded with my mother under the Dragon's tail, and my nativity was under Ursa Major, so that it follows, I am rough and lecherous.

> 1.2.126-31

It appears that we 'read' the formations of the stars as animals in order to be able to explain their supposed influence on us in terms of the already-given commonplace traits of those animals: a curiously convoluted extension of this kind of anthropomorphism which is still going strong in twentieth-century popular astrology.

It is worth noting at this preliminary stage that the commonplace traits associated with animals are not necessarily present in all contexts, nor are they necessarily consistent with each other. Take, for example, two 'worm' references in *King Lear:* in 3.4. Lear celebrates the 'unaccommodated' nakedness of the disguised Edgar:

> Thou ow'st the worm no silk, the beast no hide, the sheep no wool, the cat no perfume.
>
> 3.4.103-5

Soon afterwards, Gloucester recalls seeing the same character:

> I' th' last night's storm I such a fellow saw,
> Which made me think a man a worm.
> 4.1.32-3

In the first quotation the worm (specifically, we assume, the silkworm) has neutral or benign associations as one of the animals which provide man with clothing, whereas in the second it is assumed to be despicable or at least insignificant and pathetic—Gloucester moves quickly to the more famous analogy:

> As flies to wanton boys are we to th' gods,
> They kill us for their sport.
> 4.1.36-7

Similarly dogs, which we shall discuss at greater length below, can be associated with fawning and flattery in one instance but with truth and loyalty in another.

King Lear uses a broad range of literal and commonplace statements and assumptions about animals as a sort of base from which it can move into more heightened metaphorical language when it needs to, rather as *Troilus and Cressida* moves from an unusually dense base of literal time references into elaborate time metaphors. As many literary critics have noted, *King Lear* is particularly concerned to locate man in the hierarchy of nature and to explore what we mean when we call human behaviour '(un-) natural' or '(un-)kind'.[3] In a sense all this takes off from the grim pun whereby Edmund is the 'natural' son of Gloucester. Man is traditionally seen as being below god (or the gods) but above the animals and, in a different way, above the devils. In this play however, man's behaviour is seen as 'worse that brutish' (1.2.77) on many occasions while the beasts themselves seem to behave more sensibly and kindly than the humans. Characters frequently insult each other by direct comparisons with animals (mongrel, ass, tiger and so on), only to take themselves up and restate the insult in the form 'Even a bear/wolf/dog would not behave like you'. Humans are seen to be in danger of degenerating into beasts or worse—into fiends or monsters whose attributes and behaviour, being totally the products of human fantasy, are more appropriately and meaningfully depraved.

Kittay and Lehrer: Semantic Field Theory

In their article, 'Semantic Fields and the Structure of Metaphor', Eva Kittay and Adrienne Lehrer claim 'that in metaphor the lexical items from one semantic field are transferred to another semantic field and that the structure of semantic relations of the first field . . . provides the structure or reorganizes some previous structure of the second field' (32).[4] This is not far from such formulations as Martin and Harré's 'Metaphor is a figure of speech in which one entity or state of affairs is spoken of in terms which are seen as being appropriate to another'.[5] But what semantic field theory promises is a method of specifying how this 'speaking-of-in-terms-of' works in detail.

What is a semantic field? The expression itself is spatially metaphorical; one is to imagine 'around' each word an organized space in which other words related to it are laid out. While a word can be related to its 'neighbours' in a great number of ways, two chief varieties of relation can be distinguished. Paradigmatic relations exist among a set of words which are *like or unlike* one another in meaning in certain regular ways:

> The commonest kinds of paradigmatic relationships are synonymy (*big, large*), antonymy (*hot, cold*), hyponymy (*robin, bird*), converseness (*buy, sell*), part-whole relations (*finger, hand*) and incompatibility (*red, blue, green, yellow*, etc). (33)

50

Syntagmatic relations exist among a set of words which *go together* because they all pertain to what Lakoff and Johnson call 'experiential gestalts',[6] regularly recurring and consistently structured experiences, activities or events. Here,

> the relations are all relations which the nominal, adjectival, and adverbial phrases bear to the verb which dominates the field. Thus in the field of fishing, *the fisherman* is the *AGENT, the fish* is the *PATIENT, in the water* is the *LOCATIVE,* and *with rod and line* is the *INSTRUMENT.* Some other syntagmatic relations are the *SOURCE,* the *GOAL,* the *RESULT* and the *CAUSE.* (33)

So there is a paradigmatic semantic field of animals (relationship: incompatibility) which consists of *horse, dog, cat, sparrow, elephant,* and so forth; and there is a syntagmatic semantic field of terms to do with, say, horsemanship, including items like *horse, rider, bridle, hay, neigh,* and so forth.

Kittay and Lehrer demonstrate how metaphorical transfer works by analysing four examples: Wordsworth's sonnet 'On the Extinction of the Venetian Republic' (in Lakoff–Johnsonian terms, VENICE IS A NOBLEWOMAN); Donne's 'The Bait' (COURTSHIP IS FISHING); a passage from Plato's *Theaetetus* (THE PHILOSOPHER IS A MIDWIFE); and Shelley's 'Song to the Men of England' (WORKING MEN ARE BEES). The first three of these are described in approving detail, while the Shelley example is presented as 'what we take to be an unsuccessful metaphor' (57). Although we find this evaluation problematic, we would like to salute Kittay and Lehrer for putting it forward so vigorously and cogently; it is the sort of useful evaluative claim that focusses attention on just how the words do work.

The most elaborate transfers occur in the Donne and Plato examples, both of which Kittay and Lehrer characterize as fundamentally syntagmatic field movements. A *donor* syntagmatic field is used to restructure a *recipient* syntagmatic field; that is, the interconnections among the fishing vocabulary are transferred to courtship talk, and the interconnections among the midwife vocabulary are transferred to the description of how Socrates 'brings forth' thought from his interlocutors.[7] The method corresponds closely (though more formal linguistic detail, within a Fillmore case grammar framework,[8] is provided) to Lakoff and

Johnson's detailed discussion of how ARGUMENT IS WAR works. There, a rough breakdown of 'war' is provided (into participants, parts, stages, linear sequence, causation and purpose), and the effects of transferring all this to 'argument' are assessed (80-82). Kittay and Lehrer are dealing with specific literary texts, so it is a matter of breaking down 'fishing' and 'midwifery' into semantic roles and then demonstrating how these roles are taken up in the text under discussion. Thus 'fishing' involves certain activities, carried on in a certain manner, by certain agents, at the expense of certain 'patients' (the fish), by means of certain intruments, in certain locations. The vocabulary of the Donne poem can be divided up according to these categories. 'Midwifery' has, as a syntagmatic field, 'an embedded sentential structure'; that is, around one verb—agent—result triad, whereby *mother creates child,* another verb—agent—result triad is wrapped, whereby *midwife aids (mother—creates—child).* The conceptual intricacy of this enables Socrates/Plato to 'present an important alternative view to the traditional understanding of teaching' (56), where the standard view would involve a verb—agent—patient triad (teacher teaches student) which puts the student in the passive 'patient' position.

The midwifery metaphor gets top marks for 'cognitive interest' from Kittay and Lehrer because there remains a 'sustained difference' between the fields of education and childbirth—they speculate that 'if our understanding of the act of teaching ever approaches the one envisioned by Socrates, the metaphor will begin to lose [its] vitality' (56)—while the effect of thinking about the recipient field in terms of the donor field, going indeed beyond the analogies actually made explicit in the *Theaetetus* text, is consistently illuminating. The Donne example is also admired, but as, in at least one crucial respect, 'non—serious'. It turns out—for reasons which the detailed analysis spells out very satisfyingly—that the line 'For thou thyself art thine own bait' involves a contradiction. For our purposes, what is interesting is not the nature of the contradiction but the argument which Kittay and Lehrer come up with for not worrying about it:

what Donne has done is to create a metaphor which on the surface seems plausible, but which in fact is impossible to explicate in terms of the relations which are set up and transferred. If 'The Bait' was a serious love poem, this might be a problem. But in fact this is not a serious love poem; it is a parody and it mocks the view of courtship presented by traditional love poetry. (47-8)

Admittedly, 'might be' is not 'would be', but the thrust of the evaluation is towards a positive view of transfers which 'work out' in detail, *unless* some further generic consideration (here, the status of the text as parody) can be brought to bear on the question. There is an interesting footnote appended to 'problem' in the passage we have just quoted:

> There are, of course, many metaphors which can only be explicated in very limited ways. Of an extended metaphor such as the one in this poem, a poem written by as intellectual a poet as Donne, we can expect that the metaphor is explicable in terms of the new relations it sets up in the recipient field. (62, n. 15)

Again, while this acknowledges that in-explicable transfers exist, it would seem that the role of the 'intellectual' poet, of the cognitively-alert writer, will be to come up with something more satisfactory, or at least to be so thoroughly aware of where the contradiction in a metaphorical implication lies as to turn it into a calculated, sharable, joke.

When they turn to Shelley's 'Song to the Men of England', Kittay and Lehrer find no comparable excuse for their author. The bee stanzas are II and III:

> Wherefore feed, and clothe, and save,
> From the cradle to the grave,
> Those ungrateful drones who would
> Drain your sweat—nay, drink your blood?
>
> Wherefore, Bees of England, forge
> Many a weapon, chain, and scourge,
> That these stingless drones may spoil
> The forced produce of your toil?

Kittay and Lehrer object to this for several reasons. First, 'Shelley chooses to ignore the queen bee, certainly an important element in bee society' (58); the queen bee works unceasingly for the hive, but is aristocratic, thus presenting a paradox for Shelley's 'two class society'. (They note that someone proposing an anti-bourgeois alliance between monarch and workers—they instance the nineteenth–century German social democrat Ferdinand Lassalle in his later years—could make better use of the bee metaphor in this respect). Secondly, and fundamentally, the very notions of the drones exploiting the bees and of the bees forging weapons for the drones come not from bee-lore but from human concerns:

> Shelley's metaphor, then, lacks interest because the expressions from the donor field (bees) are simply added on to the content of the recipient field; it does not structure the content. On the contrary, the recipient field lends structure to the donor field—the field whose structure is presumably being used to enlighten us about the recipient field. This gives the metaphor its banal and contrived quality. Although all metaphors have the dual structure of donor and recipient fields, not all metaphors have much cognitive interest. The degree to which a metaphor is enlightening depends rather on how much of the donor field is going to be productive of new meaning and new insights in the recipient field.

We want to test this argument against the animal metaphors in *King Lear.* How much do the animals donate? And if we find that the answer is 'not much', does a semantic field analysis of these metaphors confirm that they are thereby without much cognitive interest?

'They flatter'd me like a dog'

Since Caroline Spurgeon discussed the issue in *Shakespeare's Imagery and What It Tells Us,*[9] it has usually been assumed that Shakespeare's attitude towards dogs was consistently negative. She pointed out that when the notion of false friends or flatterers occurs to him he frequently develops it through a 'cluster' of images involving a dog or spaniel, fawning or licking, candy or sweets of some sort, and thawing or melting. This cluster occurs briefly in *1 Henry IV* when Hotspur recalls the attitude of Bolingbroke before he became king:

> Why, what a candy deal of courtesy
> This fawning greyhound then did proffer me!
> *1 Henry IV,* 1.3.251-2

It is developed at greater length in *Julius Caesar* when Caesar rejects the suppliant Metellus Cimber:

> Be not fond
> To think that Caesar bears such rebel blood
> That will be thaw'd from the true quality
> With that which melteth fools—I mean sweet words,
> Low-crooked curtsies, and base spaniel fawning.
> Thy brother by decree is banished;
> If thou dost bend, and pray, and fawn for him,
> I spurn thee like a cur out of my way.
> *Julius Caesar,* 3.1.39 46

It comes up again when Hamlet denies he is flattering Horatio:

> Why should the poor be flatter'd?
> No, let the candied tongue lick absurd pomp,
> And crook the pregnant hinges of the knee
> Where thrift may follow fawning.
> *Hamlet,* 3.2.59-62

And in Antony's reaction to the supposed betrayal of Cleopatra:

> The hearts
> That [spannell'd] [10] me at heels, to whom I gave
> Their wishes, do discandy, melt their sweets
> On blossoming Caesar.
> *Antony and Cleopatra,* 4.12.20-3

There seems no denying the consistency of this pattern of associations, which Spurgeon attributes to Shakespeare's empirical experience of pet dogs:

> It was the habit in Elizabethan times to have dogs, which were chiefly of the spaniel and greyhound type, at table, licking the hands of the guests, fawning and begging for sweetmeats with which they were fed, and of which, if they were like dogs today, they ate too many, dropping them in a semi-melting condition all over the place. Shakespeare, who was unusually fastidious, hated the habit, as he disliked all dirt and messiness, especially connected with food. (197)

This would give us a Shakespeare who does indeed generate

metaphors according to Kittay and Lehrer's semantic field theory: he takes a number of features from the syntagmatic donor field (spoilt pet dogs) and transfers them in order to produce new insights in the syntagmatic recipient field (false friends).[11] Spurgeon ignores the extent to which the association of dogs with fawning and flattery was a commonplace one[12] rather than a result of Shakespeare's unusual fastidiousness (as indeed Kittay and Lehrer ignore the conventional nature of Shelley's bees-for-human-society metaphor). And she gives a misleadingly exaggerated notion of Shakespeare's consistency by her method of selecting compatible references across a number of plays.

Realising that for a nation of dog-lovers Shakespeare's very patriotism might be in question, William Empson came to his defence ('It is a popular but tactfully suppressed grievance that Shakespeare did not love dogs as he should . . .'), arguing that in *Timon of Athens* at least Shakespeare's attitude towards dogs is equivocal, even contradictory.[13] Certainly Timon's flattering courtiers are frequently seen as 'dogs' in an uncomplimentary sense, but, especially in relation to Apemantus, dogs are also associated with honest criticism and loyalty (as well as cynicism).

A similar ambivalence, or at least inconsistency, could be claimed for *King Lear* which has a large number of 'dog' references which are clearly not derived from a single internally consistent donor field. On the simplest level of reference, 'dog' and its synonyms ('cur', 'mongrel') can be used as straight insults, as frequently happens in relation to Oswald. Lear begins this pattern in 1.4 where he describes Oswald as 'that mongrel' (1.4.49), and later addresses him as 'You whoreson dog, you slave, you cur!' (1.4.81). Kent takes up the same theme in 2.2. when he calls Oswald 'the son and heir of a mongrel bitch . . . whom I will beat into clamorous whining' (2.2.22-3). The commonplace assumptions behind these insults seem to be that dogs belong to an inferior (and perhaps 'illegitimate') species and that they are cowardly. (We shall return to the structure of insults below. At this point we could characterize animal insults as involving a paradigmatic choice in which a non-human lexical item is applied to a human being—a 'lowering' move in itself—on the basis of highly conventionalized 'associated commonplaces' which, when transferred to the recipient, have a further degrading effect.)

Kent makes the additional point that Oswald is dog-like in his blind (and immoral) obedience to his masters in the extraordinarily animal-rich outburst he makes against Oswald and others like him in 2.2:

> Such smiling rogues as these,
> Like rats, oft bite the holy cords a-twain
> Which are t'intrinse t'unloose; smooth every passion
> That in the natures of their lords rebel,
> Being oil to fire, snow to the colder moods;
> Renege, affirm, and turn their halcyon beaks
> With every gale and vary of their masters,
> Knowing nought (like dogs) but following.
> A plague upon your epileptic visage!
> Smile you my speeches, as I were a fool?
> Goose, and I had you upon Sarum plain,
> I'ld drive ye cackling home to Camelot.
>
> 2.2.73-84

The same criticism of dogs for copying the attitudes of their masters regardless of the merits of the case is made when Edgar describes his 'madman's rags' as 'a semblance/ That very dogs disdain'd' (5.3.188-9) and in Lear's pitiful comment that

> The little dogs and all,
> Trey, Blanch, and Sweetheart, see, they bark at me.
>
> 3.6.62-3

And Regan expresses surprise and anger that a servant has forgotten both his inferiority and his obedience to the point of opposing his master when she says 'How now, you dog?' to the man who tries to stop Cornwall from blinding Gloucester (3.7.75).

But in this last example we can see a hint of the play's characteristic ambivalence about its animal insults as we observe that a 'dog' is behaving more admirably than his master. This sense of the 'unnatural' reversal of the human and the animal is present on many occasions in the play, as in Kent's remark to Regan, 'If I were your father's dog,/ You should not use me so' (2.2.136-7) and in Cordelia's comment on her sisters' cruelty in driving Lear out into the storm:

> Mine enemy's dog,
> Though he had bit me, should have stood that night
> Against my fire.
>
> 4.7.35-7

In these examples, the unnatural behaviour of the humans is emphasized by the notion that 'even a dog' deserves better treatment. But when Goneril makes the same point to Albany in her sarcastic comment on his failure to greet her—'I have been worth the whistling'—she is rebuked for the presumption of the comparison:

> O Goneril,
> You are not worth the dust which the rude wind
> Blows in your face.

> 4.2.29-31

This reversal of human and animal roles is taken up by Lear in his moralizing talk with Gloucester in 4.6:

> Thou hast seen a farmer's dog bark at a beggar? . . . And the creature run from the cur? There thou mightst behold the great image of authority: a dog's obey'd in office.

> 4.6.155-9

If we concentrate too much on the donor field in this instance we get an inappropriately positive meaning—the dog is after all being a good watchdog—whereas in fact the recipient field is the important one, giving us the absurdity of the reversal in which a man obeys a dog.

In the light of these reversals, Lear's remark earlier in this scene, 'They flatter'd me like a dog' (4.6.96-7) has a teasing ambiguity. Do we paraphrase it 'They flattered me like a dog flatters his master', or might it be 'They flattered me as if I were a dog' (i.e. the kind of dog that is obeyed in office)? The first reading is supported by Spurgeon's image-cluster analysis and by the proverbial reputation of dogs for flattery, while in the second reading Lear would be identifying himself with the dog as the innocent victim imposed upon by the wickedness of others (with a glance at the equally proverbial 'to use one like a dog', Tilley D514). It seems to us that the second reading is arguably closer to the main impulse behind this speech though the first reading is more popular.

The play's most positive dog reference is also its most apparently contradictory one, consisting in the Fool's remark:

> Truth's a dog must to kennel, he must be whip't out, when the Lady Brach may stand by th' fire and stink.

> 1.4.111-13

On the positive side, one dog here is the truth-telling cynic or critic who shows up the insincerity of the others (just like the 'dog' Apemantus in *Timon*), while on the negative side we assume that 'Lady Brach' is the flattering, insidious (and somehow sexually corrupt) type of dog.[14]

The picture that begins to emerge is much more varied than we might expect from reading Spurgeon. The notion of the image cluster implies that whenever the idea of 'dog' enters Shakespeare's consciousness, the candy-melting-fawning gestalt is apt to be triggered. That such a gestalt was available to Shakespeare and that he enjoyed working it up in elaborate ways in different contexts is clear; it is equally clear that a much more *public* linguistic and experiential network around 'dog' is there for him to tap.

It is significant in this regard that the degree of metaphoricity in these passages can change almost without our noticing. 'Truth's a dog' involves transfer from the animal field to the abstract field, quite a leap in semantic space. Calling a man a dog is clearly metaphorical, but the leap is not so great (men like dogs are, in componential-semantic terms, +CONCRETE and +ANIMATE). Less non-literal still are the dogs of the 'Knowing nought (like dogs) but following' sort. The two readings of 'they flatter'd me like a dog' could be distinguished in terms of the last two varieties: 'They flattered me like a dog flatters his master' is straight simile, while 'They flattered me as if I were a dog' embeds an 'I am a dog' self-directed animal metaphor or insult. Finally, what of the status of 'Mine enemy's dog'? Cordelia's claim may not even be hyperbole. Similarly, when Lear asks, 'Thou hast seen a farmer's dog bark at a beggar?' his auditors can answer quite unfiguratively, 'Yes'. Yet the literal phenomenon is instantly available for donor field status: 'authority' (another abstract field) is going to receive a donation from this everyday sight, and when the form of the donation gets spelled out—'a dog's obey'd in office'—it carries with it, as an extra bonus as it were, an animal-insult wording (we hear human authorities called 'dogs').

Such mobility up and down the metaphoricity scale is not only inconsistent with any automatic, symptomatic repetition of a single image cluster, it is inconsistent with maintaining a single level of 'cognitive interest' in the donor relation. If animal insults are conceptually rather predictable and routine in themselves, they have the compensating advantages of being swift,[15] pragmatically relevant (in the drama, the reasons characters have for insulting one another are important independently of the insults' wordings), and 'natural' in the sense that animal insults are a verbal game common in non-heightened, non-poetic speech. Making them more interesting on top of this *may* be done by seriously elaborating a donor-field gestalt; but there are other heightening possibilities, and the *Lear* 'dog' examples illustrate a variety of them.

Horses and Asses

Within the paradigm set of animals, we may distinguish wild animals and domestic animals; among domestic animals, there is a 'beast of burden' sub-group, including horses, asses, donkeys, mules, oxen, and so on. Donkeys do not appear in Shakespeare because the word (synonymous with and largely replacing 'ass') seems not to pre-date the eighteenth century. Mules do not turn up in *King Lear* (though there are several references to them elsewhere in Shakespeare), and oxen are present only submergedly at 3.6.37 where Lear, setting up the mock-trial of his daughters and addressing Kent and Edgar as judges, speaks of one of them as the other's 'yoke-fellow of equity'.[16] This leaves horses and asses to constitute a two-term beast of burden paradigm. We propose to look closely at four passages from this point of view, analysing the horse/ass paradigm in some detail in terms of Kittay and Lehrer's semantics-based approach to metaphor.

At 1.4.160-62, the Fool says to Lear, 'When thou clovest thy crown i' th' middle and gav'st away both parts, thou bor'st thine ass on thy back o'er the dirt'. A listener who was unfamiliar with the specific Aesop's fable which lies behind this reference[17] would still have no difficulty in grasping the point of this: Lear's division of the kingdom is equivalent to a perverse reversal of proper relations ('thou mad'st thy daughters thy mothers', says the Fool restating his point ten lines later), and this reversal can be quickly illustrated via the simplest possible form of a beast of burden syntagm, so that

VERB	AGENT	PATIENT
bears	ass	man

becomes

VERB	AGENT	PATIENT
bears	man	ass

Straightforward as this is, several further points can be made about it. First, the ass-bears-man syntagm hierarchically relates two items in paradigmatic contrast, namely ass and man (the man/beast contrast). We shall find that this contrast is always at issue in the examples we shall be discussing. Second, the grammatical 'deep structure' case relationship whereby the ass should be the agent fails to correspond[18] with what we might call the substantial agential relationship, whereby men are more agent-like than beasts, particularly than the beasts they make use of. So a fuller version of the normal syntagmatic field might look like this:

VERB	AGENT	RESULT
makes	man	

VERB	AGENT	PATIENT
bears	ass	man

Considering this, the Fool's accusation is all the more pointed: Lear's *unnecessary,* unnatural doing, as reflected in his emergence as agent in the embedded syntagm, is still his *own* doing. Third, whatever the reasons why 'ass' rather than 'horse' is the standard vocative insult (so that 'You ass'! is a much more likely locution than 'You horse'!) the line would be flatter if 'horse' were substituted for 'ass' because the insult quality would be lessened. In the reversed syntagm, the man, as bearer of his ass, has become as it were the ass of his ass—which is virtually to call the king an ass raised to the second power.

The Fool sets up a similar inversion of a simple standard paradigm at 1.4.223-4: 'May not an ass know when the cart draws the horse'? Here the basic reversal, with horse and cart switching their proper agent–patient roles, is proverbial to the point of banality. However, the proverb is embedded in a context which brings in the other element in the horse–ass paradigm. Why? Within that paradigm, the two elements are hierarchically ranked, with 'horse' superior to 'ass'. Various real-world or conventional reasons underpin the ranking: asses are smaller than horses, are not as fast or as comfortable to ride (no racing or pleasure-riding function is associated with them), are (or were) cheaper, and, most importantly in this context, are taken to be less intelligent. As the *OED* puts it, 'The ass has, since the time of the Greeks, figured in fables and proverbs as the type of clumsiness, ignorance and stupidity'.[19]

What is important in this sentence is the Fool's 'May not an ass know . . .', especially since the context is one in which hyperboles claiming non-knowledge are being exchanged by Lear and Goneril. Lear has just asked, 'Are you our daughter?' and is about to suggest 'This is not Lear', while Goneril asks Lear to lay aside 'These dispositions which . . . transport you/ From what you rightly are'. The hyperbole here consists in moving from a judgement that the perceived (Goneril or Lear) is not behaving properly to the judgement that the perceived is not what or whom it had been thought, or that the perceiver is not perceiving properly ('Where are his eyes'?), or even that the perceiver is himself not whom he had thought himself ('Who is it that can tell me who I am'?). The Fool too joins in the hyperbole game, but takes the basic situation in a different direction; for him, the behaving-improperly of Goneril does not put her or Lear's identities in question; rather, it is itself perfectly identifiable, so much so that a proverb can encapsulate it and an ass can recognize it.

The basic proverb is revitalized by the deployment of the ass–horse opposition, because its explicit reversal is thereby embedded in a context setting up two implicit reversals. The ass is stupider than the horse, but the ass as knower is agent to the horse's patient (cf. 'A cat may look at a king'), and anyway the horse has become patient to the cart's agent. Meanwhile, the beast–man opposition has been reversed in the way that always happens in animal insults (more on this in the discussion of the next example), at least to the extent that one hears the sentence as meaning 'Even you (Lear) . . .' or 'Even I (the Fool) can see that . . .'.[20] The fact that the human being to whom 'ass' is being transferred may be either the King or the Fool means that a tenuous equivalence between the horse–ass opposition and the King–Fool opposition can be felt, though probably the direction of transfer is more from human to animal here than the reverse; if so, the ass is once again valued upwards ('not altogether ass', as it were).[21]

The third horse–ass passage, spoken yet again by the Fool, is at 1.5.34; in reply to Lear's 'Be my horses ready?', the Fool replies, 'Thy asses are gone about 'em'. Here 'horses' and 'asses' are alike as beast s of burden but different in their semantic status, the horses being literal and the asses metaphorical. But the metaphor in question can hardly be described as involving a transfer from the donor field of asses to the recipient field of servants, with an asinine gestalt used to structure thoughts about servility. Rather, as in Kittay and Lehrer's discussion of the Bees of England, 'the recipient field lends structure to the donor field': we understand what is happening in terms of our already-formed sense of what servants do to get horses ready. Does this mean that the Fool's retort lacks cognitive interest?

Certainly little new is brought forward by the donor–recipient transfer that the basic insult involves: the commonplaces associated with 'ass'—'clumsiness, ignorance and stupidity'—are transferred to the human realm in a standard fashion. This standardization is, whatever its cognitive interest, presumably of the essence in everyday insult pragmatics: we are less interested in restructuring our enemy's conceptual field than in abusing him by *calling him a name* with strong, instantaneously-effective negative connotations of some sort. Playful insults are similar, with the appended higher-order message somehow conveyed, 'Don't take this seriously'; it is possible that the Fool should be heard thus on this occasion.[22] But the unquestionably present level of play here, the linguistic level, operates via the horse–ass paradigm just as in the previous example, only here it is an insult rather than a proverb which is revitalised.

The syntagmatic field which Lear and the Fool both have referentially in mind could be laid out thus:

VERB	AGENT	ACTION
order	superior (King)	

VERB	AGENT	PATIENT
make ready	subordinates (servants)	horses

Two hierarchically–ranked paradigms figure here, the one in the embedded action being the man–beast of burden opposition, the other between the two agencies being a master–servant opposition. For everything to unfold as it should, the servants must maintain a lesser status than their master in the human realm while retaining their superiority in the man–beast field. But the Fool reverses the latter hierarchy, by bringing in the sixth term necessary to complete the following diagram (A)—the one term not literally part of the action at this point—and substituting it for what had been the pivot concept 'servants'.

Diagram A: Normal Hierarchy

	1. Human Realm	2. Interface	3. Beast Realm
(Superior)	King	servants	horses
(Inferior)	servants	horses	(asses)

This has the effect of troubling the hierarchies in columns 2 and 3 in reciprocal ways, as shown in the next diagram (B):

Diagram B: Fool's Hierarchy

	1. Human Realm	2. Interface	3. Beast Realm
(Superior)	King	'asses'	(asses)
(Inferior)	servants = 'asses'	horses	horses

In the beast realm, the normal hierarchy (based not on agenthood but on differential properties—horses don't *command* asses) is reversed, as the asses are in command. In the interface realm, the servants' superiority to the horses is put in question by a renaming which maps onto their human-realm status of inferiority a beast-realm inferior name, as if the similar positions of 'servants' and 'asses' in columns 1 and 3 of Diagram A justified the substitution of 'asses' for 'servants' in column 2 of Diagram B. Nor is this disquieting effect without its echoes in the human hierarchy.

The real hierarchical worries at this point in the play are, after all, human ones: not perhaps King–servant, but certainly as embodied in Lear and his bad daughters, King–subject and parent–child (and perhaps male–female). And the question of who is to serve the King (his own knights or Goneril's household) has in fact precipitated Lear's call for his horses in the first place. These are the rich relationships; the prosaic question of men saddling horses and the commonplace paradigmatic beast of burden field are neither of them likely to restructure our thoughts about the human realm in detail. But perturbations in and between the lesser realms can be set up which, while taking structure from the greater, in turn vivify it.

Finally, in a passage which appears only in the Quarto text (see footnote 19), we leave the Fool behind and proceed to the grim concluding events of the play. After his forces have won the battle, Edmund gives written instructions to a Captain to kill Lear and Cordelia in prison and the Captain signifies his acceptance of the commission (the exact nature of which is not yet known, either to him or to the audience) thus:

> I cannot draw a cart, nor eat dried oats,
> If it be man's work, I'll do't.
>
> 5.3.38-9

This is a good example of how it need not be literal falsity which alerts us to the presence of the figurative;[23] however, the Captain's remark on his own capacities and diet do violate Gricean conversational postulates, notably the Relevance Condition.[24] Reinterpreting the sentence to make it relevant, we of course take the Captain to be saying 'I am not a horse', and by that in turn to be saying 'I will execute your orders'. But why should an animal metaphor appear here at all, especially in a grammatically negative form?

In the Captain's speech the beast of burden field is left unsubdivided: the horse–ass distinction is not exploited,[25] and the relevant paradigm opposition is that between man and beast. Within the beast field the beast of burden field is riddlingly specified—that is, the listener must infer what the (rejected) donor field is from two details (what I cannot do that it does, what I cannot eat that it does); of course the riddle is not a difficult one. The two details are not chosen arbitrarily but arise in reply to Edmund's offer:

> if thou dost
> As this instructs thee, thou dost make thy way
> To noble fortunes. Know thou this, that men
> Are as the time is: to be tender-minded
> Does not become a sword. Thy great employment
> Will not bear question; either say thou'lt do it,
> Or thrive by other means.
>
> 5.3.28-34

Edmund is offering *means of sustenance* ('noble fortunes') in return for the *doing* of an as-yet-unspecified 'it'. The overall syntagmatic scheme might be set out as:

$AGENT_1$ offers X to $AGENT_2$ in return for Y
when X is valued material of some sort, Y is an action of some sort, and $AGENT_2$ is subordinate to $AGENT_1$. Edmund's speech

specifies the elements of this scheme, with the crucial exception of Y. Given what we know of the dramatic situation and of Edmund, of course, the general nature of Y is not hard to infer, especially since its specifics *are* being withheld. However, Edmund's clues about Y are metonyms designed to minimize any sense of incompatibility between $AGENT_2$ and Y. Basically, the scheme can only be properly fulfilled if (i) $AGENT_2$ is such that he can perform Y, and (ii) Y is such that it is proper for $AGENT_2$ to perform it. These conditions overlap in that the propriety of Y could depend on the nature of $AGENT_2$. So Edmund's metonyms are designed to clarify the nature of $AGENT_2$. 'Men are as the time is'; these are violent times, $AGENT_2$ is a man, he is thereby (justified in being) violent. A captain, as a military officer, carries a sword; by synecdoche, he *is* his sword (his superior's sword), and as such it would be tender-minded Ys rather than violent Ys that would be incompatible with his $AGENT_2$ status.

Now the $AGENT_1$-X-$AGENT_2$-Y structure here is part of the literal world of the action; even the metonymies work on the basis of real, present elements (the real temporal context, the Captain's real military status, even his real sword). What the Captain now does is to evoke another field, which, *as* other, will somehow legitimate his position.

	Literal field (LF)	Field invoked by Captain (CF)
($AGENT_1$)	Edmund	(men)
(X)	noble fortunes	oats
($AGENT_2$)	Captain	horse
(Y)	? (but defined by 'times' and 'sword' metonymies)	draw a cart

CF is like LF in that it answers to the same scheme. But it is the *in*compatibility of the literal field $AGENT_2$, the Captain, with X_{CF} and Y_{CF} that the Captain is concerned to draw from the comparison. If CF is a beast field, and LF is a human field *vis-à-vis* its $AGENT_2$, then the scheme suggests that Y_{LF}, whatever it is, will be 'man's work'.

Actually, the Captain seems to reserve his judgement on this, as well he might, but it will turn out that he obeys Edmund's command; indeed we can somehow infer that he will from his invocation of the cart and the oats. Our inference here may possibly be based on inversions we have already looked at. While the Captain is unlike a horse in his capacities and diet, he is like one in his subordination. Any scheme which sets up a subordinate human as superior to a beast is ripe for inversion, since his subordination is a sign of non-superiority, perhaps even inferiority. Actually, moral inferiority is very much in question here as the audience is not for a moment carried along by Edmund's or the Captain's arguments. The ironic discrepancy between our perception and theirs is based on our realisation that an illicit collapse of what is properly a four-cell product of two paradigmatic sets is being attempted.

	Man	Beast
(Violent)	Captain	(wild beast; carnivorous)
(Non-Violent)	(ethical man)	domestic beast of burden: vegetarian

The Captain, arguing 'I am not a beast' across the diagonal, ignores another possiblity on the human side (rejection of Edmund's position; cf. the servant who gives Cornwall a fatal stroke), as well as his 'true' likeness on the beast side (some carnivore, say a wolf). What gives the Captain a certain stoic dignity, despite all this and despite (because prefiguring!) his final destiny (Lear's dismissive comment, 'I kill'd the slave that was a-hanging thee', 5.3.275) is that, in terms of the key distinction between $AGENT_1$ and $AGENT_2$, he has articulated, even while denying it, his own subordinate position.

	Man	Beast
(Non-Subordinate)	Edmund	(wild beast)
(Subordinate)	Captain	domestic beast of burden

This leaves 'man's work' radically devalued when 'work' is heard as implying subordination: 'What as a subordinate I must do, given that I am unable to subsist on what beasts do and accomplish the strenuous, pacific tasks that they do, is ''man's work'' however terrible it may be'. We are left feeling that horses are happier.

Animal Lists

The play's last and perhaps most devastating animal reference
comes when Lear, holding Cordelia's body, asks

> Why should a dog, a horse, a rat, have life,
> And thou no breath at all?
>
> 5.3.307-8

We have puzzled over these lines; why are these animals selected
and why are they put in this particular order? They constitute a
simple paradigmatic list of common animals with monosyllabic
names. They are all 'low' in comparison with man but they are not
arranged in a hierarchical order of size or utility which would
presumably be 'horse, dog, rat'. What is important here is the sense
of outrage that *even* these common creatures have more life than
Cordelia. The particularity of the animals does not seem to matter
very much; 'dog' and 'horse' do not, in this context, carry the
associations we have explored at earlier points in the play.

Yet one can link this passage with many others in which a
number of animals appear together in a single context, often in the
form of a list. Indeed, the listing of animals is a popular form of
amplification in all kinds of rhetorical contexts for obvious reasons:
the paradigmatic list itself is familiar and easily grasped, while each
item of the paradigm carries with it a rich set of syntagmatic
attachments which can be elaborated if appropriate. To begin with a
fairly simple example, when the Fool sees Kent in the stocks he
exclaims:

> Hah, ha, he wears cruel garters. Horses are tied by the heads, dogs and
> bears by th' neck, monkeys by th' loins, and men by th' legs.
>
> 2.4.7-9

Here, the simple paradigmatic list of horses, dogs, bears, monkeys
and men is elaborated in terms of the syntagmatic relation 'how
these creatures are tied'. Moreover, the Fool combines his first list
with a second paradigmatic list taken from parts of the body—head,
neck, loins, legs—which has the effect of reversing the expected
hierarchy (horses are at the top in terms of their association with
'heads', while men are at the bottom, associated with 'legs'), thus
emphasizing the indignity of Kent's position.

Clearly such lists are not 'metaphorical' in the usually accepted sense. In both examples discussed so far, the references to animals could be classed as literal rather than figurative, yet some kind of comparison is still involved and the analysis of that comparison is similar to the analysis of metaphor. As we have seen in this play, comparisons between men and animals usually have the effect of showing men up as being in some respect worse or 'lower' than the animals in question. At the very least, a man is capable of combining in himself a number of unsavoury animal traits, as when Edgar claims to be a 'hog in sloth, fox in stealth, wolf in greediness, dog in madness, lion in prey' (3.4.93-4),[26] or conversely a man can adduce a whole range of animals to illustrate a single negative characteristic as when Kent refers to kingfishers, dogs and geese to deride Oswald's spinelessness in the passage from 2.2. quoted on p.57 above.

Rarely are lists of animals neutral in *King Lear,* though Edgar's list of different types of dog—'Mastiff, greyhound, mongrel grim,/ Hound or spaniel, brach or lym', etc.—at 3.6.68-73 comes near to this. The dogs here are apparently not related to each other hierarchically or in terms of their different functions but are ordered merely by the demands of rhyme and metre.[27] Later in *Lear* it is Edgar again who uses a brief list of animals in a neutral way in his bravura attempt to persuade the blind Gloucester that they are standing on a cliff's edge:

> The crows and choughs that wing the midway air
> Show scarce so gross as beetles . . .
> The fishermen that walk upon the beach
> Appear like mice . . .
>
> 4.6.13-14. 17-18

We take it that size alone is important in this comparison: the fishermen are not being 'placed' in any more significant sense here, by contrast with Gloucester's earlier statement that the sight of the naked beggar made him 'think a man a worm' where social and moral dimensions are implied.

Other instances of lists of apparently neutral animals can occur in relation to clothing and to food (animals provide us with both) but, as we might expect by now, the wider context in *King Lear* complicates these issues. In 3.4, for example, Lear first takes pity on Edgar's nakedness—'Thou wert better in a grave than to answer with thy uncover'd body this extremity of the skies'(101-2)—but then reappraises it as somehow positive or honest: 'Thou ow'st the worm no silk, the beast no hide, the sheep no wool, the cat no perfume . . . Thou art the thing itself' (103-6). Here we have a simple paradigmatic list of animals with a secondary paradigmatic list of their respective contributions to 'sophisticated' man: the animals are the literal donors! But the simple 'back to nature' impulse is countered by the immediate context (Edgar is *not* the naked wretch he appears but a nobleman who has paradoxically disguised himself by removing his clothes rather than by the more usual method of changing them) and by the larger context of the earlier discussion of man's needs in 2.4. In that scene, Lear responds to his daughters' superficially reasonable argument that he does not need his own servants when he can command theirs by crying:

> O, reason not the need! our basest beggars
> Are in the poorest thing superfluous.
> Allow not nature more than nature needs,
> Man's life is cheap as beast's. Thou art a lady;
> If only to go warm were gorgeous,
> Why, nature needs not what thou gorgeous wear'st,
> Which scarcely keeps thee warm.
>
> 2.4.264-70

Lear's perception here that man does in fact 'need' more than the mere physical necessities of food and shelter if his life is not to be 'cheap as beast's', and his illustration of it in terms of Regan's clothing (which might be silk or fur), makes his later desire to identify with the naked Edgar seem more like regression and a retreat into nihilism.

As for the animals we eat, Edgar's listing of his diet as mad Tom is interesting as a deliberate cataloguing of animals which would not normally be considered acceptable as food. He claims to eat 'the swimming frog, the toad, the tadpole, the wall-newt and the water [-newt], . . . the old rat and the ditch-dog' (3.4.129-33). This ostensibly literal list clearly has social implications—'Tom', having fallen beneath the lowest level of ordinary society, eats creatures which are 'below' the usual categories—but there may

71

also be a religious dimension since many of these creatures are aquatic (even the 'old rat' and 'ditch-dog' are assumed to be waterlogged) and it was of course traditional for men to eat fish rather than meat as a gesture of penitential fasting. Does Edgar's diet form part of a meaningful pattern of penance and self-abasement that he has undertaken despite his innocence of the crime of which he is accused? At 2.3.9 he describes himself as 'brought near to beast', and it seems at times as if he is indeed exploring the interface between the two realms.

Edgar's social reversal is parallel to that of Lear, the 'unnaturalness' of whose plight is expressed through another list of animal references delivered by an anonymous Gentleman to Kent in response to a query about what the King is doing during the storm:

> This night, wherein the cub-drawn bear would couch,
> The lion and the belly-pinched wolf
> Keep their fur dry, unbonneted he runs,
> And bids what will take all.
>
> 3.1.12-15

This is yet another example of the 'even a beast' syndrome ('even a beast would behave more sensibly, more kindly, etc. than men are doing'). The animals chosen here, bear, lion and wolf, are normally seen as wild and violent, creatures whose behaviour might be matched with or encouraged by the storm rather than deterred by it. The bear and wolf are described as being in conditions, 'cub-drawn' (sucked dry by cubs, therefore ravenous) and 'belly-pinched', that would tend to make them even more ferocious than usual, yet they show a greater sense of self-preservation than the King. Again the natural covering of the animals ('fur') is contrasted with the relative nakedness of 'unbonneted' man.

Lear himself sees his fellow creatures as being lower than the animals in his ironic defence of the 'naturalness' of adultery in 4.6. on the grounds that

> The wren goes to't, and the small gilded fly
> Does lecher in my sight.
>
> 4.6.112-13

Yet, he claims, women are worse:

> The fitchew nor the soiled horse goes to't
> With a more riotous appetite.
> Down from the waist they are Centaurs,
> Though women all above;
> But to the girdle do the gods inherit,
> Beneath is all the fiends'.
>
> 4.6.122-7

The paradigm here of wren, fly, fitchew (polecat) and soiled (wanton with feeding on new grass) horse are chosen for their supposed lecherousness, as the Gentleman in 3.1 chooses the bear, lion and wolf for their supposed savageness, and Kent in 2.2 chooses the kingfisher, dog and goose for their supposed spinelessness. But in the animals the quality is a natural one whereas in human beings, and especially women, it is vicious and, moreover, hypocritical ('Behold yond simp'ring dame,/ . . . That minces virtue, and does shake the head/ To hear of pleasure's name . . .'). The movement to 'Centaur' is interesting, partly because Centaurs, being mythical, are not just another set of animals that can be added to the list, and partly because the locution, 'Down from the waist they are Centaurs', seems a redundant one: Centaurs are, by definition, human above the waist. In fact Centaurs are, by definition, the kind of mixture of the human and the bestial that Lear sees in his daughters.[28] The paradigm in fact becomes a more cosmic one here as Lear also takes in gods and fiends: the natural order would descend from gods through humans to animals, then monsters (unnatural animals), then fiends, but in this case the humans who are supposed to be (and pretend to be) nearest to the gods are associating themselves with the fiends through their bestial or monstrous behaviour.[29]

It is important, though, to avoid sliding from an argument involving semantic hierarchies into a too hierarchically conservative reading of the play as a whole. Sometimes critics write as if questions of degree, the Great Chain of Being, and so on, are of primary concern to Shakespeare—as if the particular human situations unfolded in *King Lear* were chosen simply as examples of the awful effects of challenging or reversing authority relations. The animal field, however, does not support such a reading as much as it might seem to. Certainly the man—beast paradigm is hierarchical, but not in such a fixed manner that further thought about it is excluded or deplored. A semantic hierarchy provides material for thought, not a final determination of it, much less a final determination of the real world.

That people behave so badly in *King Lear* is terrible, but that beasts do, or might, behave better is not deplored as an attack on degree: if they do, good for them! And within the beast paradigm, while localised two- or three-term hierarchies exist (as in the horse–ass case), the result of listing is generally to bring out the overall *lack* of a stable and principled hierarchization of animals. The 'and ... and ... and' quality of such lists is itself a demonstration of the unranked variety 'out there'. Returning to Lear's final list: we have the hierarchized man–beast opposition expressed as being inappropriately out of alignment with one of the least challengeable hierarchies of all, that whereby life is higher than death.[30] Yet in the very act of appealing for the alignment of these hierarchies (an impossible appeal: how *could* one argue that beasts' lesser nature meant that their very existence in the face of human death was an affront to the Great Chain?), Lear instantiates beastness via an unordered list. Appropriately so, since in the semantic field of mortality the paradigm of death's 'patients' is an unordered one, grouping together the whole organic ('sublunary' to Shakespeare) world—men, beasts, plants—as (com-)mutable.

Monsters

Monsters are clearly a special case. They have many similarities with actual animals but they are distinguished from them by the fact that they do not really exist. In theory this might make metaphors which use monsters as their donor field quite incomprehensible: we can refer to something in the real world when we hear or read 'He is a dog' or 'He is an ass', but how do we make any sense of 'He is a monster'? In practice, as we hope we have indicated, we do not in fact interpret dog and ass metaphors by direct reference to empirical reality but rather by reference to a series of associated commonplaces, and the same procedure can work for monsters though we have even more extreme kind of anthromorphism; monsters might themselves be metaphorical to start with.

What are the commonplace associations of 'monster'? The *OED* lists the following meanings for the word itself, all of which were current in Shakespeare's time:

1. Something extraordinary or unnatural; a prodigy, a marvel.
2. An animal or plant deviating in one or more of its parts from the normal type, . . . a misshapen birth, an abortion.
3. An imaginary animal . . . having a form either partly brute and partly human, or compounded of elements from two or more animal forms.
4. A person of inhuman and horrible cruelty or wickedness; a monstrous example *of* (wickedness or some particular vice).
5. An animal of huge size; hence, anything of vast and unwieldy proportions.

It is notable that all these are given as primary or literal meanings; according to the *OED* one is not necessarily being metaphorical at all in calling a person a monster. Let us now look at some of the 'monster' references in *King Lear* to see how Shakespeare draws upon and elaborates these common meanings.

To begin with, 'monster' and its associated terms can be used as a simple insult, as when in the last scene of the play Albany exclaims 'Most monstrous!' (5.3.160) in response to Goneril's shameless behaviour. This is clearly the adjectival form of *OED*'s meaning 4 and strictly speaking need not be metaphorical at all. Gloucester's first response to the supposed treachery of Edgar is similar—'He cannot be such a monster' (1.2.94)—but in this scene the speaker has led up to (or rather down to) the monster insult by calling Edgar 'Abhorred villain! unnatural, detested, brutish villain! worse than brutish!' (1.2.76-7). This gives us a hierarchical paradigm as Edgar descends through 'villain' (which carried a stronger sense of 'low class person' then than now) to brute to something-worse-than-brute, i.e. monster. *OED* actually cites this passage as one of its examples of meaning 4 but it is clear from the context that animal associations are present as well as human ones.

As we have already noted in our discussion of 'Centaur' above (a clear example of *OED*'s meaning 3), monsters can participate in a cosmic paradigm which begins with gods and descends in hierarchical order through humans, beasts and monsters to fiends or devils. When characters call each other monsters in *King Lear*, they often seem to have this hierarchical paradigm in mind and to be implying (as Gloucester does) that human beings are degenerating into monsters: they are in a sense doubly monstrous since their inhuman behaviour (sense 4) is threatening to turn them into deviant animals (sense 2). For example, after the blinding of Gloucester, one of the servants comments (in the Quarto text only) on Regan's role in the proceedings:

> If she live long,
> And in the end meet the old course of death,
> Women will all turn monsters.
>
> 3.7.100-2

The servant is saying first that Regan's behaviour is so monstrous (sense 4) that it will surely be punished by an early death, but secondly that, if she should in fact live to die a natural death of old age, then all women will copy her and turn into monsters (sense 2), presumably because they will no longer fear divine punishment.

Albany takes up the same theme and elaborates it in relation to Goneril in 4.2, in another passage found only in the Quarto.[31] He is shocked to hear how Goneril and Regan have treated their father, upbraids his wife through a series of 'unnatural' metaphors taken from the plant realm as well as the animal realm, and comes to a climax with

> If that the heavens do not their visible spirits
> Send quickly down to tame these vile offenses,
> It will come,
> Humanity must perforce prey on itself,
> Like monsters of the deep.
>
> 4.2.46-50

Again, an absence of divine intervention to check the monstrous behaviour of a few threatens to lead to an apocalyptic situation in which all humanity becomes monstrous, specifically by becoming cannibalistic which is presumably deviant behaviour of the kind implied by *OED* sense 2. This particular trait, supposed by Albany to belong to some quasi-mythical sea-creatures, is appropriate to

Goneril and Regan who are 'preying on' their own father. Lear himself has already commented on this:

> filial ingratitude!
> Is it not as this mouth should tear this hand
> For lifting food to't?
>
> 3.4.14-16

> Judicious punishment! 'twas this flesh begot
> Those pelican daughters.[32]
>
> 3.4.74-5

Hence the already horrific monstrosity of cannibalism (a creature eating one of its own species) is intensified by the notion of a creature eating itself.[33]

Continuing his tirade against Goneril, Albany degrades her from monster to devil:

> See thyself, devil!
> Proper deformity shows not in the fiend
> So horrid as in woman . . .
> Thou changed and self-cover'd thing, for shame
> Bemonster not thy feature. Were't my fitness
> To let these hands obey my blood,
> They are apt enough to dislocate and tear
> Thy flesh and bones. Howe'er thou art a fiend,
> A woman's shape doth shield thee.
>
> 4.2.59-67

Albany begins by saying that deformity or deviance (*OED* monster, sense 2), which is appropriate to a devil or fiend, looks more horrible in a woman, presumably because it is not appropriate. But, having used the word 'shows',[34] he takes up the question of whether her deformity is visible—whether in fact it is literal or metaphorical. By calling Goneril 'changed', he must mean 'transformed' (i.e. to a monster or devil), but 'self-cover'd' seems to imply that Goneril's true nature is in fact hidden, perhaps that she is covering her new self with her old self? Ironically, he warns her not to let her monstrosity show in her face—'Bemonster not thy feature'—lest she forfeit the chivalrous protection normally granted to women and become the victim of *his* unnatural violence.

77

The association of a monster with some kind of covering or clothing that we find here is not part of any of the *OED* meanings, nor indeed what we might predict if we elaborated a syntagmatic donor field of characteristics for mythical (sense 3) monsters: we might see them as being large and ugly, possessing teeth and claws, and so on, but do monsters have clothes? Nevertheless, this association has occurred earlier in the play, in fact in the opening scene when France comments in amazement on Lear's *volte-face* over Cordelia:

> This is most strange,
> That she . . . should in this trice of time
> Commit a thing so monstrous, to dismantle
> So many folds of favor. Sure her offense
> Must be of such unnatural degree
> That monsters it, or your fore-vouch'd affection
> Fall into taint.
>
> 1.1.213-14, 216-21

These lines are difficult and the precise connection between the monster and the clothing is obscure. Most obviously, the monstrosity of Cordelia's crime is supposed to be so great (metaphorical use of *OED* sense 5) as to disrobe or deprive her of Lear's favour, in which case the monster is in some sense removing Cordelia's (protective) clothing. But the more familiar use of clothing metaphors, coupled with the general context of hypocrisy, makes it difficult to avoid some sense that Cordelia's 'real' monstrosity is being revealed underneath her disguise, that is, that the monster is underneath the 'folds' rather than outside them—the monster is the result of the dismantling rather than the agent. Here, as in the previous example, 'monster' (or 'bemonster') is used as a verb rather than a noun ('very rare', according to the *OED,* and most of its examples are from Shakespeare), which further emphasizes that it is, as elsewhere, the recipient field of human beings which is uppermost in Shakespeare's mind rather than the donor field of monsters; he is only interested in monsters in so far as humans can be or can become monsters.[35]

France does not know at this point what Cordelia is supposed to have done, so the 'monstrosity' remains ambiguous in its reference as well as in the syntax. Later, when Lear begins to understand the truth behind Goneril's hypocrisy, he sees the ingratitude of children to their parents as being the most monstrous of actions:

> Ingratitude! Thou marble-hearted fiend,
> More hideous when thou show'st thee in a child
> Than the sea-monster.
>
> 1.4.259-61

We could read this to mean simply that 'ingratitude . . . is more hideous that the sea-monster' but editors usually take it to mean that 'ingratitude . . . is more hideous in a child than *in* the sea-monster', a reading which they support by reference to notoriously ungrateful sea-creatures but which could also be supported by Albany's parallel perception that 'Proper deformity shows not in the fiend/ So horrid as in woman'. In both passages, qualities which are appropriate (and hence not shocking) to fiends and monsters are truly horrific when they are 'shown' in a child and/or a woman.

The monster which is ingratitude (later, Lear is to exclaim simply 'Monster ingratitude'! 1.5.40) is here given coldness or lack of feeling as its dominant characteristic rather than, say, savageness. Goneril's monstrosity is evident not because her attitude to her father is overtly violent or malevolent here but because she is unmoved—mildly contemptuous at best—in the face of his heartfelt anger and 'hot tears'. Yet, as in 4.2, the context contains threats and suggestions of physical violence: Lear remembers Cordelia's supposed ingratitude 'Which, like an engine, wrench'd my frame of nature/ From the fix'd place' (1.4.268-9), he threatens that Regan will take a suitably monstrous revenge—'with her nails/ She'll flay thy wolvish visage' (1.4.307-8)—and he offers up his extraordinarily wild and shocking prayer that if Goneril ever has a child it may be 'a thwart disnatur'd torment to her' (1.4.283; cf. *OED* 'monster', sense 2) so as to make her in turn feel 'How sharper than a serpent's tooth it is/ To have a thankless child' (1.4.288-9).

Clearly, to repeat, it is not that cognitive interest is here the result of using a body of monster-lore to structure the ingratitude field; the monster field itself is created by projection onto the beast field of aspects of the abstract ingratitude field, with all the licence of hyperbole.[36] Just as the projection of the lust field onto the beast field resulted in a list which began with 'real' beasts plus their

79

associated commonplaces but continued with the monstrous Centaur, so projecting ingratitude's characteristics can equally easily evoke a real beast (the pelican, the serpent), a 'real-ish' beast (the sea-monster as sometimes glossed: hippopotamus or whale), an unreal beast (sea-monster with the stress on monster), or an entity combining two alternative below-beast concepts, the diabolical (fiend) and the inorganic (marble-hearted). Lear is not trying to understand ingratitude better, to think and talk of it in new terms which will illuminate and clarify it for himself and his listeners. He knows all about ingratitude and with great verbal energy searches through his vocabulary for items which can serve as pale equivalents for its awfulness. Once found, these equivalents 'donate back' as it were, so that the particular watery 'depth' of sea-monsters/monsters of the deep is taken up as part of the coldness and heaviness of the feeling, or the notion of a hideous appearance (perhaps based on a false etymology of the word monster, deriving it from *monstrare,* to show, rather than from *monere,* to warn) provokes speculation about visibility–invisibility, clothedness–nakedness, veiledness–unveiledness, and so on. But it is primarily the recipient field that enlightens us about the donor field rather than the other way round. This is why a reference to 'these pelican daughters' is not seriously baffling in today's theatre to an audience which has lost the associated commonplace which a Jacobean audience would have shared, and why we accept the sea-monster as a type of ingratitude although its imputed cannibalism may not come to mind when (as at 1.4.261) it is not specifically invoked.

Metaphorical Transfer

In the preceding analyses, we have been cheerfully and gratefully building upon the work of Kittay and Lehrer (and through them on a whole tradition within linguistic semantics); we have also been sniping at them over one point, the question of 'cognitive interest'. It is time to make clear just why the latter argument seems worth pursuing, but also why our disagreement with Kittay and Lehrer is not over the usefulness of their analytical framework as a whole. Our view is that it is by means of their analytical machinery that the needless restrictiveness of their evaluative stance can best be brought out.

The important advance which their donor field/recipient field terminology makes over I.A. Richards' 'vehicle' and 'tenor' seems to us to be centred on the word *field*. That is, what we have found enlightening in looking at our Shakespearean passages has been the invitation to see whole networks of associative relations, paradigmatic and syntagmatic, implicated in the words actually uttered by the characters, and to watch these networks mobilized in the course of the language's figurative heightening. But if metaphor involves some sort of transaction between two fields, it does not follow that a single account of (or metaphor for!) that transaction is to be sought: armed with the field concept, we are free to described a number of ways in which the fields can be related to one another.

It is at this point that we find Kittay and Lehrer becoming unduly confident in their judgement of what interesting metaphors must do, though they are only making explicit something implied by the whole transfer-transport tradition of metaphor;[37] whereas the relationship between the fields implied by Richards' vehicle/tenor distinction is obscure,[38] perhaps because Richards wisely chose not to pick terms which carried an implicit theory of what remained to be elucidated, the relationship between a donor and a recipient is quite precise—one of unidirectional transfer of something valuable. The clarity of this seems to us all to the good, so long as we take the obvious next dialectical step and ask, 'Does the implied directionality fit the example under discussion? And if it doesn't, wouldn't it be more reasonable to describe this alternative directionality rather than condemn it?'

Once the particular notion of transfer built into the donor–recipient terminology is firmly in one's mind, it does become difficult to see how other directionalities, or for that matter inadequate knowledge of or less than maximal exploitation of the donor field, could result in anything but slack writing. Our analyses however seem consistent with several lines of defence for alternative donation practices.

To begin with, the dramatic text does not want to be maximally 'interesting' on all levels at once. The audience's macro-level interest in diegetic questions of event, character and plot allows for, and probably requires, a good deal of straightforwardness at the verbal micro-level at times. So if one were asked to justify the cognitive interest of a straightforward animal insult, the sensible response might be a reference upwards to the action context of the remark—who is insulting whom, and why.

But our analyses, while conducted with this sort of macro-level information as background, have not been centred at that level. Our concern has been to bring out a variety of micro-level complexities which do seem interesting in their own right. We have followed critical tradition in pointing to *idiosyncratic structuring of a syntagmatic field:* Spurgeon's dogs—candy case is an example of this and the connection of monsters with garments seems to be another. In such cases, the structure of the donor field seems to come not so much from either reality or from what is culturally accepted as reality ('associated commonplaces') as from an authorial trick of thought. Semantic field theory is useful here in allowing a more exact description of verbal clusters, and also in making plain their dependency in turn on less idiosyncratic linguistic materials: we see no reason either to privilege these clusters as much as earlier criticism has done or to deny their existence. But we have devoted more attention to exploring *paradigmatic expansions and reversals,* and it is here that donation patterns furthest from those taken by Kittay and Lehrer to be normal most clearly emerge.

The Kittay and Lehrer analyses have a contiguity-based 'what-goes-with-what' emphasis, so that the 'fish' field important for them would be that involving fishing verbs, fishermen, line, hook, bait, river, and so on. Such a field can be seen, in Lakoff and Johnson's terminology, as an experiential gestalt; and it is positive enough (large enough, complex enough) to donate. But in the swiftly-moving language of the drama, what is often exploited is not a whole, complicated syntagmatic field but a relatively simple paradigm, whether as a list source or, even less substantially, as a locus of difference. In the latter case especially, donation from the tenor (i.e. the literal, the diegetic: the real power-relations among characters, for example) to establish the pertinence of the vehicle-field contrast seems natural enough. No doubt the animals give something back in turn, but it need not be, and in fact rarely seems to be, the sort of elaborated scenario which surrounds the fish in Donne's conceit.

We find then, as in our chapter on *Troilus and Cressida,* that we have been stressing the importance of the commonplace or everyday element in Shakespearean metaphor rather than the startlingly novel or idiosyncratic. The difficulty we have encountered in our analyses has been that of the familiar-heightened-to-the-point-of-paradox rather than of the strange or the eccentric. This grounding of metaphors in the commonplace, even the cliché, has obvious advantages for an audience which needs to grasp the basic meaning at once in a single hearing.

This distinction between metaphor grounded in the everyday and the novel or idiosyncratic metaphor is discussed from a slightly different viewpoint by Alastair Fowler who sees it as not so much a contrast between what is possible in drama and what is possible in poetry but between Elizabethan and Metaphysical uses of metaphor.[39] He claims, convincingly in our view though controversially, that Metaphysical metaphors or conceits are typically much simpler and more straightforward than Elizabethan ones though they are at the same time more novel and ingenious:

> . . . [If] we were to construct a model Metaphysical conceit, we would not specify complexity of comparison. The specification would be a single tenor and a single vehicle, related by a single system of analogies . . . Such metaphors can, as it were, be solved. (105-6)

This specification would fit Donne's 'The Bait' quite well and is clearly related to the simplicity of the unidirectional donor field–recipient field model. But, Fowler argues, Elizabethan metaphor (and he takes his illustrations from Spenser and Drayton as well as Shakespeare) is usually more complicated than this: Elizabethan poets enjoy establishing multiple relationships between tenor and vehicle, they 'double' and 'mix' their metaphors and allow terms to slide from one position to another and back again so that we find ourselves in doubt as to which is to be labelled 'tenor' and which 'vehicle' or even whether we are dealing with a metaphor at all. The 'monster' metaphor (discussed on p.78 above) seems to us a good example of this kind of complexity which, Fowler claims, is only possible because of the very high level of conventional or familiar content in Elizabethan metaphors and their avoidance of Metaphysical-type novelty and idiosyncrasy.

We would want to claim that this complex relationship which allows for an interchange between vehicle and tenor is at least as important an aspect of the animal metaphors we have studied in

King Lear as the one-sided 'donor to recipient' relationship perceived by Kittay and Lehrer. In the end we would see it as equally 'interesting' for a metaphor to perform an almost circular or out-and-back movement (we 'donate' qualities to animals in order to get them back as metaphors for people) as to participate in a one-way exchange. This conclusion can hardly be avoided if we agree that Shakespeare's metaphorical processes in *King Lear* are much closer to Shelley's in 'Song to the Men of England' than they are to Donne's in 'The Bait'.

Notes

1. We use the masculine pronoun as befitting the patriarchal nature of the Elizabethan/Jacobean 'world picture'.
2. As Corin explains in *As You Like It,* 3.2.67-8, perfume was derived from a substance found in the anal glands of the civet cat. The pelican was believed to feed its young on blood drawn from its own breast; hence it was sometimes seen as symbolizing the sacrifice of Christ.
3. See, for example, A.C. Bradley, *Shakespearean Tragedy* (Macmillan, London, 1904), Lecture VII; Caroline F.E. Spurgeon, *Shakespeare's Imagery and What It Tells Us* (Cambridge University Press, London, 1935), *passim;* Theodore Spencer, *Shakespeare and the Nature of Man* (Macmillan, London, 1942), pp.135-52; John F. Danby, *Shakespeare's Doctrine of Nature: A Study of 'King Lear'* (Faber, London, 1949), *passim.* A curious early contribution to this debate is that of J. Kirkman, 'Animal Nature *Versus* Human Nature in *King Lear',* *New Shakespeare Society Transactions* 1877-9, 385-405. He notes that animals are mentioned 133 separate times, mainly 'in a morally *unsavoury* relation' (p.387) and that Shakespeare's premature awareness of man's kinship with beasts has since his time been 'biologically demonstrated' by Darwin. In *Lear,* as he sees it, man 'falls back' and 'reasserts his low original' (p.401).
4. *Studies in Language,* 5 (1981), 31-63; see also Eva Kittay, *The Cognitive Force of Metaphor: A Theory of Metaphoric Meaning,* unpublished Ph.D. dissertation (City University of New York, 1978).
5. J. Martin and R. Harré, 'Metaphor in Science', in David S. Miall (ed.), *Metaphor: Problems and Perspectives* (Harvester, Brighton, 1982), pp.89-105, p.96. Other closely-related formulations include Lakoff and Johnson's 'The essence of metaphor is understanding and experiencing one kind of thing in terms of another' (*Metaphors We Live By,* p.5), Max Black's 'The metaphor works by applying to the principal subject a system of "associated implications" characteristic of the secondary subject' ('Metaphor', *Proceedings of the Aristotelian Society,* N.S. 55 (1954-55), 273-94,

reprinted in Mark Johnson (ed.), *Philosophical Perspectives on Metaphor* (University of Minnesota Press, Minneapolis, 1981, pp.63-82, p.78), and Nelson Goodman's 'A label along with others constituting a schema is in effect detached from the home realm of that schema and applied for the sorting and organizing of an alien realm' (*Languages of Art* (Oxford University Press, London, 1969), p.72).

6. *Metaphors We Live By,* p.81.
7. Compare our discussion of Lakoff and Johnson's structural metaphor CREATION IS BIRTH in relation to 'midwife' metaphors in *Troilus and Cressida,* pp.28-32 above.
8. See Charles Fillmore, 'The Case for Case', in E. Bach and R. Harms (eds.), *Universals of Linguistic Theory* (Holt, Rinehart and Winston, New York, 1968).
9. Cambridge University Press, London, 1935, pp.195-9.
10. The Folio text reads 'pannelled' here: Hanmer's emendation to 'spaniel'd' is, as Spurgeon points out (p.196, n.), given strong support by the presence of other elements of the image cluster.
11. While the general picture of a dog field donating its structure to a courtier field is clear enough in these examples, bringing the donor field into perfect focus is difficult due to what Hilda M. Hulme (*Explorations in Shakespeare's Language,* Longmans, London, 1962, p.161), discussing the *Hamlet* passage, describes as 'the paradox in which it is the begging dog which itself proffers the candy'.
12. This is evidenced by proverbs such as, 'Better to have a dog fawn on you than bite you' (Tilley, D445), 'The dog wags his tail not for love of you but for love of your bread' (Tilley, D459), 'Whores and dogs fawn upon a man no longer than they are fed' (Tilley, W327). Further proverbs on this theme are quoted in n.29 below.
13. *The Structure of Complex Words* (Chatto and Windus, London, 1951), pp.175-84.
14. It may be significant that 'Lady Brach' is feminine since it is Goneril's behaviour which is implicitly being criticized here. The dogs who seem to reject Lear by barking at him at 3.6.62-3 might also be assumed to be feminine from their names, 'Trey, Blanch and Sweetheart'.
15. Perhaps Shakespeare valued swiftness in metaphors and even associated this quality with dogs: when in the last scene of *The Taming of the Shrew* Tranio explains his role in the courtship of Bianca—'Lucentio slipp'd me like his greyhound,/ Which runs himself, and catches for his master',— Petruchio comments 'A good swift simile, but something currish' (5.2.52-4).
16. This episode occurs in the Quarto text of 1608 but not in the Folio of 1623. All modern editions of *King Lear* conflate these two early texts but recent scholarship suggests that the Folio may represent a deliberate and authorial revision of the Quarto; see Gary Taylor and Michael Warren (eds.), *The Division of the Kingdoms: Shakespeare's Two Versions of 'King Lear'* (Clarendon Press, Oxford, 1983).
17. The old man in the fable did not wish to overload his ass, and so carried the creature to market instead of making it carry him. The fable had been retold

many times; Shakespeare may have encountered it in William Warner's
Albion's England, 1586 (enlarged and reprinted 1589, 1592, 1596, 1602,
1606).

18. Of course there is no reason why it should correspond, any more than it
should correspond to grammatical surface structure when realised in a passive
construction like 'The man was borne by the ass', where 'man' has moved
into grammatical subject position without affecting the underlying case
relationships. Accounting for such non-correspondences is the whole
purpose of case grammars.

19. The following examples of Elizabethan/Jacobean horse–ass proverbs are
taken from Tilley: 'An ass covered with gold is more respected than a good
horse with a packsaddle' (A349), 'Better ride on an ass that carries me than a
horse that throws me' (A361), 'Every ass thinks himself worthy to stand with
the king's horses' (A362). John Baret comments on the phrase 'from the
horses to the asses' in *An Alvearie or Quadruple Dictionarie* (c. 1580) that it
is 'a Prouerbe applyed to those which are fallen from dignitie into a meaner
estate'.

20. On the Fool's self-insults, Empson's discussion of 'Fool in *Lear*' (*The
Structure of Complex Words*, pp.125-57) is worth consulting.

21. The delicacy of the horse–ass oppositional field comes out clearly if one tries
to combine features of 1.4.161 and 1.4.224 so as to put the horse in the
position of knowledge: 'May not a horse know when a man bears an ass o'er
the dirt'? This just doesn't work; the reason seems to be that 'horse' is flat
both as quasi-oxymoronic *vis-à-vis* 'knowing' and as lacking the insult usage.

22. Compare his playful or ironic insulting of Kent for attaching himself to the
declining fortunes of Lear in 2.4.64-76.

23. For other examples of figurative statements which are literally true, see our
discussion of Lear's reference to the farmer's dog (above, pp.58-9), our
discussion of body-part synecdoches in *Hamlet* at the beginning of chapter 3
below (pp.98-104) and our discussion of the larger metaphorical fields of
Sonnet 63 in Chapter 4 below (pp.154-9). In the present instance the fact that
the Captain's statement is cast in the negative makes it comparable to what
Ted Cohen has termed 'twice-true' metaphors such as 'No man is an island';
see our discussion of this phenomenon in Chapter 5 below (p.172 and n. 15,
p.203).

24. On Gricean conversation postulates, see above, Introduction, p.8.

25. Why then does it seem more natural to paraphrase l.38 as 'I am not a horse'
rather than 'I am not an ass'? One of the effects of the hierarchization of the
horse–ass field is to leave 'horse' as the unmarked term, in the sense that
markedness bears in linguistic semantics: 'The member of a syntactic
opposition automatically selected when choice from the semantic opposition
is inappropriate or neutralized is called the *unmarked* term, while the opposite
term is called *marked*' (Geoffrey Leech, *Semantics* (Penguin,
Harmondsworth, 1974), p.189. What 'ass' possesses as *extra* connotation
(notably the stupidity and vocative insult senses) goes beyond whatever the
listener is justified in inferring in the context.

26. The Seven Deadly Sins were often described through animal metaphors;
Kenneth Muir cites examples from Harsnett and Florio in his note on this

86

passage (New Arden *King Lear* (Methuen, London, 1952), p.113). Such metaphors could obviously be represented visually, and indeed several animals, and specific combinations of animals, carried symbolic significance in Renaissance painting. Anthony J. Lewis argues in 'The Dog, Lion and Wolf in Shakespeare's Descriptions of Night', *Modern Language Review* 66 (1971), 1-10, that this combination of animals (which is said to denote 'time' in Titian's 'Allegory of Prudence') is often used by Shakespeare in descriptions of night, but only when the possibility of death is part of the context. It is conceivable that other groups or lists of animals might turn out to have this kind of significance.

27. This might be contrasted with the catalogue of dogs cited by Macbeth (3.1.91-100) where the different breeds are carefully distinguished in terms of function and value. The notion of hierarchy *is* important in this context because Macbeth is trying to persuade two men that, in order to prove that they 'have a station in the file,/ Not i' th' worst rank of manhood', they must kill Banquo. His thinking, and his employment of the basic man—beast paradigm, is comparable with that of Edmund's Captain discussed above, pp.65-8.

28. Strictly speaking, Lear does not know of their (would-be) adulterous relationship with Edmund but the audience does, and in any case it is common for Shakespearean characters to associate any kind of 'unnatural' behaviour with lust and sexual corruption as when Malcolm surprisingly alludes to Macbeth's 'luxuriousness' and 'voluptuousness' (4.3.57-61).

29. The Fool mixes animals and people in a different way in the mock-trial scene which, as we have said, is omitted from the Folio. As part of his running commentary on the nature of madness, he tells Lear and Edgar, 'He's mad that trusts in the tameness of a wolf, a horse's health, a boy's love, or a whore's oath' (3.6.18-19). This has a proverbial ring to it and indeed some editors emend to read 'a horse's heels' because of the proverb 'Trust not a horse's heels nor a dog's tooth' (Tilley, H711). Other proverbs which relate the human and the animal in this way are: 'Who drives an ass and leads a whore has pain and sorrow evermore' (A368), 'Three things always bring cost: the fawning of a dog, the love of a whore and the invitation of a host' (T208), 'Fiddlers, dogs and flies (or flatterers) come to feasts uncalled' (F206) and 'Flatterers look like friends, as wolves like dogs' (F347). Shakespeare makes use of this proverbial tradition again for Apemantus' 'grace' in *Timon* 1.2.64-9.

30. Of course, the very unchallengeability of this gives rise to images of its transcendence, in the Christian tradition, whereby death becomes ultra-life, eternal life, and 'takes place' in an ultra-height, heaven. Little if any of this is to be found at the conclusion of *King Lear*.

31. It is not clear why either the passage in 3.7 or the one in 4.2 should have been omitted from the Folio except as part of a general cutting of the text in order to save stage time. If Shakespeare himself was responsible for this cutting one might speculate that he felt some of this was rather repetitive.

32. For the significance of the pelican, see n. 2 above. The theme of cannibalism is repeated in Edgar's final couplet in this scene: 'Fie, foh and fum,/ I smell the blood of a British man' (3.4.183-4). Michael Schmidt has noted the extended

reference to cannibalism in scene xxiv of the old *King Leir* play when Perillus (roughly the equivalent of Kent) offers his own flesh to the starving King: 'Cannibalism in *King Lear*', *Notes and Queries* 216 (1971), 148-9. It has been suggested that Shakespeare himself played Perillus: see Kenneth Muir's New Arden edition of *King Lear* (as cited in n. 26 above), p.xxix.

33. The notion that animals behave better than men in this respect is found in Edward Topsell's *The historie of foure-footed beastes*, 1607: he claims in his dedicatory epistle that 'many and most excellent rules for publick and private affaires . . . are gathered from Beasts', and asks rhetorically: 'Were not this a good perswasion against murder, to see all Beasts so to maintain their natures, that they kill not their own kind?' (A7r).

34. 'Shows' is in fact a correction found in some copies of the Quarto. Other copies and the Folio read 'seemes'. Shakespeare uses 'shows' in a very similar context at 1.4.260 (in the passage quoted on p.79), and the false etymological relation of 'monster' to *monstrare*, to show, may have influenced the correction. The meaning is the same whether we read 'shows' or 'seems', though perhaps 'shows' puts more emphasis on visual appearance. That the words could be virtually synonymous is illustrated by Hamlet's play on them: 'Seems? . . . I know not ''seems''./ . . . These indeed might seem,/ . . . But I have that within which passes show . . .' (*Hamlet* 1.2.76-85).

35. Lear becomes interested in whether the transformation is literal as well as metaphorical: 'Then let them anatomize Regan; see what breeds about her heart' (3.6.76-7), a sentiment curiously echoed later by Edgar, 'To know our enemies' minds, we rip their hearts . . .' (4.6.260).

36. As we have already seen with the 'great-siz'd monster of ingratitudes' in *Troilus* (pp.24-7 above), Shakespeare frequently saw ingratitude as monstrous. Other instances of this can be found in *As You Like It* 2.7.174-90, *Henry V* 2.2.95, *Coriolanus* 2.3.9, and *Timon* 4.2.45-6 and 5.1.65.

37. This tradition is interestingly explored by Patricia Parker in 'The Metaphorical Plot', in David S. Miall (ed.), *Metaphor: Problems and Perspectives* (Harvester, Brighton, 1982), pp.133-57.

38. At the 1983 'Theory and Text' conference at Southampton, Barbara Johnson revealed that she suggests to students trying to remember the tenor-vehicle distinction that they imagine Pavarotti emerging from a (very small) taxi.

39. 'The Shakespearean Conceit', in Alastair Fowler, *Conceitful Thought* (Edinburgh University Press, 1975), pp.87-113.

3

Metaphors of the Human Body and its Parts in *Hamlet*

Varieties of Parts and Wholes

The relationship between metaphor and other figures of speech becomes a practical problem as soon as almost any Shakespearean figure is analysed in any detail. In this chapter we shall be looking at a set of metaphors in *Hamlet* resting upon conceptual relationships which the rhetorical tradition classes as synecdochic or metonymic. But this also raises the broader theoretical question of metaphor's relationship to synecdoche and metonymy in general.

On the one hand, Roman Jakobson and others have seen the metaphor–metonymy distinction as constituting the fundamental polarity within the field of figurative language.[1] The two basic forms of 'association of ideas' which gave associationist psychology its name—association by resemblance and association by contiguity—are taken to underlie metaphor and metonymy respectively: a rose can stand for my love either because she is like it (resemblance) or because she grew it (contiguity). From this standpoint, synecdoche—the part standing for the whole, or the whole for the part—looks like a subdivision of metonymy: what could be more contiguous to a part than the whole of which it is a part?

On the other hand, synecdoche is closely related to metaphor rather than metonymy in the rhetorical tradition from the outset. Aristotle's four types of metaphor (metaphor being defined as 'the transferring to one object of a name belonging to another') are 'displacements from genus to species, from species to genus, from species to species, or by analogy', as Umberto Eco reminds us; and he goes on to point out that therefore 'Aristotle uses *metaphor* as a generic term: his first two types of metaphors are in fact synecdoches'.[2] Recently, the collective authors of *Rhétorique générale,* who sign themselves Group µ (Mu), have advanced the startling claim that 'metaphor is the product of two synecdoches, as in a different way is metonymy'.[3] Group µ's synecdocho-centrism, as Nobuo Sato has termed it,[4] is based on taking as primary not resemblance and contiguity but various forms of division and decomposition.

Before we can understand how metaphor and metonymy could be seen as grounded in synecdochic operations, some exposition of the Group µ analysis of synecdoche itself is necessary. It turns out that 'part for whole' is itself a formula which faces in two quite different directions.

The classic textbook example of synecdoche is *sail* for *ship.* The part–whole relationship here is concrete, referential. It reflects the possible decomposition of the whole ship into sail *and* rudder *and* hull *and* cabin *and* . . . Group µ, following a logical tradition[5] speak of this 'and'-related series as a decomposition of the whole into the logical Product of its parts—mode Π (Pi) decomposition for short. This is the sort of part–whole relationship which theorists have in mind when the metonymic flavour of synecdoche is stressed.

But another form of decomposition exists, in the conceptual rather than the referential realm. Here we must consider 'that model for definition, structured by genera species and differentiae, known as the Porphyrian tree'[6]—a model which Porphyry developed from Aristotle. Within a Porphyrian tree, each level of classification can be thought of as 'decomposable' into the members of the level below: each genus is composed of its species, each class of its subclasses. Here the decomposition of ship would be into kinds of ship: a ship is a barque *or* a brig *or* a ketch *or* a schooner *or*. . ..Group µ speak of this 'or'-related series, whereby the class is decomposed into the logical Sum of its subclasses, as mode Σ (Sigma) decomposition. As Eco points out, Aristotle's first two types of metaphor are synecdoches in mode Σ. The first, substitution of genus for species, may be termed a *generalizing synecdoche in* Σ; the second, substitution of species for genus, may be termed a *particularizing synecdoche in* Σ.

The movements of generalizing and particularizing operate within mode Π as well. A *generalizing synecdoche in* Π involves the substitution of the material whole for the part, while a *particularizing synecdoche in* Π involves the substitution of the material part for the whole.

How traditional this is can be seen if we turn to an Elizabethan treatment of synecdoche, John Hoskins' *Directions for Speech and Style*(1599):[7]

> SYNECDOCHE is an exchange of the name of the part for the whole, or of the name of the whole for the part. There are two kinds of total comprehensions, as an entire body and a general name; as, *Ay, my name is tossed and censured by many tongues,* for *many men,* where the part of an entire body goes for the whole. Contrariwise, *he carried a goldsmith's shop on his fingers,* for *rings; he fell into the water and swallowed the Thames,* for *the water.* So the general name for the special: *put up your weapon,* for *your dagger;* and the special for the particular, as, *the Earl is gone into Ireland* for *Earl of Essex;* the particular for the special, as, *I would willingly make you a Sir Philip Sidney,* for *an eloquent, learned, valiant, gentleman.*

The way an 'entire body' comprehends its parts corresponds to Group μ's mode Π; the way a 'general name' comprehends its species corresponds to their mode Σ. The only complication in Hoskins' account is that his Porphyrian tree is a three-level one, with a genus comprised of species and species comprised of particulars.

Interestingly, Hoskins makes it clear in passing that he considers both synecdoche and metonymy (which he treats immediately before synecdoche) as rather prosaic figures. He does not, as is his usual practice, find examples in Sidney's *Arcadia;* of his synecdoches, he remarks that he has 'because they are easy . . . exemplified [them] familiarly', while he seems positively irritated at the thought of searching for metonymies; 'No doubt better examples of this sort are in *Arcadia,* if I had leisure to look so low as where they are' (10).[8] Metonymic and synecdochic effects in themselves are seen as heightening discourse only a little.

In the passages from *Hamlet* which we shall shortly be considering, however, synecdoche becomes more conceptually interesting than usual. This is because the wholes in question are the human body and the human person, and the decomposition of these entities into parts raises a number of conceptual problems. What are a person's parts? Are they immaterial as well as material, and if so what is the relationship between the two? (Is the soul, or the will, part of you in just the same sense as an eye is?) Are you equivalent to your body, or more than it (are you what you eat, what you wear, what gestures you make), or less than it (so that your body's surface, or your surface in general, is not you, is an opacity, a lure or a lie)? What parts can operate as reliable signs for the whole (body or person) under normal conditions—and do normal conditions in fact prevail? These interdependent questions give rise to the sort of difficulty for thought that we have already seen time generate; and, as there, metaphor is forced upon the mind struggling with these difficulties. But since it is part–whole relationships which are here in question, the metaphors must have a strong synecdochic component; they are metaphors *of* synecdoche, one might say.

Group μ *on Metaphor*

In most of this chapter it will be this one particular relationship between metaphor and synecdoche that will be explored; but we have found that thinking through the more general metaphor–synecdoche link which Group μ posit has helped us grasp the conceptual moves at work in the particular case. So some exposition of Group μ's account of metaphor (and metonymy) as double synecdoche seems in order at this point. (Readers who are eager to get to *Hamlet* may skim this section quickly without undue loss).

We have already seen that Aristotle's first two classes of 'metaphor' are in fact synecdoches (genus to species, species to genus) in mode Σ. How would his third type, species to species, operate? Rather badly, if the species in question belong to a particular genus within a *proper* Porphyrian tree: 'cat' is not a good metaphor for 'dog', where both really are species of the genus mammal.[9] But what happens in metaphor is that some similarity or 'conceptual overlap' between x and y becomes the basis for an *ad hoc* Porphyrian tree. 'My love' and 'rose' are seen as species joined, not in a real genus (as they in fact are by virtue of both being organic, living things) but in the *ad hoc* genus constituted by *whatever one can make of their intersection:* both are beautiful, sweet-smelling, pink, short-lived, thorny . . .: it is up to the particular rose-lyric to exploit some of these features or to invent unexpected new aspects of intersection. This picture of how metaphor operates gives us the familiar Venn diagram:[10]

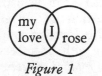

Figure 1

This can also be represented as an *ad hoc* Porphyrian tree, with I (the intersection) in the genus position:

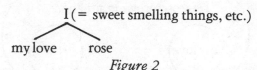

Figure 2

Group μ's derivation of metaphor from synecdoche amounts to claiming that, logically, the move from 'rose' to 'my love' involves one move upwards (a generalizing synecdoche in mode Σ: the class sweet-smelling thing standing for its member my love) and one move back downwards (a particularizing synecdoche in mode Σ: the member rose standing for the class sweet-smelling thing).

This is a logical rather than a psychological claim; clearly no one would want to argue that this upwards—downwards movement was actually carried out as a two-stage cognitive process each time we construe a metaphor.[11] But even when this is appreciated, there seems to be something odd about the synecdoches which constitute the metaphor in comparison with the usual examples of synecdoche. There are two reasons for this. The first is that we are in mode Σ, and the most vivid synecdoches are those in mode Π, where the whole is concrete rather than conceptual. The second is that our mode Σ Porphyrian tree, as *ad hoc,* is brought into being *only by the metaphoric process itself,* whereas the textbook examples of genus-to-species and vice versa always involve moving up or down a real Porphyrian tree. So while the metaphor can be seen as involving two synecdoches, the synecdoches in question are only constituted by the intersection specific to the particular metaphor.

Despite this—which is no real disadvantage once we grasp that the nub of Group μ's point lies in the diagram rather than in the 'metaphor equals double synecdoche' verbal formulation—the great attraction of the Group μ analysis is that three other forms of trope result if we explore mode Π as well as mode Σ and down–up (general–particular–general) movement, as well as up–down (particular–general–particular) movement. Let us take the metonymic reading of 'My love is a rose' first. Here, according to Group μ, we are dealing with 'membership in a material whole' (*coappartenance à une totalité matérielle*),[12] which might be Venn-diagrammed thus:

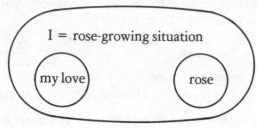

Figure 3

and tree-diagrammed thus:

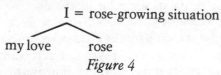

Figure 4

We are in mode Π now, where a material whole is belonged to by both the rose and the rose-grower (one such whole might be the garden): once again, the conceptual relationship can be seen as moving from part to whole and back again to another part. Thus this form of metonymy, like species–to–species metaphor, involves a generalizing synecdoche followed by a particularizing synecdoche.

What happens in modes Π and Σ if we try to reverse the generalizing–particularizing direction? Group μ claim that here it is mode Σ which fails to produce intersection and mode Π which does. In an understandable drive towards tidiness, they would like to see mode Σ as producing a form of metonymy (non-intersection) and mode Π as producing a form of metaphor (intersection)—neither, admittedly, the standard form. In fact, the down–up move made in mode Σ is very difficult to imagine, because it violates the spirit of Porphyrian tree construction, which always branches from the top downwards. One needs to think of a given item as located within two different Porphyrian trees, that is a member of two different classes; then an association between the classes might be set up on the basis of their sharing a common member. Suppose Tom, the most scholarly person you knew, were also redheaded. Then Tom becomes the whole in which two classificational modes are brought together, whether one visualizes the situation as this:

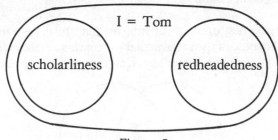

Figure 5

or this:

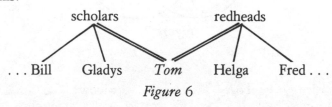

Figure 6

The trouble is that while it is easy enough to imagine this as a diagram for a process of association (so much has Tom impressed you that whenever you see a redheaded person you think of scholarship), it doesn't seem to work tropically: that you could say 'redheaded' and be understood as meaning 'scholarly', even by others acquainted with Tom, seems very unlikely.

The remaining possibility, a particularizing–generalizing movement in mode Π, is also rather strange, but it does seem to correspond to (and indeed illuminate the structure of) a real trope. Here a given item is part of two different material wholes. Group μ's example of this is *voiles,* which are a part of both *un bateau* and *une veuve.* But the untranslatability of this is instructive: the *voiles* of a boat are sails, the *voiles* of a widow are veils. (The English translation substitutes *bridge* for *voiles,* keeps to the nautical with *ship*, but fills in as another bridge-possessing object *denture*!).

95

Nobuo Sato sees the non-identity of the part as an objection to the analysis; of the *voiles* example he writes:

> We find it too difficult to understand the intermediary term as a unity. Isn't there a misleading polysemy in these *voiles?* Certainly one finds two metonymies (the first: boat—*voile* [sail]; the second: *voiles* [veils]—widow), but it still seems necessary to see another metaphor at the heart of the central term: *voiles* 1 = *voiles* 2.[13]

However, the non-unity of the intermediary term here reminds us of the *ad hoc*ness of the intermediary term class in the other case of intersection, ordinary metaphor. Diagrammatically we have this:

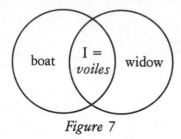

Figure 7

or this:

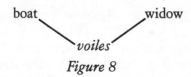

Figure 8

Now it is easy enough to think of parts which belong to more than one whole: rooms are parts of both houses and office-blocks. But this gives rise to no sense of conceptual drama, as it were; it is like the cats–dogs–mammals example above. What is needed to give surprise and delight is an *ad hoc* rather than a real unity at the intersection; and this is achieved, not by metaphorization (though that may arise secondarily—see our discussion of 'unholy suits' below), but by punning. The pun (this sort of pun at any rate) both rests upon and constitutes the double synecdoches here in mode Π in just the same way as metaphor does in mode Σ.

It is important to realize the modesty of the Group μ treatment of metaphor: to diagrammatize metaphor as in Figures 1 and 2 is not to specify how specific intersections work.[14] And, it might be objected that, in concentrating on Aristotle's species-to-species metaphor, Group μ ignore the most interesting sort, metaphor by analogy or proportion. But this would not be fair. All that changes when we move to proportionality is that our Porphyrian tree classifies not objects but relationships:

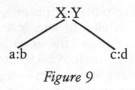

Figure 9

While Group μ have not to our knowledge developed this line of thought, it should present no insuperable difficulties for them. Similarly, we see no inconsistency between Group μ's work in situating the metaphoric structure as one of four possibilities and more detailed work on intersection (which would investigate amount and direction of transfer within the intersection, as in the approaches discussed in the two previous chapters).

However, we should stress that the discussion to follow is not concerned with demonstrating the *metaphor-dependent* synecdoches involved in the up–down movement of Figure 2. We focus, as we have said, on the *independent* synecdochic resources which get deployed in speaking of the human body and person as decomposable wholes, and on how various part–whole relationships are metaphorically mapped onto others. That is, the metaphors we are dealing with are most often of the sort diagrammed in Figure 9: four term analogies.

In the following sections of this chapter we shall be looking at a large number of passages from *Hamlet* in which part–whole relationships involving the human body enter importantly into the figurative elaboration of the text. A preliminary overview may be useful, specially as the detail of the discussion may at times obscure its direction.

Guiding our search for passages to discuss has been our sense that body synecdoches are at once routine and unsettling. This is most easily appreciated when the body is simply taken to be the skin-bound organism. To divide this body into parts conceptually is so routine, so 'natural' that we take the divisions for granted.

Thinking of the body as an assemblage of organs, limbs, areas, and so forth is required for any number of everyday practical purposes. Synecdoche exploits this commonsensical division of the body into parts, often in a low-key, virtually 'invisible' way. But the notion of the division of the body suddenly becomes horrific if any *actual* division is suggested—the nightmare of dismemberment. Tragic drama, through its concern with the dark side of what can happen, may find its synecdoches pulled in this unsettling direction.

Redefine the body as clothed and groomed, and a different combination of the routine and the unsettling emerges. In some ways the situation reverses itself. What is routine is the assumption that you and your clothing and your make-up form an indissoluble unity. Yet actually these accoutrements can be removed easily and painlessly. By the same token, they are subject to the conscious control of the person who chooses them, and this opens up the possibility of deception. What you choose to cover yourself with may be chosen in order to fool those who work on the assumption that what people wear is a dependable index of what they are. Here again the tragic text will tend to exploit the possibilities of disjunctions between the detachable part and the whole for which it claims to stand.

Body Parts

The human body is a concrete whole which lends itself to decomposition in mode Π, that is to a division into named parts. From this fact we can get some very straightforward synecdoches, as when *face, eye, hand* and so forth are used to stand for the whole person possessing them. Such synecdoches can be almost invisible for two reasons: first, they may be highly conventional, and, second, the nature of the part—whole relationship means that they are often literally true. When Hamlet speaks of disposing of Polonius' body—'I'll lug the guts into the neighbour room' (3.4.212)—he is speaking the truth, though not the whole truth: the guts are still enclosed in the rest of the body.

Conventionality and near-literality are often combined in *eye* synecdoches. Fortinbras' line 'We shall express our duty in his eye' (4.4.6), meaning 'in the king's presence', and Claudius'

98

invitation to Hamlet to remain 'in the cheer and comfort of our eye' (1.2.116), feel as little figurative as they do because to be in the presence of the king *is,* amongst other things, to put yourself before his eyes. Also, as Harold Jenkins, the Arden editor, points out in annotating the latter example, the trope is frequent, so much so that Hamlet's letter to Claudius,

> Tomorrow shall I beg leave to see your kingly eyes, when I shall, first asking you pardon, thereunto recount the occasion of my sudden and more strange return.

> 4.7.44-7

should not bother us and we should be happy to follow the punctuation of Q2 (as above) rather than adopt the Folio reading which omits the comma after 'pardon' and puts the whole phrase 'first asking your pardon thereunto' into parentheses. (The Riverside editor in fact follows the Folio here, as does Philip Edwards in his New Cambridge edition, 1985). As Jenkins says, 'The antecedent [of *thereunto*] is *your kingly eyes* and editors who find an anomaly in recounting to those ignore the conventional metonymy which uses ''eyes'' for the royal presence. Cf. *Troilus and Cressida* 1.3.219, ''Do a fair message to his kingly eyes'' (which the Folio also unreasonably emends by substituting *ears*)'.[15] The difference between Jenkin's intuition and those of the anomaly-spotting editors brings out another feature of body–part synecdoche; the part's characteristic *function* has a tendency to motivate the choice of it as a trope for the whole, and only in the case of 'dead–synecdoche', as it were, could a king who is hearing something be represented by eyes rather than by ears.

Another key synecdochic motivation is the use of the part for the whole when the state of the part is *symptomatic* of the state of the whole. Hamlet's eye functions as the organ of sight, but its status as a readable element of the human countenance is equally important. Thus when, in a famous passage to which we shall return, Hamlet give us the list of 'seems' of grief, they include the 'fruitful river in the eye' (1.2.80); weeping is a sign (but only a sign) of his 'woe'. Gertrude has shortly before this asked Hamlet to

> let thine eye look like a friend on Denmark.
> Do not for ever with thy vailed lids
> Seek for thy noble father in the dust.

> 1.2.69-71

Here we see both the conjunction of function and symptom, in
1.69, and a play on their disjunction in the following lines. To use
one's eye(s) as a friend, to look at something and see it as good, will
naturally result in one's *having* a friendly look, in one's eyes
appearing friendly. Instead, Hamlet appears depressed and hostile
through, amongst other things, his eyes being cast down. Cast-
down eyes in fact see little, but Gertrude finds an object of sight for
them: while it is Denmark (whether the state as a whole or, by
standard metonymy, its king) that should be being seen, it is the
dust that is actually in view. Dust is what dead bodies reduce to, as
the play will remind us more eloquently later (2.2.308, 5.1.203).
Yet the dead (even as corpses, much less as who they were) *cannot*
be seen in it, so the cast-down eye will never find the object it is
looking for. It is appropriate, then, that (by synecdoche or
metonymy, depending on whether we consider the eye-region as a
whole of which eyeball, eyelid, eyebrow and so on are parts, or
whether we consider the eyeball to be the eye and the eyelid to stand
for it contiguously) it should be the *lid* that seeks, that is the part of
the eye which when lowered ('vailed') actually blocks sight.[16] So
within the broad sense in which Hamlet's eyes are synecdochic of
Hamlet, both what they are and how they look can be in question,
and a delicate playing-off of these two aspects can be unobtrusively
exploited.[17]

→ At two points in *Hamlet,* characters comment on the breakdown
of the normal functioning of the human organism in terms of the
breakdown of its parts. Ophelia, distressed by Hamlet's bizarre
behaviour to her in the so-called nunnery scene, exclaims

> O, what a noble mind is here o'erthrown!
> The courtier's, soldier's, scholar's, eye, tongue, sword,
> Th'expectation and rose of the fair state,
> The glass of fashion and the mould of form,
> Th'observ'd of all observers, quite, quite down!
>
> 3.1.150-4

Editors used to assume that there was a textual error here because
the order might more logically read 'courtier's, scholar's,
soldier's, eye, tongue, sword', but there is a similar neglect of logic
in some lines in *The Rape of Lucrece*—

> For princes are the glass, the school, the book,
> Where subject's eyes do learn, do read, do look—
>
> (615-16)

and in any case Ophelia's meaning is clear: she assumes Hamlet is mad because of the apparent dislocation or disfunction of his hitherto excellent 'parts'. In this instance we find not only literal parts of the body ('eye', 'tongue') standing for larger categories of function or achievement, but also an inanimate object ('sword') standing for 'sword-arm' as well as for 'swordsmanship'.

Does some awkwardness (justified perhaps by Ophelia's confusion) remain in the integration of the synecdoches into the larger metaphor governing the sentence? A series of expressions for Hamlet's quality, with increasing stress on his visibility, moves from synecdoches (1.151) through the literal ('expectation') to metaphors ('rose', 'glass', 'mould') and back to the literal ('Th'observ'd'). And all of these are 'down'. The passage as a whole involves a Lakoff and Johnson orientational metaphor (SICKNESS IS DOWN)[18] and perhaps an ontological metaphor: certainly for a mind to be something that can be 'o'erthrown' it must be some sort of object. But this is the problem: what is the entity which all the phrases in apposition express? From 'expectation' onwards, despite the hendiadys effect,[19] there is no real trouble: Hamlet is all these things (and so what is ontological is the sum of Hamlet's splendid and visible qualities). But how can 1.151 be read as in apposition to the other phrases and as meaning 'Hamlet'? Yet despite the syntax the figure seems to work—as making explicit, via a mode Π decomposition, what are the parts of an exemplary figure such as Hamlet *used* to be. *To be* the mould of form is *to have* the courtier's tongue, the soldier's sword, the scholar's eye.

Later Hamlet, while denying his own madness, accuses his mother of suffering a similar dislocation of the functions of her various parts, as evidenced by her switch of affections from his father to his uncle. He accuses her of having

> Eyes without feeling, feeling without sight,
> Ears without hands or eyes, smelling sans all.[20]
>
> 3.4.78-9

These lines contrast interestingly with an equally synecdochic

101

passage earlier in the play where Claudius speakes to Laertes of the high regard in which he holds Polonius:

> The head is not more native to the heart,
> The hand more instrumental to the mouth,
> Than is the throne of Denmark to thy father.
> 1.2.47-9

This is a simile wherein the proportion *King of Denmark* (via conventional metonymy): *thy father* is paralleled with two body—part relationships, *head: heart* and *hand: mouth*. Not only do the parts meet smoothly in a single body in each of the two vehicle relationships, but it feels as if all four are joined together in an image of 'the human organism, with the interdependence of its various mechanisms' (Jenkins): a sort of recomposition in mode Π. (The only aspect of the figure that may jar faintly is the 'low' physical-appetite nature of the second proportion in relationship to the first). These are synecdoches of integration whereas Hamlet is accusing Gertrude of having somehow disintegrated. Now each body part, rather than joining with others in a single whole, becomes its own little whole from which in turn parts have been taken away.[21] That the 'wrong' sense is described as lacking in the case of the first two personified parts (we might expect 'eyes without sight' and 'hands without feeling') adds to the sense of dislocation, as does the move backwards and forwards between organ and sensory modality. Almost as shocking as the ears' lack of hands or eyes is the thought of an ear free-standing and person-like enough to have them.

Ears do in fact figure rather largely in *Hamlet,* presumably because the method by which Claudius actually murdered Hamlet's father can be seen as adding to both their literal and their metaphorical functions. The Ghost describes how his murderer 'in the porches of my ears did pour/ The leprous distillment [i.e. the poison]' (1.5.63-4)[22] and this scene is re-enacted both in the dumb show (stage direction at 3.2.135) and in 'The Murder of Gonzago' itself (stage direction at 3.2.260). Modern medicine tells us that such a method would not actually be effective, but Shakespeare seems to have been inspired by this bizarre detail in one of his sources to produce a long train of associated references.

The Ghost himself punningly foreshadows his account of his own murder when he begins by telling Hamlet that 'the whole ear

of Denmark/Is . . ./Rankly abus'd (1.5.36-8) by a false version of
events put out by Claudius. Presumably the audience does not, on
first hearing this, suspect that this fairly familiar metaphor is about
to be literalized before their very eyes. Neither, we must assume,
should the characters themselves seem to be aware of the
implications of their own choice of metaphors; Claudius can hardly
be consciously alluding to his own crime when he remarks that the
newly returned Laertes 'wants not buzzers to infect his ear/ With
pestilent speeches of his father's death' (4.5.90-1).

Many of the play's references to ears pursue this association by
concentrating on the notion of acts of aggression performed against
ears, resulting in disease or damage. Apart from the question of ears
being 'abused' or 'infected' by lies (Hamlet also accuses Horatio of
'doing violence' to his ears when he thinks he is lying to him,
1.2.171), they are attacked by unwelcome news, as when Barnardo
insists on repeating the story of the Ghost's appearance to the
sceptical Horatio: 'let us once again assail your ears,/ That are so
fortified against our story' (1.1.31-2); Gertrude seems less well
fortified against Hamlet's accusations in the closet scene: 'These
words like daggers enter in my ears' (3.4.95).[23] Despite the
existence of the idiom 'to close one's ears' to something or
someone, we cannot literally close our ears as we can close our eyes,
so they are more vulnerable to literal and metaphorical assault.

Even when the 'intake' is in itself untroublesome, the ears can be
hurt by the sheer volume of noise. Hamlet both deplores the
tendency of bad actors to 'split the ears of the groundlings'
(3.2.10-11) and half-envies the First Player's supposed ability to
'cleave the general ear with horrid speech' (2.2.563). This latter
example gives us a two-stage synecdoche combined with a
metaphor: the crowd becomes a single person who becomes a single
ear which becomes something that can be 'cleft' by speech-seen-as-
a-sharp-intrument. The ear is both inexpressive and passive; as well
as being attacked by noise it can be 'taken prisoner' as in the case of
Pyrrhus (2.2.477), causing the motion of the entire body to be
arrested.[24]

By contrast, the face is a vehicle for serious synecdoche *par
excellence,* expressive and active in a way which *should* express the
person 'behind' it but *may* be part of that person's deceptive
activity. Lakoff and Johnson have pointed out how everyday the
face-for-the-whole-person synecdoche is:

103

If you ask me to show you a picture of my son and I show you a picture of his face, you will be satisfied. You will consider yourself to have seen a picture of him. But if I show you a picture of his body without his face, you will consider it strange and will not be satisfied. You might even ask, 'But what does he look like'?[25]

We assume, reasonably enough, that the face both functions as that part of the body which expresses meaning and can be 'read' as so doing. We expect to be able to interpret a person's face as a set of signs indicating their thoughts or feelings. Thus when Ophelia reports Hamlet's distraught and intensely questioning reaction to her rejection of his courtship she says

> He falls to such perusal of my face
> As 'a would draw it.
>
> 2.1.87-8

Hamlet seems equally fascinated by the inscrutability and apparent deceptiveness of Claudius' face or facial gestures:

> My tables—meet it is I set it down
> That one may smile, and smile, and be a villain![26]
>
> 1.5.107-8

The face is of course an extremely complex 'part' of a person. In fact it is not a single part but an assembly of features some of which, the eyes, the mouth and the forehead, for example, can be expressive while others, the ears and the nose, for example, are more passive. Moreover it can, as we shall see, have its overall expressiveness affected by various sorts of natural and artificial colouring or marking.

Skin

The skin is a 'part' of the human body which can stand in a familiar synecdochic relation to the whole. We can speak of 'saving one's skin' or 'keeping one's skin whole' when we mean 'staying alive' or 'keeping the life *in* one's body'.

So, while being part of the body, the skin can also be seen as a container for the body, that which both distinguishes it and protects it from the 'outside' world. In answer to Hamlet's rather morbid question, 'How long will a man lie i'th' earth ere he rot?' (5.1.163-4), the Gravedigger replies that 'A tanner will last you nine year . . . [because] his hide is so tann'd with his trade that 'a will keep out water a great while' (5.1.168-71). The term 'hide' reminds us that, in comparison with other living creatures, human beings have very fragile or 'thin' skin, easily damaged or penetrated; at the end of the play, Laertes emphasizes that he has only to 'scratch' Hamlet, or 'gall him slightly' with his poisoned rapier in order to kill him (4.7.140-8).

The relationship between skin and body is readily available as a metaphor for any relationship between something 'outer' and something 'inner' respecting a person. In Lakoff and Johnson terms, this means that X IS SKIN metaphors are commonly generated where X is either some other species of material covering (for example, clothing) or something more abstract which can be thought of as having a covering function (for example, appearance). We could picture this in mode Σ thus:

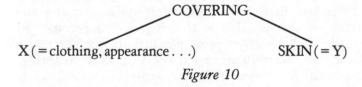

$$\text{X}\,(=\text{clothing, appearance}\ldots) \qquad \text{SKIN}\,(=\text{Y})$$

Figure 10

Other forms of covering can take the position of SKIN in this schema (let us call it the Y position), but whichever Y one has, its own distinctive *manner* of being a covering will get (to a greater or lesser extent) carried over into the field of X. This is what makes a certain reading of the metaphor-as-double-synecdoche account unsatisfactory, as Group μ themselves have cautioned: if *all* that goes on is the dropping of semes in moving from skin to covering and the addition of new semes in moving from covering to X, then the carry-over of any of Y's peculiarities to X would be unexplained.

The problem can be seen concretely at a point where we feel, though it could be argued that skin doesn't come into the picture at all, that a submerged skin metaphor is present. Hamlet is addressing Gertrude:

Leave wringing of your hands . . .
And let me wring you heart, for so I shall
If it be made of penetrable stuff,
If damned custom have not brass'd it so
That it be proof and bulwark against sense.

3.4.34-8

On the face of it, the Y position here is occupied by 'brass': the surface of Gertrude's heart may be, but hopefully is not, so 'brazen' as not to let in the 'sense' (let us ignore the rich meanings of 'sense' for present purposes) which Hamlet is about to offer. On this reading, 'custom' would have to be a personified agent, an artificer who puts the brass on hearts. However, there is one sort of covering which becomes naturally thicker, more impermeable from particular 'custom' or use: the skin. (A specialized version of this is presented by the tanner's skin.) If in everyday metaphorical terms the fear about Gertrude is that she is 'hardened', the process by which such a thing happens is most easily figured forth by a skin-based metaphor. We would then have a multi-stage metaphor whereby Gertrude-as-a-whole-person is her heart (synecdoche); the heart, to protect itself from assault (of which wringing and penetration are species), has a covering, which becomes its symptomatic and effective part (ontological metaphor plus synecdoche): the heart's covering is brass (X IS Y 'covering' metaphor with X non-material); but brass is skin (X IS Y 'covering' metaphor with X and Y equally material but with different properties). The result of all this is that a skin like aspect of covering is carried over as part of the analysis of how habituation works at the same time as a harder covering is explicitly presented as the metaphoric vehicle.

It is worth noting in passing that the question of the 'skin' of the heart redoubles a surface—substance thematic, in that the heart itself is a beneath-the-skin organ, in contrast to hands. Hamlet is, as we say, trying to 'get under Gertrude's skin', but once 'there' the same problem threatens to replay itself—there may be skins beneath the skin, as it were.

The skin is of course a much more intimate form of body-covering than armour, clothes, paint or make-up; human beings cannot 'shed' it until death.[27] Since it is the outward, visible part of the person, endowed with certain capacities for variation, its colour or condition can be taken as indicative or symptomatic of the state of the whole body; we can literally go pale with fear or red with anger, for example. Equally, the skin can be a literal indicator of the body's state of health; the Ghost of Hamlet's father describes the effect of poison on his skin in dramatic but, presumably, tenor-rather-than-vehicle terms:

> And a most instant tetter bark'd about,
> Most lazar-like, with vile and loathsome crust,
> All my smooth body.[28]

> 1.5.71-3.

Bodily states—the expressiveness of the body as well as its overall health—inevitably get used as metaphors for mental (spiritual, psychological) states. Such metaphors seem natural because not only are thoughts and feelings ripe for general 'ontologization' in Lakoff and Johnson's sense, but in our culture we are used to thinking of our thoughts and feelings as being as much 'inside' us as our brains and hearts are. The skin then becomes the figure not so much for *keeping* out (foreign substances) but for *letting* out (information). To find that your resolve is being interfered with by your thoughts can thus be 'embodied' metaphorically by saying that 'the native hue of resolution/ Is sickled o'er with the pale cast of thought' (3.1.83-4), where the natural skin-colour of either the resolute man or of Resolution itself, personified—presumably red given the 'sanguine' basis of resolve in Elizabethan humours theory—is replaced by pallour, and this testifies to (spiritual) illness. (If Resolution is personified, to lose his proper colour is to be sick almost to oxymoron!) Similarly, Gertrude is made to see the state of her soul as akin to a diseased skin:

> Thou turn'st my eyes into my very soul,
> And there I see such black and grained spots
> As will not leave their tinct.

> 3.4.89-91

But any figure for information must be able to allow for the possibility of misinformation. The condition of one's skin can, like one's clothes and gestures, be a false indicator as easily as it can be a true one, though its deceptiveness is of a different sort (not being replaceable, nor, except through make-up, under the actor's control). The skin can lie either through over- or under-indicating. Hamlet compares the Danish fault of drunkenness with a 'mole' on the skin which has a disproportionate effect on the judgement of outsiders, perhaps because it is assumed to be the visible sign of a more general state of imperfection:

> So oft it chances in particular men,
> That for some vicious mole of nature in them,
> As in their birth, wherein they are not guilty
> (Since nature cannot choose his origin),
> By their o'ergrowth of some complexion
> Oft breaking down the pales and forts of reason,
> Or by some habit, that too much o'er-leavens
> The form of plausive manners—that these men,
> Carrying, I say, the stamp of one defect,
> Being nature's livery, or fortune's star,
> His virtues else, be they as pure as grace,
> As infinite as man may undergo,
> Shall in the general censure take corruption
> From that particular fault; the dram of ev'l
> Doth all the noble substance of a doubt
> To his own scandal.[29]
>
> 1.4.23-38

Conversely, it is possible for the skin to appear smooth and perfect when the body 'underneath' is in fact corrupted or diseased. Here the skin is sinister both as indicator and as container; in covering over the disease, it both hides it from sight and makes it worse. Hamlet warns Gertrude:

> Lay not that flattering unction to your soul,
> That not your trespass but my madness speaks;
> It will but skin and film the ulcerous place,
> Whiles rank corruption, mining all within,
> Infects unseen.
>
> 3.4.145-9

Claudius uses similar terms when reproaching himself for not treating Hamlet as the dangerous illness he really represents:

> We would not understand what was most fit,
> But like the owner of a foul disease,
> To keep it from divulging, let it feed
> Even on the pith of life.
>
> 4.1.20-3

Here 'divulging', and how it has been avoided, remains unspecified in detail. But somehow a covering-over of the disease has, in containing it, encouraged it to eat not outwards but inwards. Perhaps we can think either of an infection working inwards from beneath the skin or, more gruesomely, of the Spartan boy's fox eating through the skin and into the heart, hidden beneath the boy's clothing.[30]

Finally, in an age when branding was a common punishment for a number of offences, a fair skin could be artifically (officially) 'marked' in such a way as to make the 'divulging' of inner or moral corruption unavoidable. Hamlet refers to the (potentially) literal practice[31] of branding prostitutes when he accuses his mother of having done a deed which

> Calls virtue hypocrite, takes off the rose
> From the fair forehead of an innocent love
> And sets a blister there.
>
> 3.4.42-4

Laertes also invokes this practice in his hyperbolical justification of his passionate response to the death of his father:

> That drop of blood that's calm proclaims me bastard,
> Cries cuckold to my father, brands the harlot
> Even here between the chaste unsmirched brow
> Of my true mother.
>
> 4.5.118-21

The skin of a person's forehead would be particularly apt to stand for the whole person since it can be thought of as the 'front' of something (the face) which is already the 'front' of the rest of the body. Hence, apart from its sheer visibility (the forehead is rarely clothed), its significance in this context and in the related one of the endless 'horn' jokes of the literature of this period.

Paint

The coloration of the skin may result from natural causes such as fear, anger or sickness, or it may be due to artificial means, specifically painting or make-up. Hamlet himself takes the standard moral line against make-up when he generalizes his attack on women to Ophelia:

> I have heard of your paintings, well enough. God hath given you one face, and you make yourselves another.
>
> 3.1.142-4

As Harold Jenkins puts it in his note on this passage, 'In attacks on the vanities of women cosmetics excited particular indignation as being in principle a blasphemy against God and in practice an accompaniment of easy virtue'. Later, Hamlet seems to take a certain glee from the fact that painting will not protect the skin from its inevitable decay: soon after the conversation about the superior (but relative) protective qualities of the tanner's 'hide', he addresses Yorick's skull:

> Now get you to my lady's chamber, and tell her, let her paint an inch thick, to this favor she must come.
>
> 5.1.192-4

The human head must finally be reduced to the skull, shedding its coverings of flesh and skin as well as paint.

The relationship between the two surface-layers of a face, the skin and the paint, is used by Claudius as a metaphor for the relationship between ('inner') deed and ('outer') word. Responding to Polonius' comment on the hypocrisy of setting up Ophelia with her prayer book to entrap Hamlet,

> We are oft to blame in this—
> 'Tis too much prov'd—that with devotion's visage
> And pious action we do sugar o'er
> The devil himself—
>
> 3.1.45-8

Claudius takes up the link between 'visage' and 'sugar o'er':

110

> O! 'tis too true!
> How smart a lash that speech doth give my conscience!
> The harlot's cheek, beautied with plast'ring art,
> Is not more ugly to the thing that helps it
> Than is my deed to my most painted word.
>
> 3.1.48-52

These are hard lines to understand if, as in every production of a Shakespeare play involving prostitutes we have seen, the prostitute's make-up is itself presented as ugly-making or failed. But the point must be that the make-up is a success. The skin's ugliness is truly representative of the harlot's 'inner' condition, either spiritual or physical (there might be a causal link implied whereby the skin has been made ugly by a sexually-transmitted disease), but a new surface has been superimposed on it which makes it beautiful. Reading 'to' as 'compared to' and 'thing' as 'paint or make-up',[32] we find a careful simile set up: the cheek is as ugly compared to its mask of paint as Claudius' acts (themselves truly representative of his spiritual state) are compared to his words (which presumably stand in synecdochic relationship to his behaviour as a whole).

Something remains odd about the lines nevertheless. The difficulty lies in the way in which the 'beautied' version of the cheek seems self-standing, a wholly separate thing from the real cheek (as separate as words are from the deeds that contradict them). This is only the same point made in 'God hath given you one face, and you make yourselves another', plus a particularizing synecdoche (from face to cheek); yet that particularization brings out the strangeness of separating the make-up from the cheek while still allowing it the shape, the beauty, of a cheek. As it happens, the Variorum edition records a nineteenth-century objection to Claudius' 'cue'—Polonius' comment as quoted above—which reveals sensitivity to this strangeness. Samuel Bailey wrote,

> Can anything be more preposterous than to talk of *sugaring over* the devil with a *visage?* What Shakespeare meant to say is clear enough: we too often disguise the devil himself with devout looks and pious acts. To express this, read: 'with devotion's *vizard* . . . we do *figure* o'er', etc.[33]

What Bailey is unwilling to allow is that a visage can be thought of as substantial and other than what lies behind it in just the way that

111

a vizard is—even though its shapely substance is a strange combination of an opposite substance (the devil, the ugly cheek) and shapeless matter (the sugar, the paint).[34]

'Paint' can form an intersection point for the opposite-to-the-usual metaphorical possibility envisioned by Group μ (see above, Figures 7 and 8) whereby a mode Π decomposition allows us to move from whole to part and back to another whole sharing the same part (in some sense): it is part both of the made-up face and of the painted canvas.

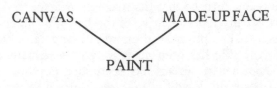

Figure 11

Whether or not one's intuition supports this as a schema for metaphor as such, there is no doubt that the conceptual relationships it captures are exploited in *Hamlet*. The key speech here is that quoted by Hamlet concerning the killing of Priam by Pyrrhus:

> The rugged Pyrrhus, he whose sable arms,
> Black as his purpose, did the night resemble,
> When he lay couched in th' ominous horse,
> Hath now this dread and black complexion smear'd
> With heraldry more dismal: head to foot
> Now is he total gules, horridly trick'd
> With blood of fathers, mothers, daughters, sons.
>
> 2.2.452-8

Both Pyrrhus' colours express rather than hide the truth: his armour is as black as his purpose (coincidence between inner and outer), and over it and himself is smeared the red of his victim's blood (causal link between action and coloration). No doubt editors are correct to point out that 'complexion' here is more generally 'colour, appearance, not necessarily of the face only, and here applied to the whole armed figure',[35] but it would not be wholly outside the spirit of the semantic relationships involved to say that Pyrrhus' 'heraldry'[36] is also his make-up.

When the First Player takes up the speech, he describes how Pyrrhus hesitated just before killing Priam; distracted by the crash of the falling citadel, he stood for a while motionless:

> for lo his sword,
> Which was declining on the milky head
> Of reverent Priam, seem'd i' th' air to stick.
> So as a painted tyrant Pyrrhus stood
> And, like a neutral to his will and matter,
> Did nothing.
>
> 2.2.477-82

Pyrrhus is 'painted' here in a double sense; he is still painted with blood but, because he is motionless, he is also like a mere representation or painting of himself. In this second sense, the paint of the painted tyrant is not secondarily expressive of him but substantially constitutive of him. But with this comes immobility and the draining-away of real substance (only for a moment within the Trojan diegesis, but of course more disquietingly both within the *Hamlet* diegesis, where Pyrrhus is a parallel for Hamlet, and as meta-discourse on art). Thus this notion of painting moves from referring to a surface *over* a substance to designating a surface which is merely a surface. Claudius uses such a metaphor in his efforts to incense Laertes against Hamlet:

> Laertes, was your father dear to you?
> Or are you like the painting of a sorrow,
> A face without a heart?
>
> 4.7.107-9

More sadly, he uses the same metaphor to describe Ophelia's madness:

> poor Ophelia
> Divided from herself and her fair judgement,
> Without the which we are pictures, or mere beasts.
>
> 4.5.84-6

The surprising analogy between pictures and beasts works because both, like Ophelia, lack 'godlike reason' (4.4.38) which is seen as the essential defining characteristic of human beings. But 'Divided from herself' may remind us of Pyrrhus' 'like a neutral to his will and matter'. The broad metaphorical equivalence is somehow between lacking a dimension (being a mere representation) and finding oneself split, divided, doubled.

The play actually makes use of portrait paintings as stage properties in 3.4 when Hamlet forces Gertrude to compare 'The counterfeit presentment of two brothers' (3.4.54).[37] Although 'counterfeit' in the sense of being mere representation, the portraits must be true enough as likenesses (unbelievably truthful in the 'warts and all' sense in the case of Claudius). Here the divisions and differences between the two men, and Gertrude's double marriage, cause Hamlet to accuse *her* of being in effect 'Divided from herself and her fair judgement', which as we have seen he expresses as a schizophrenia of the senses:

> .What devil was't
> That thus hath cozen'd you at hoodman-blind?
> Eyes without feeling, feeling without sight,
> Ears without hands or eyes, smelling sans all,
> Or but a sickly part of one true sense
> Could not so mope.[38]
>
> 3.4.76-81

Clothes

'The apparel oft proclaims the man', says Polonius (1.3.72), advising his son how to dress during his sojourn in Paris. Clothes can be seen as 'part' of a person in the sense of being a covering or surface which conveys information about what is underneath. Unlike skin, but like paint in the make-up sense, the covering can be assumed or detached at will. Like both skin and paint it can convey true or false information about the person ('oft', not 'always').

Most simply, we can be recognized by our clothing ('How should I your true-love know/ From another one?/ By his cockle hat and staff,/ And his sandal shoon', 4.5.23-6), either as an individual or as a type: Claudius contrasts the 'light and careless livery of youth' with the 'sables and weeds' of age (4.7.78-81).[39] Hamlet assesses people's characters by the clothing they *ought* to be wearing when he says of Polonius, 'that great baby you see there is not yet out of his swaddling-clouts' (2.2.382-3) and when he describes Claudius as 'A king of shreds and patches' (3.4.102).[40] His own literal *déshabille* as described by Ophelia in 2.1 ('Lord Hamlet, with his doublet all unbrac'd') is presumably an accurate expression of his state of mind.

Yet clothing can equally conceal or even deliberately distort the wearer. When Francisco asks Barnardo to 'Stand and unfold yourself' at the very beginning of the play, his metaphor suggests that Barnardo's identity is hidden by a cloak or some such garment. Polonius uses a similar but more complex metaphor when he advises Ophelia not to put too much faith in Hamlet's courtship:

> Do not believe his vows, for they are brokers,
> Not of that dye which their investments show,
> But mere implorators of unholy suits,
> Breathing like sanctified and pious bonds,
> The better to beguile.
>
> 1.3.127-31

The vows are personified. If you believed them, it would be because they are acting as themselves, autonomously; but actually they are acting on behalf of (as brokers for, implorators for) some other personified verbal entities, namely Hamlet's suits—his (imputed) requests for sexual favours. The vows act like (breathe like—a sort of particularizing action synecdoche) yet a third group of personified verbal entities, bonds. (One loses this link in the chain if, with editors from Pope in 1728 to Jenkins in 1982, one emends by reading 'bawds' for 'bonds'. This reading would however set up yet another triplet: brokers ('go-betweens in love affairs') –unholy suits–bawds, a sexual corruption triplet).[41] The vows–suits–bonds triplet gives what we take to be the passage's main sense. Counterpointed against it, though, are two other triplets. There is the more strongly financial association which, while not really articulated by the syntax, arises from brokers–investments (modern sense)[42]–bonds. And there is the clothes triplet: dye–investments (vestments)–suits. Dye and investments are operating in the usual synecdochic way within the basic personification. The dye opposition that is understood is presumably black *versus* white: the vows' clothing fails to express

115

their real nature (as acting for the unholy suits) in being the colour of sanctity and piety. (Jenkins notes that 'the only other instance of *investment* in Shakespeare (*2 Henry IV* 4.1.45) also refers to vestments of a colour which belies the wearer's inward character'). This leaves 'suits' as a pun. Jenkins speaks of the pun sharpening 'the disparity between [the vows'] *investments* and their *suits*'. Again we could diagrammatize this via a mode Π decomposition whereby a sense of equivalence is set up between the two wholes of which 'suits' are parts.

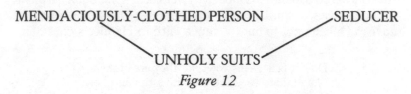

Figure 12

'Unholy suits' are appurtenances both of the seducer and of the person who is dressed up to appear other than he or she is; but it is clearer than it was in the case of 'paint' that the 'suits' in question are identical only verbally.[43] On the other hand, the fact that the dissembler and the seducer are species of the genus 'bad person' bolsters the equivalence set up by the pun via an implicit mode Σ decomposition:

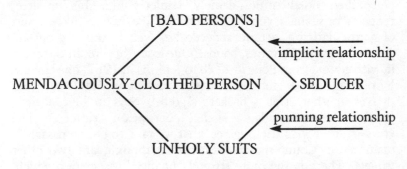

Figure 13

However intricate the micro-level semantics of the passage, its assumptions about clothing and honesty are very straightforward. But the capacity of the part to change as well as to express the whole to which it belongs can lead to a different line of thought. In 3.4 we find Hamlet in the surprising and paradoxical position (given his famous rejection of 'seeming' on his first appearance at 1.2.76-86) of actually recommending deceit in terms of a clothing metaphor. Having deplored his mother's second marriage at some length, he says to her,

> Good night, but go not to my uncle's bed—
> Assume a virtue, if you have it not.
> That monster custom, who all sense doth eat,
> Of habits devil, is angel yet in this,
> That to the use of actions fair and good
> He likewise gives a frock or livery
> That aptly is put on. Refrain tonight,
> And that shall lend a kind of easiness
> To the next abstinence, the next more easy;
> For use almost can change the stamp of nature.
> 3.4.159-68

Gertrude is recommended to 'put on' the garb or appearance of virtue on the grounds that it will help her to become genuinely virtuous: she will become what she seems. It is as if the mere 'trappings and the suits of woe' scorned by Hamlet earlier might eventually turn a person into a genuine mourner. (See below, pp.121, for a longer discussion of this related passage.)

Dodging the vexed question of whether to read 'devil' or 'evil' in 1.162[44] let us concentrate on the link between 'habits' and 'livery'. The same coupling is found in Hamlet's 'vicious mole' speech about Danish drunkenness (see above, p.108). There, a mode Σ decomposition of the category 'defect' (expressed, as we have seen, by 'mole') gives rise to three species of defect in men, occurring (1) 'in their birth', (2) 'By their o'ergrowth of some complexion', (3) 'by some habit'. 'Complexion' here, bearing an Elizabethan humours theory sense,[45] is more an 'inner' than an 'outer' term, though since the humours were supposedly readable in skin-coloration a 'surface' meaning is not distant. 'Habit' in context clearly bears its ordinary modern sense of 'settled practice'. But such practice *is like clothing*—via the more usual Elizabethan meaning of 'habit', today restricted to ecclesiastical contexts—so it, like birth or humour blemishes, is 'nature's livery'. What you normally do intersects with what you wear (1) as direct synecdoche: what you wear is part of what you normally do (one of Hamlet's habits in the modern sense is to wear black): (2) metaphorically with an embedded synecdoche: the two sorts of habits are similar in that each is in a (comparably problematic) synecdochic relationship to the whole of the person.

Returning to Hamlet's exhortation to Gertrude, we find him claiming that virtue is 'assumable' (something you can put on) even if you 'have it not' (are not intrinsically virtuous). There is a mild puzzle here (How can you put on what you haven't got?) which the receiver automatically negotiates by understanding something like 'the appearance of' or 'the garb of' virtue for 'virtue', while reverting to virtue proper as the antecedent of 'it'. But now the way is open for an argument to the effect that the part that is distinct from the whole is by custom rendered co-substantial with the whole (*aptly* put on). The remaining puzzle is that the same sort of things—acts—seem to constitute both virtue's surface and virtue's substance: one might feel that if Gertrude does not go to bed with Claudius she is *being* virtuous, not just pretending to be virtuous. Presumably Hamlet means that true virtue would consist in wanting to refrain rather than just making oneself refrain. At any rate, if habits (in the modern sense of customary behaviour) consists of acts, and acts are given by custom an apt 'frock or livery'[46] then the latter conceptually rather peculiar surface is, in the clothing sense, habit's habit.[47]

Shapes

Human beings can change their clothes in order to deceive others, but supernatural beings can effect more radical transformations between their real selves and their outer appearances. When the Ghost first appears it is described as coming 'In the same figure like the King that's dead' (1.1.41) and Horatio challenges it:

> What art thou that usurp't this time of night,
> Together with that fair and warlike form
> In which the majesty of buried Denmark
> Did sometime march?

Later Hamlet decides 'if it assume my noble father's person,/ I'll speak to it' (1.2.243-4). In all these expressions, the Ghost as a supernatural being is seen as having the power to put on ('usurp', 'assume') the entire body and appearance ('figure', 'form', 'person') of the dead King, not just his clothes.

Traditionally, such apparitions were thought to tend towards extremes of beauty or horror according either to their own moral status ('spirit of health' or 'goblin damn'd', 1.4.40) or to their desire to seduce or horrify their beholders: Horatio suggests to Hamlet that the Ghost may tempt him to a cliff

> And there assume some other horrible form
> Which might deprive your sovereignty of reason,
> And draw you into madness.
>
> 1.4.72-4

Later, Hamlet reminds himself to be cautious because

> The spirit that I have seen
> May be a dev'l, and the dev'l hath power
> T'assume a pleasing shape.
>
> 2.2.598-600

Supernatural beings thus terrify not only because of their radical insubstantiality *per se* ('for it is as the air, invulnerable,/ And our vain blows malicious mockery' (1.1.145-6); compared to the insubstantiality of the painted figure, this is an active, taunting insubstantiality) but because this allows for unlimited shape-changing. Of course, the moral status of the observer comes into the equation too. So the Ghost himself, while drawing on this tradition to comment on Gertrude's 'falling off' from himself to Claudius, is sure that the virtuous person can resist the *apparently* good shape, while the vicious person gets bored even with the *really* good shape:

> But virtue, as it never will be moved,
> Though lewdness court it in a shape of heaven,
> So lust, though to a radiant angel link'd,
> Will sate itself in a celestial bed
> And prey on garbage.
>
> 1.5.53-7

The rather abstract theme of 'shape' suits the abstracting figure whereby an attribute is taken from a particular person or class of person and is then itself personified. The Ghost, finding lust in Gertrude, proceeds to talk about Lust as a human Gertrude-like figure. Hamlet and Ophelia together perform a similar abstractive operation when they are talking about Ophelia's beauty and honesty. Ophelia herself moves into the abstractive–personification mode in rejecting Hamlet's recommendation of a kind of purdah ('if you be honest and fair, your honesty should admit no discourse to your beauty' 3.1.106-7): the 'persons' she evokes ought, she thinks, to consort well together: 'Could beauty, my lord, have better commerce than with honesty?' (3.1.108-9). Hamlet retorts in the same mode with an intricate formulation:

> Ay, truly, for the power of beauty will sooner transform honesty from what it is to a bawd than the force of honesty can translate beauty into his likeness. This was sometime a paradox but now the time gives it proof.

3.1.110-14

Beauty and Honesty, personified, each have a power or force to exert on the other. Honesty is the superior virtue; as such, the power he should have is to 'translate' into his likeness whoever looks at him, to make his shape mirrored. But this power is less, if the viewer is Beauty, than is Beauty's power, *even* when the viewer is Honesty. And since Honesty's nature is to be at one with himself, any change from him must be in the direction of dishonesty. ('Bawd' respecifies the sort of dishonesty most typically associated with beauty). If Hamlet's 'time' demonstrates the truth of this, it must be because honesty's force (the 'radiant angel', i.e. the Ghost) failed with Gertrude while Gertrude's beauty was transforming Claudius' honesty to something else. (The underlying identification of Hamlet's father and Claudius with Honesty and Gertrude with Beauty explains our choice of pronouns above.) Honesty, then, fails to shape his likeness; Beauty, herself (mere) 'shape', so always potentially opposed to honest 'substance', in attempting to re-shape, succeeds in misshaping.

Here again 'the power of beauty' is presumably a mere shape or show *because* it has no necessary connection with moral perfection or 'honesty'. But back at the human level the 'transformation' will not necessarily be expressed outwardly or visibly. If Ophelia is 'dishonest', this might not appear in her face (she can still, after all, present the same 'picture' even when she is mad).

Shape or appearance is the genus, the species of which Hamlet runs through at some length on his first appearance. In response to Gertrude's request that he 'cast [his] nighted color off' (1.2.68) and her query as to why the experience of death, which is common, 'seems . . . so particular with thee' (1.2.75), he explodes:

> 'Seems', madam? nay, it is, I know not 'seems'.
> 'Tis not alone my inky cloak, good mother,
> Nor customary suits of solemn black,
> Nor windy suspiration of forc'd breath,
> No, nor the fruitful river in the eye,
> Nor the dejected haviour of the visage,
> Together with all forms, moods, shapes of grief,
> That can denote me truly. These indeed seem,
> For they are actions that a man might play,
> But I have that within which passes show,
> These but the trappings and the suits of woe.
>   1.2.76-86

Clothes and behaviour 'indeed seem' (in deed seem?). They are fakeable; this does not mean they are necessarily a fake—in fact, a mode Π breakdown of Hamlet into an inner griefstricken essence and an outer set of grief symptoms would reveal no discrepancy between the two—only that they are other than some sort of central, unfakeable identity. That this identity still *needs* its trappings and suits to identify itself is a paradox which may account for some of the anger in the passage. What Hamlet wants to establish is that 'I am woe' (or 'woe is me' as the idiom puts it); woe is inner, and the whole varied set of its symptoms are nothing *but* its clothes, its shapes—nothing without it.

Grief's shape, however, seems as ineffectual as that of Honesty or that of the radiant angel; and very soon Hamlet declares his intention to 'put an antic disposition on' (1.5.172).

'To divide him inventorially': Laertes' Parts

At this point some recapitulation may be in order. We have moved from body parts through skin, paint and clothes to shapes as such.

As it happens, in discussing clothes we found that we were led to consider characteristic actions (habits), while in discussing shape the question of non-material parts of the person, namely attributes (lust, beauty, honesty, woe) arose. This gives us seven sorts of parts. Our argument has been that each sort of part enters into synecdochic relationships with a whole, and that it is the fact that these relationships are sufficiently similar to one another which allows one sort of relationship to be used as a metaphor for another sort. At the same time, it is the differences among these part-whole relationships that keep the metaphors from collapsing into identities, or into the stale 'appearance *versus* reality' thematic to which many of them might seem to reduce. That thematic, in fact, operates at a level of generality too great to have much purchase on our examples.

What has emerged repeatedly is the sign-reliability problem: can I take this (part) as a sign of that (whole)? Co-substantiality is only one (but a very important) guarantee of sign-reliability: if you give me part of something and truthfully assure me that the rest of it is of the same material, then my identifying the part's material gives me the material of the whole. But what is the whole of a person, and what is a person's substance? We are already in the realm of ontological metaphor, whereby such 'things' as one's honesty, sincerity and consistency are materialized in terms of inorganic integrity or organic health.[48]

Having moved over to the material side, we find ourselves in the realm of everyday synecdoche—not on its own one of the most striking or conceptually challenging of figures. But in so far as, in much the same way as we saw in the previous chapter, the supposedly recipient field 'donates back' its preoccupations to the donor field, the material synecdoches become charged with some of the play's wider themes. Whether parts are detachable or not, whether they can be thought of as free-standing or not, takes on new significance in the light of puzzles about the 'detachability' (hence replaceability, hence unreliability-as-sign) of acts, shapes and attributes of persons, and about the consequent conceptual possibility of these non-material parts standing up against, being opposed to, the persons to whom they should belong. On the latter point, it is important to be clear about where the notion of free-standingness comes from in this field. None of the material sorts of part are much good as literal free-standers; the non-detachables certainly are not, and even clothes on their own fall in a heap![49] But in synecdoche the part, in standing for the whole, takes over from the whole the latter's capacity to stand alone and act. That it has the potential to stand against the whole follows simply from the conceptual structure of the figure. In a context in which at the macro-level questions of characters' 'difference from themselves' is so important, this aspect of synecdoche becomes more interesting.

However, it may be as useful for the text to keep the ontologizing side of synecdoche under control as to exploit it. Complimenting Horatio on his even-temperedness, Hamlet declares:

> Give me that man
> That is not passion's slave, and I will wear him
> In my heart's core, ay, in my heart of heart.
>   3.2.71-3

Here we have in a s᾿ t space the externalization and personification of an attribute (passion) so as to put it at the same ontological level as 'that man'; the depersonification of 'that man' into something that can be worn (perhaps a jewel, as when Laertes decribes Lamord as 'the brooch indeed/ And gem of all the nation', 4.7.93-4); the re-internalization of the wearable thing, rather paradoxically, since wearing should be outer rather than inner; the insistence on this paradox by splitting the heart, synecdoche for the inner man, into something which itself has an inner core; the doubling of synecdoche whereby *that* core becomes a second heart; and the re-externalization and personification of the worn thing via simile as Horatio himself. Yet none of this is dwelt upon as 'troubled'; the sentence registers as spontaneity and clarity itself (especially after some dense passages earlier in the same speech—'No, let the candied tongue lick absurd pomp,/ And crook the pregnant hinges of the knee/ Where thrift may follow fawning', etc.; see above, pp.54-6). This must be because each of the synecdochic moves here is utterly conventional, and even the operation of so many moves at once barely registers upon us as complex. The language is held to a minimally heightened level, so that the audience-member, who didn't quite grasp what was going on with the candied tongue, is nevertheless left in no doubt about Hamlet's feelings for Horatio.

As the play draws to its conclusion, the 'part' that Claudius deploys against Hamlet belongs to Laertes. It is a particular sort of habit, a skill; Claudius likens it to clothing—'A very ribbon in the cap of youth' (4.7.77). It is, says the King to Laertes

> a quality
> Wherein they say you shine. Your sum of parts
> Did not together pluck such envy from him [Hamlet]
> As did that one.
>
> 4.7.72-5

Not until twenty lines later is this quality finally identified: Claudius has heard Laertes praised

> For art and exercise in your defense,
> And for your rapier most especial.
> 4.7.97-8

Laertes, who has already declared his hope that Claudius, setting up Hamlet's death, 'could devise it so/ That I might be the organ' (4.6.69-70), has it in his power to lure Hamlet by virtue of a shining part, or in other terms a surface whose shine can be applied like paint: as Claudius proposes,

> We'll put on those shall praise your excellence,
> And set a double varnish on the fame
> The Frenchman gave you.
>
> 4.7.131-3

Hamlet will finally excuse himself to Laertes in terms of the most radical of decompositions, one in which from the whole person no less than the 'proper' whole is taken away, leaving a free-standing attribute standing against not only Laertes but Hamlet himself:

> If Hamlet from himself be ta'en away,
> And when he's not himself does wrong Laertes,
> Then Hamlet does it not, Hamlet denies it.
> Who does it then? His madness. If't be so,
> Hamlet is of the faction that is wronged,
> His madness is poor Hamlet's enemy.
>
> 5.2.234-9

But before this Hamlet has to confront Laertes' varnished, conveyed to him by Osric.

This relaxed and funny episode (which is severely cut in the Folio), with Osric trying for a high style which goes over the top, contains two moments in which Laertes' parts are in question. Osric avers that

> he is the card or calendar of gentry; for you shall find in him the continent of what part a gentleman would see.
>
> 5.2.109-11

'Continent' here, in Osric's affected diction, is the container; to the arithmetical metaphor of a man being the 'sum' of his parts, as Claudius straightforwardly puts it, Osric adds the equally material or commercial metaphors of the 'card' (literally a chart or map, as at 5.1.138) and the 'calendar' (literally a register or directory). The map sense of 'card' makes it inevitable that 'continent' should register as a pun—perhaps not quite under Osric's syntactic control?—so 'part' is a desirable region as well as a desirable ability or quality. But, as the language threatens to escape from Osric's grasp, a comic flattening of Laertes seems to take place, via the two-dimensionality of 'card', 'calendar' and (geographical) 'continent'.) It is a bathetic replay of the reduction to shape or surface which Hamlet has seriously proposed before Osric's entrance, when he declares of Laertes that 'by the image of my cause I see/ The portraiture of his' (5.2.77-8).

Hamlet responds with a spirited parody of Osric's style:

> Sir, his definement suffers no perdition in you, though I know to divide him inventorially would dozy th'arithmetic of memory, and yet but yaw neither in respect of his quick sail; but in the verity of extolment, I take him to be a soul of great article, and his infusion of such dearth and rareness as, to make true diction of him, his semblable is his mirror, and who else would trace him, his umbrage, nothing more.
>
> 5.2.112-20

Picking up the metaphors from commerce and from travelling, Hamlet, while seeming to agree with Osric's inflation of Laertes, in fact implies a reduction of him to his own mirror image or shadow (surface again).[50] But from the point of view of this chapter, the interest is in Hamlet's open presentation of a mode Π decomposition as a painful rhetorical exercise. To think of all these parts: the mind dozies![51]

Notes

1. The key text in this tradition is Jakobson's 'Two Aspects of Language and Two Types of Aphasic Disturbances' in Roman Jakobson and Morris Halle, *Fundamentals of Language* (Mouton, The Hague, 1956; also in Jakobson's *Selected Writings* II, Mouton, The Hague, 1971). Jakobson's work is developed and criticized by Albert Henry in *Métonymie et métaphore* (Klincksieck, Paris, 1971); by Michel Le Guern in *Sémantique de la métaphore et de la métonymie* (Larousse, Paris, 1973) (on these as well as Jakobson, see Paul Ricoeur, *The Rule of Metaphor,* Routledge and Kegan Paul, London, 1978); by Michael and Marianne Shapiro in *Hierarchy and the Structure of Tropes* (Indiana University Press, Bloomington, 1976); by Christian Metz in 'Metaphor/Metonymy, or the Imaginary Referent' , in *Psychoanalysis and Cinema: The Imaginary Signifier* (Macmillan, London, 1982); and by Donald Rice and Peter Schofer, *Rhetorical Poetics* (University of Wisconsin Press, Madison, 1983).
2. Umberto Eco, *Semiotics and the Philosophy of Language* (Macmillan, London, 1984), p.91.
3. Group μ is also sometimes known as the Groupe de Liège (after their university) and as Dubois *et al.* (after Jacques Dubois, credited as 'first author' on most μ material). *Rhétorique générale* (Larousse, Paris, 1970) has been translated by Paul B. Burrell and Edgar M. Slotkin as *A General Rhetoric* (Johns Hopkins University Press, Baltimore and London, 1981). On some problems with the translation, see Roger Fowler's review in *Criticism* 24 (1982), 273-7, as well as Grimaud (see below, n.11) footnote 1. We give page references below both to the original (*RG*) and to the translation (*GR*). The passage just quoted is at *RG* 106/*GR* 107.
4. Nabuo Sato, 'Synecdoque, un trope suspect', *Revue d'Esthétique* no.1-2, 1979 (published as a book under the title *Rhétoriques, Sémiotiques*), 116-27.
5. Logical sum and logical product are notions which date from the work of the nineteenth-century British logician, George Boole. Group μ's use of them may be somewhat idiosyncratic. For a standard exposition, see for example P.F. Strawson, *Introduction to Logical Theory* (Methuen, London, 1952), pp.105-6.
6. Eco, p.46; see also the whole chapter, 'Dictionary *vs.* Encyclopaedia' (pp.46-86), as well as the remarks on the Porphyrian tree in his 'Metaphor' chapter (pp.87-129).
7. Hoskins' manuscript *Directions* has been edited by Hoyt H. Hudson (Princeton University Press, 1935). It was not printed as such until this edition but Jonson incorporated a portion of it into *Timber* (1641) and it appears 'almost in full but without acknowledgement' (Hudson, p.v.) in Thomas Blount's *Academy of Eloquence* (1654).

8. The distinction between metonymy and synecdoche seems shaky in Elizabethan theory: Hoskins gives 'the city met the Queen' as an example of metonymy ('city' for 'citizens'), p.10, but George Puttenham in *The Arte of English Poesy* (1589), gives a very similar sentence, 'the town of Antwerp were famished' as an example of synecdoche ('town' for 'the people of the town'), p.163 in the Scolar Press facsimile edition (London, 1968).

9. This point about the need for distance between tenor and vehicle is also made, in different ways, by Eva Kittay in her thesis (see Chapter 2 above, n. 4, p.84), p.242, and by Stephen Ullmann in *Style in the French Novel* (Cambridge University Press, Cambridge, 1957), p.214.

10. 'The basic idea of using circles in this way was due to the eighteenth-century Swiss mathematician Euler. Some . . . refinements . . . are due to the nineteenth-century British logician Venn [J. Venn, *Symbolic Logic,* London, 1881]'—Patrick Suppes, *Introduction to Logic* (Van Nostrand, New York, 1957), p.195 n.

11. For an exceptionally wide-ranging survey article which begins as a review of *A General Rhetoric* and argues that μ's a-psychological ('mindfree') approach badly needs to be complemented by recent work in cognitive psychology, see Michel Grimaud, 'Mindful and Mindfree Rhetorics: Method and Metatheory in Discourse Analysis', *Semiotica* 45 (1983), 115-79.

12. *RG* 118/*GR* 121.

13. Sato, p.124. Sato also makes some very shrewd remarks about difficulties in the Group μ analysis of mode Π decomposition which would need to be taken into account in a more extended treatment of their thesis. Curiously enough, Sato is happiest with Group μ on the mode Σ front, which is where they have been attacked most recently by Bernard Meyer, 'Synecdoches du genre?', *Poétique* 57 (1984), 37-52 (see also Nicolas Ruwet, 'Synecdocques et métonymies', *Poétique* 23 (1975), to which Group μ have responded with some asperity in an essay, 'Rhetorical Mirrors: Seven Years of Reflection', appended to *GR*). For our purposes the Group μ analysis is illuminating enough to work with as it stands; but our feeling is that, given the nature of the μ project, Sato's criticisms are more to the point than Meyer's.

14. In their later, still untranslated, *Rhétorique de la poésie* (Editions Complexe, Brussels, 1977), Group μ show themselves keenly aware of the dangers of oversimplifying the dynamics of the intersection: see especially pp.64-6.

15. Harold Jenkins (ed.), *Hamlet* (The Arden Shakespeare, Methuen, London, 1982), p.366. As with *Troilus and Cressida* and *King Lear,* the textual situation is complex. We shall take account of variants where necessary. It is not part of our project to attempt to explain the differences between the variant texts. The most radical as well as the most lucid recent account of the textual situation can be found in Philip Edwards' Introduction to the New Cambridge *Hamlet* (Cambridge, 1985).

16. A slight muddle in the annotation of the Penguin edition (ed. T.J.B. Spencer, 1980), shows the synecdoche at work at this point. If we agree that 'vailed' means 'lowered' and not 'veiled', then is it the lids that are lowered or the eyes? Practically it comes to much the same thing; but only in the latter case does 'lowered' mean 'downcast'. So when Spencer gives 'downcast eyelids' as a paraphrase of this expression the effect is of a mild solecism.

17. How the eye looks can be taken more concretely or less. A good example of how this matters is afforded by Claudius' use, as part of a series of oxymoronic characterizations of his grief and happiness at marrying his brother's widow, of the phrase 'with an auspicious and a dropping eye' (as Q2 puts it, 1.2.11). Jenkins cites as a similar passage the woman yielding her maidenhead in Elyot's *The Governour* 'with an eye half laughing half mourning', where the appearance of the eye is a synecdoche for a divided reaction on the part of the whole person rather than being literally contradictory in appearance. But Claudius' line, *if* we envisaged it more concretely, could amount to cross-eyedness; and as it happens the Folio text moves us in that direction, so that, as Spencer points out, 'The comic or repulsive image (one eye smiling, the other weeping) is stronger in the Folio reading: "With one Auspicious, and one Dropping eye".' Here it could be part of a comic or grotesque effect that Claudius has slightly mismanaged his own synecdoche. For a further discussion of eye synecdoches, see Chapter 5 below, pp. 168-70 and n. 10, p.202.

18. *Metaphors We Live By*, p.15.

19 Hendiadys, a figure in which 'and' joins two related but in some respect *not* parallel words, such as 'expectation and rose' here, has been shown by George T. Wright in a brilliant article ('Hendiadys and *Hamlet*', PMLA 96 (1981), 168-93) to have been a favourite of Shakespeare's especially in the plays of his middle period, and nowhere more so than in *Hamlet*. According to Wright, Shakespeare's use of hendiadys 'usually elevates the discourse and blurs its logical lines, and this combination of grandeur and confusion is in keeping with the tragic or weighty action of the major plays' (171). The blurring comes about because 'if we take the words one by one, it is hard to make them and their syntax add up to [the required] meaning' (169). Wright suggests that we often hear hendiadys as if it resolved itself into a more normal adjective-noun phrase, so that we would have not two appositions but one in 3.1.152: 'The rosy expectation of the fair state' (182). While this is no doubt generally true, one might prefer in this case, given the consistent inconsistency of entities in the passage as a whole, not to move to that 'easy translation' too quickly. Incidentally, the same habit of mind which would delight in hendiadys proper might be expected to be prepared to work with hendiadys-like longer appositional not-quite-parallels, which is precisely what we have in the passage under discussion.

20. These lines do not appear in the Folio text. See below, pp.114 for further discussion of this passage.

21. Or—a slightly different reading, though it comes to broadly the same thing—each part, and its associated sense, is still part of Gertrude; what it is 'without' is communication with the other parts. On this reading we do not need to personify each of the parts; indeed the passage becomes literal (or at most hyberbolic). Telling against this less figured reading are Hamlet's next words, 'Or but a sickly part of one true sense/ Could not so mope' (3.4.80-1), where the notion of each sense having 'parts' in turn (even having sickly parts, *versus* lacking parts altogether) seems inescapable.

22. In this passage the unity of the body is expressed first through the metaphor of a building ('porches') and then through the metaphor of a city as the Ghost

goes on to describe the poison running through 'The natural gates and alleys of the body' (1.5.67). The reversed form of this metaphor—the city or state seen as a human body—was of course widely used during this period although it is not especially prominent in *Hamlet*. For a general study, see David G. Hale, *The Body Politic: A Political Metaphor in Renaissance English Literature* (Mouton, The Hague, 1971). Hale claims that Shakespeare used this metaphor more extensively than any other playwright of the time, especially in his Roman plays. See also David G. Hale, *'Coriolanus:* The Death of a Political Metaphor', *Shakespeare Quarterly* 22 (1971), 198-202, and John Anson, *'Julius Caesar:* The Politics of the Hardened Heart', *Shakespeare Studies* 2 (1966), 11-33.

23. Also in this scene we find Hamlet describing Claudius as 'like a mildewed ear,/ Blasting his wholesome brother' (3.4.64-5), where the primary reference is to an ear of corn, but there is surely an unconscious pun on the other kind of ear.

24. See below, pp.112–13, for further discussion of this passage.

25. *Metaphors We Live By*, p.37.

26. For further comments by Shakespearean characters on the inscrutability of the face, see *Macbeth* 1.4.11-12, and *Cymbeline* 5.5.62-5.

27. Some commentators see a skin metaphor behind Hamlet's reference to death as 'When we have shuffled off this mortal coil' (3.1.66), assuming that Hamlet sees us shedding mortality as snakes shed their skins.

28. Literal discussion of the condition of the skin is rare in Shakespeare. It is interesting that it is done here through a tree metaphor ('bark'd').

29. The last lines of this extract constitute one of the most notorious textual difficulties in the play; see the commentary in the Variorum edition, ed. H.H. Furness, 1887, and in Jenkins, pp.449-52. This entire speech, after the first three and a half lines, does not appear in the Folio. Philip Edwards argues (New Cambridge edition, p.14) that it was discarded by Shakespeare himself during the composition of the play.

30. Shakespeare might have known this story from Plutarch's *Life of Lycurgus* XVIII.

31. As Philip Edwards points out in his note on 3.4.42-4 (New Cambridge edition, p.176) prostitutes were not in fact branded in the face in Elizabethan England though this punishment was threatened by Henry VIII in 1513 and again by the Commonwealth in 1650. He therefore reads 'blister' in 3.4.44 as indicating a literal disease, while he accepts 4.5.119-20 as figurative.

32. We are not convinced by Spencer's suggestion in the Penguin edition (p.207) that 'the thing' refers to the servant who 'helps' the harlot with her make-up.

33. *On the Received Text of Shakespeare's Dramatic Writings and Its Improvement*, 2 vols, 1862-66, II. p.341. Quoted in the Variorum *Hamlet*, p.204. A similar conflation of 'visage' and 'vizard' could be said to occur in *Othello* when Iago praises the behaviour of servants who 'trimm'd in forms and visages of duty,/ Keep yet their hearts attending on themselves/ . . . throwing but shows of service on their lords' (1.1.50-2).

34. Edward A. Armstrong has some interesting thoughts on painting and discusses both 5.1.192-4 and 3.1.48-52 in *Shakespeare's Imagination* (Lindsay Drummond, London, 1946), pp.66-8. See also Chapter 16 'The Painted Walls', in John Erskine Hankins, *Shakespeare's Derived Imagery*

(University of Kansas Press, Lawrence, Kansas, 1953), pp.208-18.

35. Jenkins, p.264.

36. Jenkins again has an excellent note on the synecdoche and metonymy involved in the use of 'heraldry', p.264. The symbolic use of black and red in a martial context is reminiscent of Marlowe's *Tamburlaine*, Part 1, 4.1.49-61.

37. For a discussion of the type of portrait likely to be used on stage, see Jenkins, pp.516-19.

38. Hamlet uses the idea of the double portrait again in 5.2 when he says,

> But I am very sorry, good Horatio,
> That to Laertes I forgot myself,
> For by the image of my cause I see
> The portraiture of his.
>
> 5.2.75-8

Here the double portrait stands in synecdochic relationship to the double plot itself. On the question of doubling and dualisms in the play, see Ann Thompson, 'Who Sees Double in the Double Plot'?, in D.J. Palmer (ed.), *Shakespearian Tragedy* (Stratford-on-Avon Studies, vol.20, Edward Arnold, 1984), pp.47-75; and George T. Wright, 'Hendiadys and *Hamlet*', *PMLA* 96 (1981), 168-93.

39. The practice of recognizing or mistaking characters by their clothing or other 'parts' is of course essential to many of Shakespeare's plots, as for example in *Much Ado About Nothing* where Margaret is mistaken for Hero because she is wearing her clothes. Desdemona's handkerchief might in this way be considered as a synecdoche (or metonymy) for its owner, and the device runs riot in *Cymbeline;* see Ann Thompson, 'Philomel in *Titus Andronicus* and *Cymbeline*', *Shakespeare Survey* 31 (1978), 23-32.

40. Editors take this to mean (1) Claudius is a makeshift sort of apology for the ideal or complete king; (2) he ought to be wearing the motley or parti-coloured clothing of the Fool or Vice.

41. The passage is discussed at length, and the reading 'bonds' rather than 'bawds' defended, by Thomas Clayton in 'The Quibbling Polonii and the Pious Bonds: the Rhetoric of *Hamlet* I.iii', *Shakespeare Studies* 2 (1966), 59-94.

42. On the difficulty of determining when 'investment' did take on its modern financial meaning, see the entry in *OED*.

43. Or that, in Ross's terms, the two 'suits' are related 'by mere equivocation'. See below, Chapter 4, pp.137−9. Equivocation in *Hamlet* is explored from a more literary viewpoint by M.M. Mahood in *Shakespeare's Wordplay* (Methuen, London, 1957), pp.111-29. She analyses the 'vicious mole' speech amongst other examples.

44. Long notes on this will be found in the Variorum *Hamlet* and in Jenkins. Fortunately, this textual crux does not affect our argument. Much of this speech does not appear in the Folio. Again, Philip Edwards assumes in the New Cambridge edition (pp.10-13) that Shakespeare himself made the cuts.

45. 'Complexion' in Elizabethan humours theory refers to the mixture or

combination of the four humours (blood, choler, melancholy, phlegm) in a person's physical constitution and hence to their temperament or character.

46. Another link between this passage and the 'vicious mole' speech in 1.4 is that there 'nature's livery' is in apposition to 'the stamp of one defect'.

47. Shakespeare takes a gloomier view of the power of habit in sonnet 111 which uses metaphors of branding and dyeing.

48. Polonius uses this materializing type of ontological metaphor when he cautions Ophelia against Hamlet's 'tenders' of affection:

> think yourself a baby
> That you have ta'en these tenders for true pay
> Which are not sterling.
>
> 1.3.105-7

49. Similarly in the visual tradition of the emblem books, the portrayal of an eye or a hand on its own strikes us as bizarre or surreal.

50. We find a similar decomposition-as-comic deflation, this time using food metaphors, in *Troilus and Cressida* when Cressida responds to Pandarus' enthusiastic listing of all Troilus' good qualities as 'the spice and salt that season a man' by calling him 'a minc'd man' (1.2.251-7).

51. We have also discussed Group μ's approach to metaphor in our paper, 'To look so low as where they are: Hand and Heart Synecdoches in *Othello*', delivered at the 1985 Annual Conference of the Renaissance Society of America in California, and published in *Southern Review* 19 (1986), 53-66.

4

Making Sense in 'Sonnet 63'

J.F. Ross: Analogy in Language

J.F. Ross's *Portraying Analogy*[1] is a dense, intricate and somewhat idiosyncratic work of philosophical semantics. It offers a new picture of how both everyday and heightened language work, based on taking as central certain phenomena of language which other accounts forget or are embarrassed by. We think that this picture brings out features of Shakespearean language which are apt to be obscured in the more static picture which is standard, though these features may *in practice* be clear to careful readers, attentive spectators and conscientious editors. In this chapter, after giving an outline of those of Ross's concepts which are most pertinent to our own purposes, we shall apply what he has taught us to reading a Shakespearean sonnet.

Portraying Analogy is not an easy book to summarize. Its key concepts are interdependent in ways which make it difficult to find the best point of entry. Analogy is Ross's central theme, that is, that regular process in language whereby the same word in different contexts adjusts so as to mean different but analogous things. But his framework turns out to take account of certain linguistic operations where analogy precisely does *not* hold (as in 'mere equivocation'), and in addition to offer an account of metaphor—hence our interest—situating it as a particular sort of analogy ('asymmetrical meaning—related equivocation'). And the intellectual roots of his enterprise are in his long study of a philosophical tradition of speculation about analogy stretching from Aristotle to the medievals (Aquinas and Cajetan) but thereafter submerged. From that tradition he takes some

132

terminology and some illustrations, but he considers it to have erred fundamentally in a number of ways (see pp.19-27), most notably in seeking to locate an explanation for the phenomenon of analogy in the nature of reality rather than in the workings of language.[2]

Aristotle was interested in such issues as how ' "to be" differs in meaning according to the category of the things that are said to be' (20), a concern which scholastic philosophy applied to the question of how the 'exists' of 'God exists' can be related to the same word's sense in 'This book exists'. But Ross accuses classical analogy theory of having 'failed to grasp that the underlying phenomenon is *differentiation*' (20) and that this is a linguistic process which is at work in much humbler contexts, indeed is omnipresent in natural language use:

> Everyone who speaks one of the relevant natural languages . . . from the youngest speaking children through the least intelligent persons capable of coherent discourse and the most sophisticated masters of the language, characteristically and automatically uses the same words in different meanings, sometimes related (*see*/light, *see*/point: *collect*/books, *collect*/friends, *collect*/debts, *collect*/barnacles), and sometimes unrelated (*charge*/enemy, *charge*/battery, *charge*/ account).(4)

Differentiation is Ross's term for this process. The word 'drop', for example, means something rather different, but not totally different, according to whether what is being dropped is a brick, a stitch, a friend or a hint; Ross would say that 'drop' differentiates accordingly. Extralinguistic context can enter into the picture (imagine 'dropping a friend' in a hanging-out-of-a-window scenario or a trapeze act), but the linguistic context very often handles the situation on its own, as in the more expected sense of 'dropping a friend'. When this happens, Ross speaks of a relation of *dominance* existing between the relevant context-word and the differentiating word; 'friend' dominates 'drop'.

Ross's basic framework for describing and accounting for same-word polysemy is this. The meaning of the same word will vary, systematically and in a lawlike manner, according to its context. This can be brought out by experimenting with *sentence frames,* that is, sentences needing only one element in order to complete them; it will often happen that a different completion-word gives us the clue we need to choose amongst the meaning-possibilities of one or more words in the frame:

> Consider the sentence frame: 'He cancelled the (noun phrase)', completed with 'cheque'[3] and completed with 'appointment'. 'Cancelled' adjusts its meaning to the completion noun. So too, with 'He wrote for a (noun phrase)' completed as: 'He wrote for a living' and 'He wrote for an appointment'. The reverse occurs as well: 'He (verb phrase) for living', (i) 'He wrote for a living'; (ii) 'He married for a living'. (That of course, is ambiguous between 'as an occupation', and 'to avoid having to work'.) Adjustment, (in the sense of 'fit') occurs in the single concatenation of words, the meaning of 'for a living' in (i) is not *altered* in (ii), or vice versa, but rather *what* 'for a living' means in (i) and (ii) is (within a range of possibilities) *settled* by what words it is combined with. (48)

The process whereby 'cancelled' and 'for a living' here demonstrate different meanings according to how the frame-sentence is differently completed is what Ross means by *differentiation*.

The words that caused 'cancelled' to differentiate as it did were 'cheque' and 'appointment'. This is what Ross calls a relation of *dominance:* 'cheque' and 'appointment' dominated 'cancelled'. Sometimes it may be unclear without further context which word or words dominate in a given expression: this would be the case in those ingenious examples of metaphor in which it is uncertain which element of the sentence is to be taken as literal. In 'The stone smiled', for example, either literal 'stone' dominates 'smiled' so that its meaning differentiates to something like 'looked pleasant', or literal 'smiled' dominates 'stone' so that the latter's meaning differentiates to something like 'the stone-like individual'. But it would require considerable care (of the sort demonstrated, for example, in the poetry of John Ashbery) to construct verbal environments in which dominance relations were kept systematically ambiguous.

With 'dominance' we see how a certain energy metaphor enters Ross's vocabulary, of which he is both aware and unashamed (see his justification on pp. 3-4). Accordingly, he speaks of a principle of *linguistic inertia,* meaning by this that *unless* something differentiates same-words they will mean exactly the same thing; and, more importantly for our purposes, he posits a countervailing principle of *linguistic force:*[4]

> Generally, *words resist combining unacceptably in the linguistic
> environment, until forced to.* That is *linguistic force.* In other words
> grammatical strings will not go together unacceptably (as 'not English')
> if there is any step-wise adaptation of word meanings (comparatively to
> their other occurrences in the corpus) which would result in an
> acceptable utterance and is not prevented by the environment. (10)

It is characteristic of Ross's approach that he grants language and
its sentences a force prior to and to some degree independent of the
forces we can ascribe to speakers (intentions) and to the world; this
is nicely illustrated by his striking formulation, *'sentences make
what sense they can'* (11).

Before going on to look at Ross's categories of differentiation, it
might be well to clarify the relationship between his purposes and
ours. In fact, Ross has several ends in view as a philosopher. He is
interested, as were his medieval intellectual forebears, in blocking
an argument against theological language whereby the patent
difference between what some words must mean in a theological
context (as descriptive of God, say) and in other contexts is claimed
to be so great as to render them meaningless in the former case.
About this motive for his enquiries we shall have nothing more to
say.

Secondly, and more broadly, he is concerned to provide an
account of how language works which differs crucially from that
which prevails in most current philosophical conceptions of
meaning. Here the focus of his attention is on the most everyday
kind of language, and on effects of meaning that speakers rarely
notice. To make these effects visible, it is necessary to juxtapose
possible expressions so that differentiation of same-words across
the range of examples can be experienced. It is the investigator who
brings together the bricks, stitches, friends and hints to
demonstrate the differentiation of 'drop'. There is nothing
particularly rich or noteworthy in any of the cases singly; what they
testify to as a group, however, is a richness in the potential of the
language *as a whole and over time* which is much greater than the
standard accounts recognize: given what 'drop' can already be
shown to do, there seems virtually no limit to what might be
intelligibly, but differently, 'droppable'.

Thirdly, and more narrowly once more, Ross aims to show that
his explanatory terminology allows for a better description of what

happens specifically in figurative speech than do other accounts. This enterprise is advanced, albeit rather briefly, in his Chapter 6, 'Figurative Discourse'. The central claim here is this:

> The meanings of salient words in figurative discourse can be hypothetically constructed as a shortest sequence of stepwise adaptations from typical same words in nonfigurative discourse. (142)

In other words, in the heightened discourse of poets, we find double or multiple differentiation at work; analysis can hypothetically reconstruct how the *strikingly* differentiated word arises as a combination of 'moves' each of which taken singly would be prosaic enough. (Just what this means will only become clear once we have seen the kinds of differentiation—and hence the kinds of 'moves' that Ross distinguishes.) These claims are illustrated not only via made-up examples but with 'Some Examples from Poetry' (pp.153-7), and what Ross is doing here comes much closer to what close-reading literary critics have always done, except of course that it is done within a new explanatory framework.

Our own purpose is to investigate Shakespearean language in the light of Ross's notions of differentiation and dominance. As in previous chapters, we shall be examining how Shakespeare exploits and builds upon an aspect of everyday language—in this case, the same word's ability to take on a wide variety of meanings, analogically or metaphorically related to one another, in different contexts in a regular and generally unnoticed manner. Heightening language here will involve combining a number of analogical or metaphorical 'moves' to produce more complex figures, and also setting up the syntax so that real puzzles about dominance relations can provide the reader or hearer with a string of noticeable, and even debatable, differentiations.

We find Ross's approach illuminating not only for what it tells us about the nature of heightened language in itself but also for what it tells us about how we understand heightened language. Our competence as readers depends on our being able to make sense of complex patterns of differentiation and dominance. Sometimes, as we shall see, the sense that a modern reader can make of a Shakespearean sentence is not the same as the sense that an Elizabethan reader might have made of it: words differentiate differently over time. Also, it becomes easier to pinpoint what is happening when readers disagree over what sense they make of a Shakespearean sentence; often this is a matter of discrepant perceptions of how individual words differentiate. In what follows we shall be looking at some examples of critical disagreement in this light.

We begin by describing the three main divisions into which Ross groups the differentiation phenomena. Collecting together some 'same word different meaning' cases from the Shakespearean corpus as a whole, we distinguish cases where the differentiation happens so invisibly as to seem hardly an interesting fact about the text (as opposed to being an interesting fact about the workings of language) from cases where the text itself plays upon more than one differentiation possibility. We then turn to a single text, Sonnet 63, and explore it with Ross's help. At this point, we find Shakespeare taking syntactic and semantic chances which suggests that he would have found 'sentences make what sense they can' an endorsable slogan. We find too that combining features of Ross's account with a less purely verbal concept of metaphor enables us to explain why 'impossible' readings of words and phrases sometime—not always—are enabled to linger as 'part of the meaning of the poem'.

Equivocation, Analogy and Metaphor

In his discussion of the ways in which same-words are differentiated in everyday language, Ross defines three kinds of meaning relationship which we think are relevant for our purposes: equivocation, analogy and metaphor.[5]

Mere equivocation covers words which are identical in spelling and sound but which are *completely unrelated in meaning*. Examples are 'charge' (as in the paragraph from Ross quoted in p.133 above), 'pen' which can indifferently mean 'writing instrument' or 'enclosure for animals', and 'bank' which can indifferently mean 'verge of a river' or 'depository for valuables'. The lack of a relation in meaning can be demonstrated by the fact that there is no synonym or near synonym of the one occurrence which will also serve as a synonym of the other (unless of course it too occurs merely equivocally). The fact that the same word is used for such totally different meanings appears to be simply an arbitrary accident of natural language and this phenomenon of mere equivocation can and should be distinguished from cases where some overlap of meaning (i.e. some analogy) is involved.

Analogy covers words which are identical in spelling and sound and which have *different but related meanings.* Examples are 'see' and 'collect' (as in the paragraph from Ross quoted on p.133 above), 'drop' (as in 'drop a stitch/'drop a friend') and 'give' (as in 'give a present'/'give a hand'/'give a speech'). That the meanings, though different, are related, can be demonstrated by the fact that in these cases some near synonyms of one occurrence can also be near synonyms of the other. We could for example, substitute 'perceive' for 'see' ('perceive a light'/'perceive a point'), or we could substitute 'gather' for 'collect' ('gather books'/'gather friends', etc.). Although the different meanings are readily distinguishable, there is a certain overlap or analogy involved.

Ross distinguishes two types of analogy: *analogy of proportionality* and *denominative analogy.* For the sake of expository simplicity, we are largely going to ignore this distinction in what follows. But for the record, the examples just given are of analogy of proportionality, where related differentiating words change, roughly at least, 'in proportion to' the change between one dominating word and the next. (That is, the difference between gathering books and gathering friends is roughly the same as that between collecting books and collecting friends.) Denominative analogy comes into play when same-words differ in the manner in which 'what is predicated inheres in what is predicated of' (7). Thus in 'Napoleon is wearing a hat', 'hat' differentiates according to whether the 'Napoleon' in question is flesh and blood or a two-dimensional patch of paint respectively. Another sort of case in this category, according to Ross, is the way in which ' ''He plays the piano'' can *attribute* a proclivity, an ability or an occupation, and so forth' (7-8). The distinction is taken over by Ross, with modifications, from the scholastic analogy tradition.

Metaphor, finally, means for Ross much what it means to other writers, though distinguishing it formally from analogy is tricky. What he insists on is the presence of an asymmetry between same-words: one is metaphorical, and the other literal. Such an asymmetry does not exist between analogous pairs. For Ross, 'drop' is no more and no less literal in stitch-talk than in friend-talk.

(Herein lies a key difference between his approach and that of Lakoff and Johnson, for whom probably both dropped friends and dropped stitches would be seen as involving an orientation metaphor grounded in the experience of dropping medium-sized physical objects). But in cases of metaphor, *some but not all* of what would be implied by a literal use of the word is implied by the metaphorical use of the word, *but not vice versa:* this is the asymmetry. Consider the two sentences, 'The workman swept the halls' and 'The clouds swept the moon'. According to Ross, we feel that some but not all of what 'swept' means in the workman—halls frame is implied in the clouds—moon frame. (What is lost is the extent to which 'sweeping' means 'physical-action-by-a-person-for-purposes-of-cleaning'.) But we do not, symmetrically, feel that 'swept' in the former case has lost some of the meaning it bears in the latter case: we do not see the workman's sweeping as having lost, as an implication of 'swept', the fact that it is done by distant aerial entities.

Some Shakespearean Same-Word Sets

The differentiation-under-dominance phenomenon, and the way in which groups of same-word occurrences are internally related either as mere equivocation (which is effectively no relation, unless the author creates one punningly) or as analogy, or as metaphor, can be observed very easily by working with a concordance. The sort of discoveries one makes bear on the Shakespearean text and its meanings in a number of different ways. Here are just a few.

1. Typical cases of merely-equivocal pairs of same-word occurrences can be instanced abundantly. The completely unrelated meanings of the word 'pen' can be seen by comparing Slender's reference to 'how my father stole two geese out of a pen' (*The Merry Wives of Windsor,* 3.4.40-1) with Dogberry's command to Seacole to 'bring his pen and inkhorn to the jail' (*Much Ado About Nothing,* 3.5.58-9). Likewise, the different meanings of 'charge' can be seen at work in Salisbury's report that the French army is in the field 'And will with all expedience charge on us' (*Henry V,* 4.3.70) and Diomedes' remark that Helen has cost both parties in the

Trojan war 'a hell of pain and world of charge' (*Troilus and Cressida*, 4.1.58). These examples illustrate how easily and automatically differentiation works; one is not tempted to reverse the meanings for a moment, indeed the 'other' pen or charge simply doesn't enter one's mind, given the specific dominance relations prevailing.

2. Armed with the knowledge that a merely-equivocal relationship between instances of a given word exists today, we can check if this was so for Shakespeare, and sometimes the evidence will suggest that it was not. For example, Shakespeare never uses the word 'bank' to mean 'depository for valuables'; all the thirty-five instances of 'bank(s)' cited in the Harvard concordance refer to the bank of a river, a bank of flowers, and so on. We thus learn a difference between Elizabethan English and ours.[6]

3. Contrariwise, we sometimes find that Elizabethan English contained a merely-equivocal pair of words, one of which has now disappeared. The word 'beetle', for example, could mean then, as it does now, an insect ('The crows and choughs . . ./ Show scarce so gross as beetles' (*King Lear*, 4.6.13-14)), but it could also mean a wooden hammer or mallet, which is the sense relevant to Falstaff's 'if I do, fillip me with a three-man beetle' (*2 Henry IV*, 1.2.228)—a 'three-man beetle' being one that required three men to lift it. This meaning of beetle has now become obsolete as far as most speakers are concerned, though it may survive in specialized contexts.

4. In the cases considered so far, no relationship between two mere equivocals has been deliberately set up by Shakespeare. But of course the Shakespearean pun exploits unrelated senses of some same-word pairs unmercifully. This was particularly easy to do in an oral medium where more words would *sound* the same than would be spelt the same. Consider Gratiano's pun at the sight of Shylock whetting his knife on the sole of his shoe: 'Not on thy sole, but on thy soul, harsh Jew,/ Thou mak'st thy knife keen' (*The Merchant of Venice*, 4.1.123-4).[7] It might be interesting to ask why Shakespeare felt there was mileage to be had in organizing the juxtaposition of some mere equivocals and not others.

5. Next we enter the realm of ambiguity, whether poetic or simply puzzling, when at a particular point in a text the dominance

relationships are such that *either* of two merely equivocal senses of a word might be chosen. We have discussed above (pp.115-16) the difficult passage in *Hamlet* where Polonius says to Ophelia that Hamlet's vows are 'mere implorators of unholy suits' (1.3.129)—here 'suits' could mean either 'requests' or 'sets of clothing'—or, as sometimes happens in these cases, both.

6. In identifying instances that fall under categories 4 and 5 above, we need to remember that words which for us have quite distinct sounds were sometimes identical in Elizabethan pronunciation, thus allowing for both punning and puzzlement in an oral medium. A pun that occurs more than once in the canon depends on the identical pronunciation of 'room' and 'Rome' as in Cassius' bitter remark, 'Now it is Rome indeed and room enough,/ When there is in it but one only man' (*Julius Caesar,* 1.2.156-7).[8]

7. Conversely, there are some words which sound identical in modern English but were pronounced differently by the Elizabethans. It would seem, on the evidence of Shakespeare's failure to exploit an attractive pun, that the words 'morn' and 'mourn' would not have sounded the same to his audience, though negative evidence of this kind is of course much more debatable.[9]

8. Particularly tricky cases involve words which are merely equivocal when heard but not so on the page. The most obvious example in Shakespearean texts is the oral equivocation possible on 'ay' meaning 'yes' and 'I' meaning 'me'. Sometimes it may be possible for an actor to speak the word so as to leave both meanings open, as when Richard II responds to Bolingbroke's question, 'Are you contented to resign the crown?', by saying:

> Ay, no, no ay; for I must nothing be;
> Therefore no no, for I resign to thee.
> (*Richard II,* 4.1.201-2)

The Folio text here reads 'I, no; no, I': but the Elizabethans frequently wrote 'I' for 'ay'. Most editors choose to print 'ay' twice but it would be perfectly possible to print 'Ay, no, no I', since Richard's speech for the next twenty lines explores his loss of identity.

141

9. Spelling change can also affect what needs to be perceived as part of the equivocation phenomenon. For the Elizabethans, the spellings 'travel' and 'travail' were quite interchangeable, allowing the meanings of 'journey' and 'labour' to arise equivocally very frequently, whereas modern spelling has tied the 'journey' meaning to the 'travel' spelling and the 'labour' meaning to the 'travail' spelling so that equivocation is no longer possible. Again the editor of a text has to choose which spelling to print; we shall discuss below the implications of this choice in the case of Sonnet 63 where the poet anticipates the time when his lover's 'youthful morn/ Hath travell'd [or travail'd] on to age's steepy night' (lines 4-5). [10]

10. Just as we have moved from textually unrelated same-word pairs demonstrating mere equivocation (1-3), to cases where the existence of different meanings *matters* to the interpretation of a particular moment in a Shakespearean text (4-9), so we can collect pairs within which analogy or metaphor form the basis of differentiation and use them either to learn something about the language in general (our language and/or the language of the Elizabethans) or to help with the understanding of specific passages. But now the full subtlety of the differentiation process comes into clearer view. In the case of mere equivocation, senses differ on a sharply either/or basis: 'pen' is either a writing instrument or an enclosure. Examples of genuine ambiguity, like the use of 'suits' and the 'ay/I' problem we have quoted above, tend to occur rarely and then only as part of deliberate wordplay; ambiguities of this kind which were *not* deliberate would probably be perceived as incompetence on the part of the writer. Once analogical or metaphorical relatedness between the same-word senses is in question, however, one finds these senses, while still distinguishable, shading into one another.

A grasp of analogical or metaphorical differentiation in action helps us to understand how Shakespearean language can so regularly register upon us as full of 'period' quality (the differentiations are not quite the same as those provided for by the language today) while remaining broadly comprehensible. Take the word 'bend'. Bending the body (stooping) is a different, but analogous, action compared with bending the knee (kneeling).

'Bend' correspondingly differentiates straightforwardly between Don Pedro's 'I would bend under any heavy weight' (*Much Ado About Nothing*, 5.1.277) and Aumerle's 'Unto my mother's prayers, I bend my knee' (*Richard II*, 5.3.97). But whereas bending under a weight is idiomatic contemporary English, bending a knee for us out of context might be more likely to suggest physical exercise or physiotherapy (knee-bends). This simply reflects the fact that kneeling to figures of authority has, outside of church-going, become a virtually obsolete gesture. No audience will have any difficulty with Aumerle's line, but it gives off a period flavour. Even more so do expressions like 'his goodly eyes . . . now bend, now turn' (*Antony and Cleopatra*, 1.1.2-4) and 'I do bend my speech' (*Measure for Measure*, 1.1.40), because neither *bend*/eyes nor *bend*/speech is currently in common usage. This may be because a sense of 'bend' meaning 'to direct or aim' has lost currency, though this sense survives in the substantive 'one's bent' meaning 'one's inclination' and in the idiom 'bent upon', meaning 'directing oneself towards'. The *OED* entry for 'bend' makes it clear that the early history of the word is tied up with thoughts about weaponry; a number of senses (grouped under category III) are variants of the meaning 'To direct, aim (as a bow bent for shooting)' and bent speech or bent eyes follow on analogically from this usage. The analogy of the bow is also behind the otherwise paradoxical-seeming injunction by Henry V to his soldiers to 'bend up every spirit/ To his full height' (*Henry V*, 3.1.16).

Having introduced Ross's categories and suggested some of the ways in which they bear on our reading of Shakespearean language, we propose now to discuss Sonnet 63 in this light. Starting from an examination of the operation of differentiation and dominance at the level of individual words, we shall move on to consider how our findings relate to the Sonnet's larger metaphorical fields. We should perhaps stress that we are not attempting a *complete* reading of this sonnet but merely analysing some selected examples of the phenomena in which we are interested.

Sonnet 63: Differentiation and Dominance

In speaking of differentiation and dominance in the Sonnets, it seems to us useful to consider individual words (and phrases) under three categories:

1. Cases where differentiation is straightforward and unambiguous. While the word could be used with a different meaning elsewhere (always a possibility, Ross would say), the dominance relationships and the overall context ensure that all readers would agree what the meaning is here.
2. Cases where differentiation is eventually unambiguous but only after all the evidence is in. That is, there is for the reader a moment of uncertainty which can be a significant factor in reading.
   This category can be subdivided into two types:
   (a) Cases where the wrong meaning simply drops away and is forgotten once the right meaning is established;
   (b) Cases where the wrong meaning somehow seems to linger and to remain part of the experience of the reading even though it has been formally ruled out.
3. Cases where the dominance relationships do not determine a single meaning: differentiation is uncertain or impossible, and ambiguity results.

We have chosen to look at a sonnet rather than at dramatic language in this context out of a sense that the Sonnets, which were presumably written to be read rather than to be heard, are able to make wider use of Category 2 and Category 3 constructions than the plays can. The reader of a sonnet is able to look back and re-read in the light of later information: this is not possible in quite the same way in the theatre. However, there may not be as much difference between Shakespeare's practice in the two modes as one would expect. If, as Ross argues, we are *normally* engaged in a continuous process of computing differentiation of some subtlety in understanding and producing everyday language, we can be expected to experience less difficulty in obtaining meaning from even the more syntactically curious or textually crux-ridden moments of the plays (that is, in finding the sentences making what sense they can as they flash by) than would be predicted by most other views of how language works.

Sonnet 63
Against my love shall be as I am now
With Time's injurious hand crush'd and o'erworn,

When hours have drain'd his blood and fill'd his brow
With lines and wrinkles, when his youthful morn
Hath travell'd on to age's steepy night,
And all those beauties whereof now he's king
Are vanishing, or vanish'd out of sight,
Stealing away the treasure of his spring;
For such a time do I now fortify
Against confounding age's cruel knife,
That he shall never cut from memory
My sweet love's beauty, though my lover's life.
His beauty shall in these black lines be seen,
And they shall live, and he in them still green.[11]

In Sonnet 63, as in other sonnets we have looked at, surprisingly few words are instances of Category 1; the general tendency of the style is to exclude the most straightforward kind of differentiation. Even words which seem to be straightforwardly differentiated by their immediate contexts get drawn into more complicated patterns of meaning by the time one has read the whole poem. The word 'Against' in line 10, for example, clearly means 'in opposition to': no commentator on this sonnet allows for any other meaning. Yet this straightforward and unambiguous usage cannot be considered in isolation from the usage of the word in line 1 where all commentators feel it is necessary to point out that 'Against' does *not* mean 'in opposition to' (its 'normal' modern meaning) but 'in anticipation of (in preparation for) the time when'. These two meanings of 'against' are sufficiently distinct to be covered by Ross's term 'equivocation'.

Similar complications arise over the word 'lines' which also occurs twice. On both occasions it differentiates straightforwardly enough in its immediate context: the 'lines' in line 4 (*lines*/brow) are wrinkles on an ageing human face, while 'these black lines' in line 13 (*lines*/[write]) are those of the poem itself. But the proximity of the two occurrences alerts us to the larger pattern whereby Shakespeare is setting up the contrast between Time's hand 'writing' the lines on his lover's brow which witness his mortality while his own hand, as poet, is writing the lines which will confer eternal life. The amount of overlap between the two kinds of lines (both are horizontal rows of markings on a smooth surface, etc.) would lead us to call the two uses of 'lines' analogous in Ross's terminology rather than equivocal or metaphorical (both

145

foreheads and poems do literally, though differently, *have* lines—there is no element in the respective meanings of 'line' which needs to be suppressed in either case).

Sonnet 63 does however exhibit several examples of our Category 2a: cases where differentiation is ultimately straightforward but where the reader is not immediately certain and has a moment of suspension between right and wrong readings before the right one finally asserts itself. Some of the uncertainty is caused, for the modern reader, by diachronic changes in usage. For example, the word 'confounding' in line 10 has, as a regular Elizabethan sense, 'destroying', noted as obsolete by the *OED*. Hence the modern reader might at first assume the weaker sense of 'confusing', but is usually put right by an editorial gloss. Similarly, the intransitive use of 'fortify' in line 9 can produce a wrong reading for the modern reader who is used to the word being used transitively and starts to search for its object.

These examples raise the important question of the authority both of editorial glosses and the *OED,* which is worth a digression at this point. It is not as though 'confound' cannot mean 'confuse' in Elizabethan English (in the way that 'car', for instance, cannot mean 'automobile'): indeed 'confound' can mean 'confuse' *in differentiated senses* (*OED v.* 4, 'To throw into confusion of mind or feelings'; *v.* 5 'To throw (things) into confusion or disorder': cf. also *v.* 6 and *v.* 7). In some frames, 'confound' differentiated for the Elizabethans just as it does for us. The *OED* puts before us other frames which demonstrate 'confound' differentiating so as to be broadly synonymous with 'defeat', 'destroy', 'spoil' or 'waste'. The chronological distribution of these examples, plus our own intuitions, suggest that the language no longer allows for this possibility; hence the *'obsolete'* or *'archaic'* characterization. The *OED* is such an invaluable resource because of the generosity of the evidence it provides (frame exemplification) and the sensitivity of its groupings and paraphrasings (differentiation explication).

As for editors, as wide readers in the period of the text they are editing, they will have become sensitized to differentiation possibilities which are no longer current; furthermore, they will devote time to assembling frames, especially Shakespearean frames, which attest to the possibility of the frame they propose (that is to say, that for them the frame they are annotating imposes). The effect of all this readerly *activity* is rather covered over by brief notations of the sort found in Ingram and Redpath's edition of the Sonnets ['confounding] destroying. Cf. 5.5-6 and 60.8')[12], or, virtually identically, in Stephen Booth's edition.[13] Only if one consults Booth's 'Index to the Commentary' and tracks down his (brilliant) discussion of 'confound' and its environment in Sonnet 8. 5-8 ('Often Shakespeare's use of language is such that a reader can make no paraphrase that both follows the syntax of the lines and says what he knows the lines mean . . .'), is the potential openness of the question of 'confound' brought home to one. This is not to argue that brief paraphrases are illegitimate: the brief paraphrase does put the reader right (it is genuinely unprofitable to try to hold onto 'confusing' as the meaning of 'confounding' in Sonnet 63, and parallel passages open the mind to the not-now-current alternative possibilities). But a Ross-type account of the differentiation process keeps us alert to the complexity of the experience of which the brief paraphrase is the residue.

A somewhat different sort of wrong reading occurs in the case of the verb 'filled' in line 3,[14] mainly because it occurs in close proximity to its antonym 'drain'd': we are at first ready to assume that both words carry an implied reference to liquid—'drain'd' certainly does in 'drain'd his blood'—but by the end of the line this assumption has been corrected in so far as 'fill'd' has been dominated by 'brow'—a move which makes it possible for 'lines' in the next line to be unambiguously differentiated.

Uncertainties of this kind can also arise with larger units of speech. Sonnet 63's opening phrase, 'Against my love', could mean a number of things until the correct meaning is established by the larger context which allows us to deduce (a) the right sense of 'Against', and (b) the proper referent of 'my love': it is perhaps not absolutely clear that the poet is talking about 'the man I love' rather than 'my feelings of love' until we come to 'his' in line 3—hence 'his' dominates 'love'.

Likewise the phrase in line 8, 'the treasure of his spring', could be ambiguous according to whether we assume 'treasure' dominates 'spring' or vice versa. This phrase in isolation is like 'The stone smiled (see above, p.134), except that instead of having to decide whether one term is literal and therefore dominates the other one we have the further complication that both terms might well be metaphorical. If we take 'treasure' as a literal term dominating metaphorical 'spring', the phrase might mean 'the money he made in his youth'. If we take 'spring' as literal dominating metaphorical 'treasure' (and continue with the seasonal sense of 'spring') the phrase might mean 'whatever of value (seen as a rich object) he acquired this spring'. Both meanings are blocked; literal 'treasure' fails to connect with anything else in the sonnet,[15] and literal 'spring' is more immediately made unlikely by 'his' (individuals do not possess seasons; note how much more likely a literal-season reading becomes if we substitute 'this' for 'his'). So it becomes likely that both terms are metaphorical. But we still have a choice of meanings once 'treasure' and 'spring' have metaphorically differentiated. 'The treasure of his spring' could mean something like 'whatever of value he acquired in his youth' (an old man might refer to his daughter thus), or it could mean 'the valuable object which *is* his youth'. (Between the two readings, the word which differentiates is 'of'.) Once again, even a metaphorical 'treasure' distinct from 'his youth' is eliminated for lack of any indication elsewhere in the sonnet as to what it could be. This leaves 'treasure' and 'spring' bound to be coextensive and mutually defining, effectively the second of the all-metaphor readings.[16]

All the examples considered so far (i.e. ones we would assign to Category 1 and to Category 2a) seem to us instances where the differentiation is straightforward and hence the right meaning is apparent immediately or after a little further reading and thought. We would expect most commentators and readers to agree that these are indeed the right readings, and we would probably not take very seriously any suggestion that 'lines' could refer to instruments for catching fish or that 'spring' could refer to a part of a watch. As we move on to Category 2b and Category 3 we move into the realm of potential debate and disagreement.

We have defined Category 2b as covering cases where the wrong meaning, instead of being totally discarded as soon as the right meaning is established, lingers and becomes part (even if only a very subsidiary part) of the final reading. Obviously it is possible for readers to disagree about such cases. Some readers might even want to redefine some of our Category 2a examples as Category 2b examples. For instance, although most readers might regard it as simply wrong to read the sonnet's opening phrase 'Against my love' as meaning 'In opposition to the man I love', it would be possible for a reader who takes a very dark view of the relationship described in the Sonnets to see this as a significant and meaningful suggestion at some subtextual level. One might argue that there is something rather ambiguous about the whole treatment of the immortalizing theme since it seems to be *the poet* who, through his work, aspires to (and of course has achieved) immortality, while his subject has in some important ways been forgotten. Gerald Hammond provides a rather chilling reading of Sonnet 63 from this point of view, noting that 'where the octave presents an aged poet and a young subject, the sestet presents the poet still alive and the subject dead—or at least his beauty dead which, for him, is the same thing'.[17] In this sort of reading, 'Against my love' might be said to carry a hint of hostility which is not entirely discarded.

What is involved in the claim, basic for our Category 2b, that a meaning can be ruled out on syntactic or domination grounds and yet persist to be part of the 'meaning' in a broader sense? One might contrast the two most fully annotated modern editions of Shakespeare's Sonnets, that of Ingram and Redpath (1964) and that of Booth (1977) by saying that, on the whole, Ingram and Redpath are reluctant to admit the lingering presence of 2b-type readings while Booth tends to welcome them. Ingram and Redpath prefer to choose a single right reading and ignore or specifically reject other wrong ones, whereas Booth is more likely to allow for multiple possibilities. This can be illustrated in Sonnet 63 by contrasting the ways in which the two editors annotate lines 11-12, 'That he shall never cut from memory/ My sweet love's beauty, though my lover's life'. Ingram and Redpath do not gloss any words individually but provide a paraphrase for the whole of these two lines: 'i.e. The beauty of him whom I love will never be forgotten, though he will no longer live to love me'. In this reading, 'My . . . love' is assumed to refer unequivocally to 'him whom I love' and Time's threat is confined to the mere fact of mortality. Presumably Ingram and Redpath rejected as wrong the additional possibilities offered by Booth who gives two glosses for 'love's' – '(1) of my beloved; (2) of the affection I feel' and two more for 'though my lover's life': '(1) even though his life be cut off; (2) even though his life be forgotten'. Taking Booth's secondary glosses together, one reads something like, 'The beauty of the love I feel will never be forgotten, even though the life of the object of that love should be forgotten even by me'. This is an 'impossible' reading because of 'His' and 'he' in the next two lines (substitute

'Its' and 'it' and it becomes the only possible reading). But it seems to linger on in the air to much the same degree as the adversary sense of 'Against my love' does.

It is a familiar habit of editors to list several readings in the way that Booth does, implicitly in order of priority. In fact this is one of the ways in which 2b-type wrong readings can be as it were officially permitted to linger, having been classified as 'secondary' or 'auxiliary' meanings of some kind. Both Ingram and Redpath on the one hand and Booth on the other agree that the primary meaning of 'black' in the phrase 'black lines' in line 13 is literal, referring to the black colour of ink, but both also want to retain on a subsidiary level the associations of connotations of ugliness, night and death. Ingram and Redpath do not go on to gloss 'green' in the final line but Booth has an interesting note reading

> The primary meaning of *green* is metaphoric: '[be] youthful, lively'; its literal meaning, which is operative only because *black* precedes it, acts only to add a casual auxiliary paradox to those by which *black lines* preserve what *lines and wrinkles* destroy and by which the dead and forgotten beloved will live remembered forever.

There is an air of special pleading about this, especially evident in the two 'onlys': Booth seems to be admitting that to understand 'green' literally is wrong, but he nevertheless wants to retain that reading.

We shall advance some suggestions below about how Ross's framework of analysis might help to make Category 2b phenomena seem less puzzling and exotic. But first let us turn to some more overtly puzzling Category 3 aspects of Sonnet 63.

It is in fact Category 2b phenomena that cause commentators to disagree most sharply. As we move into Category 3 we find more agreement even if it is a rather unusual kind of agreement: commentators are united on their inability to find a single straightforward meaning. We take this to result, in Ross's terms, from the poet having set up the dominance relationships in such a way that normal differentiation is impossible and ambiguity results. Again it is of course possible for commentators to disagree on the *range* of permissible meanings.

One example in Sonnet 63 concerns the meaning of the word 'travell'd' or 'travail'd' in line 5. Ingram and Redpath print 'travail'd' whereas Booth prints 'traveled'. As Ingram and Redpath point out, they are restoring the reading of the 1609 Quarto (which prints 'trauaild') and rejecting the modern editorial tradition which prefers 'travelled'. As we have said above, the spellings 'travail' and 'travel' were interchangeable for the Elizabethans, allowing the meanings of 'labour' and 'journey' to arise equivocally, whereas modern spelling has restricted the 'travail' spelling to 'labour' and the 'travel' spelling to 'journey'. Thus in choosing a spelling the editor in this case is choosing a meaning. Some modern editors, such as John Dover Wilson in the Cambridge New Shakespeare edition (1966) and G. Blakemore Evans in the Riverside (1974), print 'travell(e)d' without any gloss, thus implying that the 'journey' meaning is the primary or even the exclusive meaning. By contrast and despite their choice of what to print, Ingram and Redpath, and Booth both agree that both senses are relevant and make this clear in their notes. The dominance pattern does not help to restrict the meaning since in either case 'travail'd' or 'travell'd' is dominated by 'his youthful morn'. The basic idea is of the young man (or his state of youth) seen as the sun (which is in turn personified) labouring or travelling from morning (youth) to night (old age). Since travel can be hard work, and labour can be seen as a journey (as when one asks oneself 'Is all this work getting me anywhere?'), whichever sense the differentiating process brings forward first for any particular reader, the other sense might be said to be implied by it. It is nevertheless interesting that one or other sense *must* 'come first' in a given reading experience; which that will be is largely determined by the spelling chosen by a particular editor.[18]

A laudable editorial wish not to allow the reader to settle on a sense prematurely is also displayed in line 8, where most modern editors emend the Quarto's 'Spring' to 'spring'. As Ingram and Redpath explain,

> *Spring*. . . in modern typography, would *confine* the sense to the season. But 'spring' (without the initial capital) could still, at least till the mid-seventeenth century, mean 'young growth' and its freshness, and that meaning seems also to be present.

Ingram and Redpath are here implicitly referring to *OED's* SPRING sb.9, and a glance through the *OED* examples certainly sensitizes one to the possibility of such a reading. We have seen above that 'treasure' and 'spring' are in a relationship of mutual dominance,[19] ensuring that both are read metaphorically; but there is still room for 'spring' to achieve more than one metaphorical differentiation, since 'treasure' taken metaphorically is compatible with several sorts of 'spring'. It feels easier to accept 'young growth' as a meaning here than, say, 'a source or origin, as of a stream', because there is, as with travail/travel, a relationship of implication between the young-growth sense and the seasonal sense (young growth emerges in the spring) which does not hold between the season and water. But it remains true that 'young growth' is a meaning quite distinct from the seasonal meaning, although it happens to be compatible with it.

Both Ingram and Redpath, and Booth agree that 'stealing away' in line 8 has more than one meaning, and they agree that some sense of 'disappearing' is present as well as a sense of 'purloining', but they differ interestingly on how they arrive at or justify their readings. Ingram and Redpath again employ an historical argument, glossing 'Stealing' thus:

> We of today have lost so much the vital sense of many common words that we may easily overlook the element of secrecy in 'steal' = 'take dishonestly *and secretly*'. Shakespeare's diction retains that vitality and the sense of imperceptible removal is definitely present here.

This is essentially to alert the reader to a diachronic change of meaning for the word 'steal' itself. Booth's gloss relates to the larger phrase 'Stealing away' and reads as follows:

> At first glance 'Stealing away' seems to be a synonym for 'vanishing' in line 7; it comes to mean 'pilfering' only when the developing syntax of the line presents an object of theft: 'treasure'.

This is not an historical reading but rather a reading in terms of differentiation and dominance: 'Stealing away' first differentiates as if dominated by 'vanishing', but then comes under the influence of 'treasure' so as to differentiate otherwise. 'Imperceptible removal', the suggestion that Ingram and Redpath want to retain by appealing to a rather mystical 'vital sense' of 'steal', is made part of the moment-by-moment reading process by Booth, with the proviso (Category 2b) that the rejected reading lingers on in some way. But on the Booth reading it is the beauties themselves that do the imperceptible removing, that steal away, whereas for Ingram and Redpath the imperceptible remover is Time (though it is actually syntactically difficult to find a grammatical subject for 'Stealing away', clear though the object of the theft is).[20]

Finally we should like to consider the word 'steepy' in lines 4-5; 'when his youthful morn/ Hath travell'd on to age's steepy night'. This seems usually to be read as poetic (dissyllabic) variant on 'steep': Booth cites a usage in Golding's Ovid which clearly has this meaning and the *OED* cites Sonnet 63 in its list of several figurative uses of 'steepy' meaning simply 'steep, precipitous'. But presumably 'steepy' must be dominated by 'night' and we are left with the question of what 'steepy [or steep] night' actually means: how does 'steepy [steep]' differentiate in this context? It may be fanciful to offer a 'subtextual' reading of Ingram and Redpath's note; they say of 'steepy night', 'Some modern explanations, eg. 'the dark and steep descent of old age', give insufficient weight to the sun metaphor. Age plunges into dotage and oblivion, as the sun to its setting'. It seems to us that the word 'plunge' is significant here, recalling, albeit only implicitly, the classical myth (often cited in Elizabethan poetry) whereby the sun-god, Apollo, descends at night into the sea to sleep with Thetis.[21] This suggests another possible sense for 'steepy' though as far as we know no commentator mentions it. As well as being an adjective meaning 'precipitous', 'steep' can also, merely equivocally, be a verb meaning 'to immerse or dip in liquid'. One could argue, as in the previous three cases, that both meanings, while distinct to the point of incompatibility, are in some sense 'present' in this passage. The 'precipitous' sense is uppermost if we assume the whole phrase is dominated by 'travel/travail' (Compare Edgar's 'Look how we labor ... Horrible steep', *King Lear* 4.6.2-4), while the 'immersion' sense is present in so far as the phrase is dominated by the sun metaphor. In support of the latter reading, since it is a novel one, we might cite a comparable use of 'steep' in *A Midsummer Night's Dream* when Hippolyta reassures Theseus that 'Four days will quickly steep themselves in night' (1.1.7).

Sonnet 63: The Larger Metaphorical Fields

Having looked in detail at a number of cases of words differentiating more or less straightforwardly in their immediate environments, we now need to stand back and consider how these operations play their role in the metaphorical structures of Sonnet 63 as a whole.

Here is a wholly non-metaphorical paraphrase of Sonnet 63's argument: 'When my love has aged, indeed when he is dead, he will be remembered by me and by others because I have written about his youthful beauty in these poems'. At the *conceptual* level as (for the moment, and for purposes of analysis) distinct from the verbal level—the syntax and semantics of the actual words on the page—we can identify a number of operations for 'heightening' this argument which involve metaphor.

1. The process of the young man's ageing and eventual death is represented as the work of a personified Enemy, variously identified as (a) 'Time', (b) 'hours', (c) the thief who steals the 'treasure' in line 8, (d) 'age'. Each of these versions of the Enemy is given a different hostile action to perform.
2. The young man's youthful attributes are themselves represented as entities capable of 'leaving' him in various ways. (a) his 'morn' travels/travails on, (b) his 'beauties' vanish, (c) his 'treasure' is stolen. The attributes are thus personified[22] (made an agent: (a)), ontologized (made an object: (c)), and treated literally (vanishing can literally be predicated of beauties (b)). What leaves can however return or be restored: 'still green'.
3. The effects of ageing are themselves treated metaphorically, in terms of (a) being 'crush'd and o'erworn', (b) being fatigued by 'travel' or 'travail', (c) having something stolen from one, (d) being 'cut' (cut from memory or from life). They are also described literally (the sparse blood and the lined brow) and, importantly, rendered through a comparison with the poet's own looks ('as I am now').[23]
4. A human life is treated as a day ('morn', 'night') or a year ('spring', implying autumn and winter).
5. Personifying the Enemy produces a cast-list of three for the sonnet as a whole. The relationship implied by the contrast young man/Enemy is straightforwardly hostile. That leaves two other contrasts: Enemy/poet and young man/poet. The former

contrast is, officially, no less hostile: M.M. Mahood speaks of 'Time . . . and the poet working in competition with one another'.[24] The metaphor for the poet's resistance to the enemy is based on 'fortify'. The young man/poet contrast is, officially, anything but hostile. The poet is one of the two Friends who are to counteract the Enemy's action. The other Friend is the (black) 'lines', the poems, who are personified or rather animated enough to 'live' in line 14. On the other hand, the poet and the young man are conceptually 'opposed': initially as old/young but eventually, in a curious reversal (as we have already mentioned), as alive (or life-giving)/dead.

Looking back at our literal paraphrase of the argument, it is clear that the sonnet's *essential* metaphorical move has involved the use of a donor field structured in Enemy/Friend terms to restructure a recipient field wherein such a structure was barely visible. This restructuring can 'work' *even when exactly what the Enemy is doing remains uncertain when the concepts are verbalized.* In other words, the essential metaphors are effective at the conceptual level regardless of a certain amount of difficulty or ambiguity at the level of syntax and semantics.

For example, we know, broadly, what 'crush'd and o'erworn' in line 2 means, but we might, with Steevens, worry that 'this is like saying a man is first killed and then wounded'; and we might get around this by imposing a tighter differentiation on the phrase, finding a semantic field in which the two participles do not seem temporally reversed.[25] So Ingram and Redpath, following earlier editors, speak of Steevens missing 'what is probably the image—that of a cloth whose nap is pressed upon and worn away'. Some readers may find that contemplating a person (Shakespeare) being or feeling crushed and worn out is more acceptable (since 'crushed' can obviously differentiate so as to mean something less terminal than Steevens supposed) than confronting the horrific image, worthy of an M.R. James ghost story, of Shakespeare looking like a crumpled cloth. However, the whole debate can feel curiously irrelevant (Booth ignores it) given the strong general sense the line conveys of a hostile hand of Time doing harm.

Similarly, it can be argued that we do not seem to need a syntactically retrievable subject for 'Stealing'. The Enemy is sufficiently firmly established that we know (conceptually) who is doing the stealing, although the sentence as such cannot be made to say. And the same sort of point can be made about other moments in the Sonnet which we have discussed above (pp.148–53) as belonging to Categories 2b and 3: the reader is secure enough about the overall argument of the Sonnet (or becomes so over a number of re-readings) that he or she can *afford* (to enjoy, to ignore) these puzzles about just how the actual words used are differentiating and dominating.

To distinguish a conceptual level from a verbal level of metaphorical operation also helps to clarify how the lingering-on of a 'rejected' verbal differentiation is sustained (Category 2b). A sense will linger to the degree that it is felt to pertain to one of the conceptual fields (either donor or recipient) which is active *elsewhere in the poem* (or even, though we do not have space to discuss this, elsewhere in the sequence of which the poem is a part). Thus 'Stealing away' does almost certainly differentiate so as to become one of the things the Enemy does, as in metaphor 1 above. But the picture presented by metaphor 2, of the youthful attributes themselves leaving, is one to which 'Stealing away' *could* have made a contribution, had it been dominated otherwise, and our sense of this is what allows the rejected meaning to linger on.

We can illustrate more fully the interplay between verbal and conceptual metaphorical levels by considering the verb 'cut' in line 11. In the first place, on the verbal level, 'cut' is differentiated from literal senses as simple metaphor: there is an asymmetry between how a memory or a life can be cut and how a thread or a piece of meat can be cut. Furthermore, 'cut' is, still on the verbal level, an example of zeugma, a figure which Ross describes as 'an important part of the *proof* that verbal dominance exists':

> It is usually explained as the kind of structure where an adverb modifies two verbs or a verb governs two nouns when it is directly only logically connected with one, 'the modifying or governing being conceded to *alter* meaning slightly' [italics added], as applied to the second. (Notice how someone had sensed the *dominance*.) That device allows more differentiated meanings than there are tokens of the word and allows pronouns to function in place of differential words: 'You have your way and I'll go mine', (the kind of examples John Fowles used). Other examples, 'He opened his door and his heart to the homeless', He governed himself and his province'. (151)[26]

'Cut' in Sonnet 63 is dominated by both 'memory', which age cuts *into,* and 'life', which age cuts *off.* Despite this piece of word-play, one would feel, simply on the basis of lines 9-12, that 'cut' is so dominated as to be unambiguously a hostile act by the Enemy, performed as with a knife.

M.M. Mahood, however, writes of the sonnet as a whole:

> Time defaces the young man's beauty by scribbling upon it or overscoring it, at the same time as the poet is making of it a speaking picture for posterity. This theme of writing or engraving is implicit in the subsidiary meanings of *hand* in line two, *lines* in line four, and *cut* which can mean engrave ('This figure that thou here seest put, It was for gentle Shakespeare cut').[27]

Now it seems to us impossible to argue that 'cut' can mean engrave in the actual sentence that constitutes lines 8-12. There, 'cut' is what Time/Age does, and why would Time/Age of all 'people' want to engrave from memory a portrait of the young man? However, as one moves back from the verbal to the conceptual level, one sees that Mahood has a point. The activities of the Enemy and the poet are opposed. This means that the semantic field of the poet's activity can be used to structure the field of the Enemy's activity *antithetically,* and vice versa. (An explicit example of this antithetical structuring in the form of a simile would be 'My mistress' eyes are nothing like the sun'.) What the poet is literally doing is writing about the young man, an activity which involves holding a pen in the *hand, draining* an inkwell, inscribing black *lines* upon a page. Mahood's argument postulates that this field is metaphorically restructured, in a familiar way, by a donor field based on engraving (*ut pictura poesis:* A POEM IS A PICTURE) to an extent that sets up a background engraving meaning for 'cut'—although it exists as itself, we might add, in providing a background writing meaning for 'drain'd' and 'lines'. The only point where the conceptual field around engraving or picturing actually finds a verbal differentiation-point to carry it is line 13's 'seen'; however, since the 'beauty' of the young man has been so much in question, and beauty is a visual matter, the field has in fact been at work throughout.

Similarly, the lingering adversarial sense of 'Against' in line 1 is sustained by how, at the conceptual level, the donor fields structure the experiences of ageing and writing in adversarial terms. Booth makes a related point about the Sonnet as a whole:

> The key word in this poem is *Against.* In both substance (the first eight lines concern a life that continues after beauty dies; the last six concern beauty that lives on after death) and fabric . . . this is a poem of paradoxical oppositions, fused pairs of contraries that cancel each other out. (244)

More specifically, the contrasts in the conceptual field outlined in point 5 above suffice to keep a this-against-that sense of 'against' in play. The darker reading of the sonnet could be summarized by saying that some of its details raise doubts about just who is against whom.

The analytical technique which we have been developing is not precisely that which Ross demonstrates in his chapter on 'Figurative Discourse'. There he shows how, between a complex figurative use of a given word and a non-figurative use of the same word, one can always construct a hypothetical 'adaptation pathway' whereby the complex figurative sense could have been achieved one step at a time. This is not a claim about what goes on in readers' or writers' minds, nor is Ross 'offering to diagnose the meanings of passages we do not understand' (156). Rather 'the explanation [afforded by such a hypothetical step-by-step construction] discloses *continuities* among meanings we know'. And the motivation for undertaking such constructions is principally to get a feel for the ubiquity and power of the differentiation phenomenon:

> Once we construct such complex adaptations (by writing out a few decompositions into atomic adaptations), we gain insight into the infinite polysemy available in natural language and the unlimited expressive power that can be achieved by interplaying variations of reference (supposition, designation), sense, rhythm, predicate schemes, predicate modes and connotation. *No matter how complex the relatedness, if one understands the meaning of the 'final' occurrence, one can map out its stepwise adaptation from any not merely equivocal same word (whose meaning is also known).* (147)

In the case of Sonnet 63, 'steepy' might be a focus for such a construction: what 'atomic adaptations' are necessary to get one from the sense (whichever it is) of 'steep' here to the most straightforward sense?

In the context of Ross's argument his examples of these constructions are illuminating, though he acknowledges that to develop them fully would require more machinery than he has yet established. ('Reference, supposition and the ways verbal environments dominate the modes of reference are matters for a separate inquiry, theoretically subsequent to the present one' (143).) We doubt, however, that such constructions represent the most important contribution that Ross makes to the understanding of literary metaphor.

The micro-level linguistic sensitivity which we have found encouraged by our reading of Ross is, rather, a matter of systematically testing the possible dominance relations and consequent differentiation of meanings in a rich text virtually word by word. Ross's picture of language allows one to grasp both how effortlessly everyday differentiations are achieved and how artfully Shakespeare can play with this process for heightening effects. We propose one major extension of Ross's picture. If, 'behind' the particular words in a text at a given juncture, we are aware of donor and recipient semantic fields (as defined by Kittay and Lehrer) in action conceptually, we can understand how readings which dominance renders 'impossible' can retain a ghostly life within the poem or speech. They are rejected hypotheses, but they are *conceptually pertinent* rejected hypotheses, and that pertinence is what makes entertaining them a proper part of the experience of reading or listening.

Notes

1. Cambridge University Press, Cambridge, 1981. For a discussion of Ross's book by a linguist, sympathetic overall but raising a number of detailed problems about aspects of Ross's exposition, see D.A. Cruse's review in *Journal of Linguistics* 20 (1984), 351-9.
2. 'Aquinas and Aristotle apparently thought that the natural language so closely reflects reality that the final step in explaining any meaning relationship must always lie in some entitative relationship. They did not look to the language for the explanation of the meaning relationships (analogy, mere equivocation and metaphor), but looked *through* the language, to what they regarded as ultimate'. (18-19)

3. In order not to introduce a complication not intended by Ross, we have substituted the British spelling 'cheque' for his 'check' here. Also we have expanded 'N.P.' and 'V.P.' to 'noun phrase' and 'verb phrase'.

4. Note that this sense of 'linguistic force' has absolutely nothing in common with a widespread use of 'force' in post-Fregean philosophy: 'Frege held that an adequate account of language requires us to attend to three features of sentences: reference, sense, and force' (Donald Davidson, *Inquiries into Truth and Interpretation* (Oxford, Clarendon Press, 1984), p.109. Here the notion is that sentences sharing the same propositional content share it differently, with different force, according to whether they are being used to assert, question, command, etc. So 'The door is open', 'Is the door open?' and 'Open the door!' differ with regard to force.

5. See *Portraying Analogy,* Chapter 4, pp.86-120.

6. The usage of 'bank' to refer to a financial institution did not really develop until after this period: see *OED* sb III 7(a). Marlowe uses the form 'banco' just just once in *The Jew of Malta* (4.1.77).

7. The Folio has the spelling 'soale . . . soule'.

8 The Folio has the spellings 'Rome . . . Roome'.

9. Homophonic puns are discussed at length by Helge Kökeritz in *Shakespeare's Pronunciation* (Yale University Press, New Haven, Connecticut, 1953), pp.53-157. In a more recent study, *Shakespeare's Works and Elizabethan Pronunciation* (Clarendon Press, Oxford, 1981), Fausto Cercignani suggests that there *may* be a pun on 'morn' and 'mourn' in Sonnet 132 (p.193), but this seems to be a unique instance and it is significant that it occurs in a context where it would be read rather than spoken, implying that the pun could be visual rather than aural. On the other hand, the aural identity of the two words is clearly exploited by the modern poet George Barker at the end of his sonnet 'To my Mother': 'and so I send/ O all my faith, and all my love to tell her/ That she will move from mourning into morning' (*Collected Poems 1930–1955,* Faber, London, 1957).

10. Stanley Wells has discussed the editor's responsibility in this area in two recent books, *Modernizing Shakespeare's Spelling* (published with Gary Taylor's *Three Studies in the Text of 'Henry V'*, Clarendon Press, Oxford, 1979) and *Re-editing Shakespeare for the Modern Reader* (Clarendon Press, Oxford, 1984).

11. We quote the text of *The Riverside Shakespeare* as usual. The sole authority for the text of Sonnet 63 is the (probably unauthorized) Quarto of 1609. No major emendations have been suggested, but significant editorial choices of spelling, capitalization and punctuation will be discussed below. It is generally agreed that the Sonnets were actually written during the 1590s—hence our use of the term 'Elizabethan' in relation to their language.

12. *Shakespeare's Sonnets,* ed. W.G. Ingram and Theodore Redpath (Hodder and Stoughton, London, 1964).

13. *Shakespeare's Sonnets,* ed. Stephen Booth (Yale University Press, New Haven and London, 1977).

14. The Quarto text actually reads 'fild' here but all modern editors accept the spelling 'fill'd' or 'filled' first printed in Bernard Lintott's edition in 1709.

15. Apart from anything else, our general sense of the decorum of the form blocks

the literal meaning of 'treasure': one does not expect a love sonnet to discuss the *actual* money or jewels possessed by the loved one.

16. Ingram and Redpath have a note justifying their own and other modern editors' decision to print 'spring' rather than follow the Quarto's 'Spring' on the grounds that the latter form 'in modern typography, would *confine* the sense to the season'. See below, pp.151–2.

17. Gerald Hammond, *The Reader and Shakespeare's Young Man Sonnets* (Macmillan, London and Basingstoke, 1981), p.76. Hammond does not in fact make this particular point about the meaning of 'Against', but it would not be incompatible with his dark though impressive reading of the whole sequence.

18. Booth rather ingeniously suggests that we should take the two senses in chronological order: 'The differing connotations of the two senses of *traveled* helped Shakespeare to conflate the images of the sun climbing, toiling, up to noon, and descending, traveling on, to night. He presents climb and descent not as two stages in passage but as a single progress in one fixed direction'. Shakespeare does of course pun on the two meanings elsewhere, as when Pandarus says 'I have had my labor for my travail . . . gone between and between, but small thanks for my labor' (*Troilus and Cressida*, 1.1.70-2).

19. Ross does allow for this possibility: see *Portraying Analogy*, pp.51-2.

20. Again, Shakespeare elsewhere puns on the two meanings of 'steal', as when Pistol decides to become a cutpurse: 'To England will I steal, and there I'll steal' (*Henry V*, 5.1.87). See also the comparable uses of 'steal' in Sonnets 77, 92 and 104. William Empson comments on several examples of grammatical ambiguity in the Sonnets (though not on this one). He argues that it is a device which gives a 'fluid unity, in which phrases will go either with the sentence before or after' (*Seven Types of Ambiguity*, Chatto and Windus, London, 1930) p.50. This seems very similar to what Ross would call a shifting or doubling of the dominance pattern. In an important but neglected book, *A Grammar of Metaphor* (Secker and Warburg, London, 1958), Christine Brooke-Rose studies literary metaphor from a syntactical viewpoint, with examples taken from fifteen poets ranging from Chaucer to Dylan Thomas, and frequently stresses that the originality and complexity of the Shakespearean examples (which she takes from *Antony and Cleopatra*) lies in their syntax rather than in their ideas or 'content'. We have explored the resources and limitations of Brooke-Rose's method in 'Shakespeare's Metaphors: The Syntax of Metaphor in *Cymbeline*', delivered at the 1986 International Shakespeare Association Conference in West Berlin.

21. This story is ingeniously re-told in *Salmacis and Hermaphroditus*, an anonymous erotic narrative poem of 1602, attributed to Francis Beaumont; see lines 562-78.

22. This personification is kept up by the implications of 'king': the 'beauties' are on one level the king's subjects.

23. John Dover Wilson links 'crush'd and o'erworn' in Sonnet 63 with 'Beated and chopp'd' in Sonnet 62 and comments: 'Shakespeare is [in both instances] describing his own face: have we any other self-portraits?' (*The Sonnets*, ed., (Cambridge University Press, Cambridge, 1966), p.168).

24. *Shakespeare's Wordplay* (Methuen, London, 1957), p.104.

25. Francis Berry in *Poets' Grammar* (Routledge and Kegan Paul, London, 1958) notes the variety of tense, voice and participle in Sonnet 63 and associates this with the poet's detachment as well as his consciousness of time (p.46).
26. Ross continues: 'You can easily see that zeugma logically requires differentiation because it is a relation *between* word meanings and requires the number of same-word meanings to exceed the number of actual word occurrences. (So, too, with syllepsis.) The way the differentiation is achieved is, of course, quite elementary under the general principles of the analogy theory. You simply surround a word with a pair of differentially *dominating* completion expressions in a frame where either would be acceptable alone (where there is no logical or semantic exclusion of both together had you repeated the differentiated word); then just leave out the second occurrence or use a pronoun' (151). (The John Fowles reference is to the novel *Daniel Martin* from which Ross takes a number of examples.)
27. *Shakespeare's Wordplay*, p.104. The notion of a brow being 'engraved' occurs again, with a merely equivocal pun, in *The Two Noble Kinsmen* when Emilia is comparing the facial characteristics of her two competing lovers and remarks that 'Palamon/ Has a most menacing aspect, his brow/ Is grav'd, and seems to bury what it frowns on' (5.3.44-6).

5

Meaning, 'Seeing', Printing

The Trouble with Imagery

In this chapter we consider metaphors drawn from the field of books and printing. They will be explored for their own sake, but also used as a body of examples against which to test the arguments put forward recently by Donald Davidson against there being any such thing as metaphorical meaning.[1]

But before assembling some printing metaphors or expounding Davidson, we want to begin by making a few critical points about the notion of 'imagery' still widely used in discussing the figurative in literature. Our readers may have noticed our reluctance so far to use the term. Perhaps this reflects an over-literal view on our part of what speaking of imagery and images implies. But we need to lay out our broad objections at this point, since later we will be asking whether Davidson, and writers influenced by him, run the risk of echoing at a more sophisticated level the mistake we believe to be involved in any treatment of metaphor as imagery.

What is supposed to be going on in a piece of language that is 'rich in imagery'? On the face of it, such language must prompt *mental images* in profusion. The reader is provided with a number of stimuli for the visual imagination. To speak of metaphor as a species of imagery is to claim that it is primarily concerned with the evocation of mental pictures. The best metaphors become those which make one 'see' something, 'picture' something. Similarly, the best vehicles, or the best donor semantic fields, become those which lend themselves to visualization, and the best readers are those who discover or are taught how to maximise this inner-eye effect in responding to metaphor.

163

We are not making a very original point when we reply to these assumptions that such an account turns one of the things that *can* happen as the result of encountering a metaphor into metaphor's defining characteristic.[2] An account of mental picture-making as part of the literary reading process would be a very interesting study in its own right. What makes it difficult is the well-known difference between visualizers and non-visualizers: some people report a vastly fuller inner-eye 'accompaniment' to the reading process than others do. It is not at all clear that non-visualizers are greatly disadvantaged when the text before them is a metaphorical one. On the other hand, it *is* necessary to visualize when reading descriptive prose such as the leisurely scene-setting paragraphs in the novels of Sir Walter Scott, if one is to enter into the experience of reading which makes the most of the text's power. What seems perverse about 'imagery' as a term is that it is applied to metaphors and withheld from Scott.

Of course, defenders of the term sometimes use it in an expanded sense whereby it is no longer confined to the visual. When luckless students are invited to count the 'images' in a poem, they are sometimes asked to classify them according to the sensory modality in question, so we hear of 'auditory images', 'tactile images', and the like.[3] To some ears (including ours) phrases such as 'tactile image' sound ill-formed: an image *is* something visual. But we would admit that, working back from 'imagination' (which clearly is not restricted to the visual: there is no problem about imagining a thunderclap or imagining the feel of polished wood), one might want to use 'image' in a specialized way so as to cover inner-ear, inner-taste, inner-smell and inner-touch phenomena as well. (There does seem to be a lexical gap here since 'imagined sense datum' is so cumbersome.) However, the same argument still applies against equating an all-senses notion of imagery with the figurative: the appreciation of Burns' love-as-rose simile no more depends on the reader's ability to summon up an imagined rose before his or her inner nose than upon the ability of the inner eye to picture woman plus rose, woman as rose (how?) or whatever a visual account of the figure as 'imagery' implies.

Once a *necessary* relationship between figure and visual or sensory image is denied, the way is open to investigate *particular* relationships that may pertain. What do we in fact 'see' in grasping the point of a particular metaphor? A plausible answer might be:

just what fleeting and diagrammatic (and perhaps internally inconsistent) visualization is helpful to that end. A reader attempting to understand one of the more complex time metaphors in *Troilus and Cressida* may very well need to spatialize time in some inner-visual way, but to speak of an image forming as a result of that process seems overly reifying, as if some Dali-esque illustrated version of the text were the text's *raison d'être*. But the denial of the primacy of such 'images' does not require us to deny that spatialization and indeed picturing (who is Time? where is his wallet? where is Oblivion?) can contribute to our grasping the *semantic* or *conceptual* analogy the reader or hearer is presented with.

People are Books

Our first group of printing-based metaphors will bring out how a donor field which is intrinsically eminently visual can nevertheless be used in a way which discourages detailed visualization.

The Elizabethans, like ourselves, were fond of using a PEOPLE ARE BOOKS everyday structural metaphor.[4] What do books as a donor field allow us to appreciate about people? Books are readable; by passing the eye over their print we receive messages, ideally truths. They have covers, and are kept closed when not in use. Although a whole book is a lengthy and often complex message, its general character and particular contents are revealed synecdochally by special parts, namely the title-page and the index. Similarly, people can be 'read': their appearance and their behaviour are semiotic. This process can require—for those who are not already 'open books'—some opening or revealing process (compare the fairly recent idiom 'He finally opened up to me'). Equally, parts of a person's appearance or behaviour can be indicative of the whole of his or her character.

A quick run-through of some Shakespearean and non-Shakespearean examples reveals some of the possibilities for using PEOPLE ARE BOOKS either straightforwardly or with some elaboration.[5] In Webster's *The Duchess of Malfi* Cariola denies betraying her mistress and declares 'when/ That you have cleft my heart, you shall read there/Mine innocence' (3.2.114–16): 'heart' is synecdochic for the whole person, and can be broken, but here the breaking would also amount to the opening of the book wherein Cariola's truth will be found written. In Marston's *The Insatiate Countess* the Countess herself asks 'Is not the face the index of the mind?' (Act 2, p.30, 1.24): face is to mind as index is to the whole book.[6] In Heywood's *A Woman Killed with Kindness* the wronged husband Frankford represents their children to his wife Anne as 'these young harmless souls,/ On whose white brows thy shame is character'd' (sc. 13. 120-1). This evokes the less happy side of the open book analogy: looking at the children, innocent though they be, the community will be able to 'read' Anne's infidelity (shades of *The Scarlet Letter!*). Earlier in the same play, Wendoll, Frankford's friend and Anne's lover, has claimed that all of her reproaches are 'recorded/ Within the red-leav'd table of my heart' (sc. 6. 126-7); perhaps here the insistence on the colour of the 'table' (= writing tablet) is a trifle unfortunate. Closely related, however, is Hamlet's promise to preserve the Ghost's 'commandment . . ./ Within the book and volume of my brain' (*Hamlet*, 1.5.102-3).[7]

In these latter two examples the permanence of the printed or written, as opposed to the transitory nature of spoken language, is relevant and the 'coveredness' of heart and brain, like the 'coveredness' of books, is seen as helpful. If you think of covers as most exciting when opened, however, consider Orsino telling Cesario-Viola 'I have unclasp'd/To thee the book even of my secret soul' (*Twelfth Night*, 1.4.13-14). Book covers with clasps represent the ultimate form of external protection for the message. On the 'open book' side, a more complicated Shakespearean example occurs in *King John* when John asks the French king, 'If that the Dolphin there, thy princely son,/ Can in this book of beauty read, ''I love'' '(2.1.484-5). The book of beauty is John's niece Blanch. What seems odd here is that the text which the Dolphin is to read in Blanch is not her declaration of love to him but his to her—a reversal not inappropriate to the cynical calculations of state upon which the whole idea of the match depends.[8]

Thus the face, the heart and the brain can all be 'seen as' (thought of as) books or parts of books. But what does it mean to 'see' a person 'as' a book? How far is the metaphor visual and how far is it purely conceptual?

Consider Northumberland in the opening of *2 Henry IV*

predicting (accurately, as it turns out) that Morton is bringing bad news: 'Yea, this man's brow, like to a title-leaf,/ Foretells the nature of a tragic volume' (1.1.60-1). Here the point of resemblance is spelt out; the man's brow is not like a title-leaf because it literally looks like one but because it has a similar capacity to 'foretell' a story. There is also an underlying synecdoche here: the brow is the 'front' of the person as the title-leaf is the 'front' of the book.[9] But the potential for strictly visual similarity between the brow of a person and the title-leaf of a book (for example, the possibility that both might have 'lines', as suggested in Sonnet 63 and discussed in Chapter 4 above) is not developed. The resemblance depends primarily on the conceptual point that the expression of the brow or face is like writing in so far as both are sign-systems which can be 'read' by those possessing the necessary skill.

The semiotics of facial expression involve the sense of vision, obviously, just as writing does, but the conceptual likenesses between writing and facial expression seem much more interesting and intricate than the visual one. Information, in both cases, is acquired by the 'reader', but only if he or she possesses the code or language in which the information is couched. The link between vision and understanding can be broken in two ways: the face can be seen but not understood (lack of code), or understanding may derive not from the face at all but from previous knowledge projected onto the face by the viewer (surplus of message). Morton's brow functions as an effective sign because those who see it can associate its configuration with bad news. Similarly, in *A Woman Killed with Kindness,* when the guilty heroine asks, 'Can you not read my fault writ in my cheek?' (sc. 17.56), we assume she is alluding to a visual signifier—a blush—that bears a determinate signified in the context. By contrast, in Chapman's *Byron's Conspiracy,* Savoy, referring to the inscrutability of the banished La Fin, speaks of 'those strange characters writ on his face/ Which at first sight were hard for me to read' (1.1.170-1): only with practice can Savoy pick up La Fin's facial code, though the face itself does not become more visible. And we have already quoted an example of the other disruption of the vision–understanding link from *A Woman Killed with Kindness:* the 'white brows' of the children are only 'character'd' with their mother's shame for those who already know her guilt, rather in the same way that the faces of contemporary celebrities come to signify the known facts about them.

How the PEOPLE ARE BOOKS metaphor can be elaborated in ways which demonstrate both kinds of vision–understanding disruption is well illustrated by two passages from Shakespeare's *The Rape of Lucrece*. After the rape, Lucrece's fear is that she is all too easily readable. She implores Night to linger:

> 'Make me not object to the tell-tale Day:
> The light will show, character'd in my brow,
> The story of sweet chastity's decay,
> The impious breach of holy wedlock vow;
> Yea, the illiterate that know not how
> To cipher what is writ in learned books,
>   Will quote my loathsome trespass in my looks'.
>   (806-12)

Yet, ironically, her own vulnerability was earlier seen to be due to her inability to read or decipher the lust in Tarquin's eyes:

> But she that never cop'd with stranger eyes,
> Could pick no meaning from their parling looks,
> Nor read the subtle shining secrecies
> Writ in the glassy margins of such books.
>   (99-102)

She could not 'read' Tarquin, for all his visibility. Now to be visible for her is to be read as ravished, where it is clearly the fact of the rape once known that will lend meaning to her looks. (In her distraught rhetoric there is a sense of some more direct, natural-sign communicability of her plight, so that it could be 'read' as directly as a blush can be 'read', but what sort of brow-configuration could, on its own, say 'rape' is hard to guess.)

It is certainly possible and arguably desirable to form a mental image of Tarquin on the basis of ll. 99-102, with some help from cultural stereotypes of 'lustful looks'. But is this directly facilitated by the figuration, or is it independently achieved once the point of the metaphors has been grasped? If the latter, we would be dealing with an 'image' that is closer to that evoked by a novelistic descriptive paragraph than to 'imagery' as usually understood. And this seems to be the case; or at least the visualization (or spatialization) involved in working out the metaphor is of a quite different sort from that which produces a reasonable Tarquin-picture. This is shown especially in the development of the metaphor in one detail: if faces are books, eyes are margins. Visually and spatially, the likeness between eyes and margins is downright negative, eyes being in the middle of the face (presumably if we looked for the most visually marginal part of Tarquin's face we would choose his ears). But of course the resemblance is a conceptual one, based on the notion that what eyes and margins have in common is a capacity to carry commentary (or perhaps to provide emphasis, as with the little hands pointing to 'notable sentences' in Elizabethan books).

Shakespeare liked the EYES ARE MARGINS metaphor well enough to use it again in *Love's Labour's Lost* and *Romeo and Juliet*. We shall be returning to the former passage, in the course of which Boyet describes the effect on King Ferdinand of seeing the Princess: 'His face's own margin did quote such amazes/ That all eyes saw his eyes enchanted with gazes' (2.1.246-7). The word 'quote' reappears; in the passage from *Lucrece* (1.812), the Riverside editor glosses it as meaning 'notice, observe', while here the gloss is 'indicate'. The verb seems to oscillate betwen referring to the reader's interpretative action and referring to the giving-off of information on which that action is based. Boyet describes a man whose eyes not only function (see) but reveal (signify): he is seen by all to be seeing in a particular way. So two different registers of the visible are in play—yet the metaphor animating them does not itself depend on, or even allow, visualization.[10]

As for the *Romeo and Juliet* margin, it is evoked in the course of Lady Capulet's encouraging Juliet to take interest in Paris:

> Read o'er the volume of young Paris' face,
> And find delight writ there with beauty's pen;
> Examine every married lineament,
> And see how one another lends content:
> And what obscur'd in this fair volume lies
> Find written in the margin of his eyes,
> This precious book of love, this unbound lover,
> To beautify him, only lacks a cover.
> The fish lives in the sea, and 'tis much pride
> For fair without the fair within to hide.
> That book in many's eyes doth share the glory,

169

That in gold clasps locks in the golden story;
So shall you share all that he doth possess,
By having him, making yourself no less.

(1.3.81-94)

Here the donor field of the book is fully explored for what likeness it can provide for Paris's merits—so fully in fact as to constitute a 'high' complement to the humour of the Nurse's 'low' approach to the question of marriage. Paris is to be 'read as' delightful, with his eyes (reciprocally?) providing a commentary which Juliet will find easier to read. At this point, however, the 'cover' aspect of books is taken in an unusual direction: Paris's lack of a wife leaves him incomplete; in this donor field the figure for the incomplete is the book without a cover. Another field is evoked briefly to lend elucidation: the sea surrounds the fish as necessarily as a book's cover binds its pages (or—with the container–contained relationship moved further away from the concrete towards the abstract—as a book encloses its contents). Juliet is to be Paris's completing environment, and as a beautiful object herself is 'golden' enough for the purpose.[11]

Any attempt to describe the 'image' or picture of Paris-as-book evoked by this passage seems bound to result in disaster. Not only are there the difficulties involved in visualizing eyes as margins or faces as written-on which have already been considered. The picture is even more radically incoherent because of the shift from Juliet-as-reader to Juliet-as-cover. Add to this the sudden undeveloped 'appearance' of the fish in its sea, and the speech seems to be revealed as a grotesque mess. Abandon the picturing strategy, however, and the speech, while still a little strained conceptually, is so well within the limits of its comic context: Lady Capulet can be recognized as speaking floridly without seeming to be uttering nonsense.

Davidson's Argument

In 'What Metaphors Mean', Donald Davidson argues elegantly and subtly for the thesis that 'metaphors mean what the words, in their most literal interpretation mean, and nothing more' (32). His paper might appear on a careless reading to be a radical attack on all interpretation of metaphor—an attack which literary scholars would feel obliged to resist. But the profession can relax: while 'a metaphor doesn't say anything beyond its literal meaning', nevertheless 'this is not, of course, to deny that a metaphor has a point, nor that that point can be brought out by using further words' (32).

Davidson's account of how metaphor works depends on drawing a clear line between meaning and use. A standard example of the meaning–use divergence is the use of a declarative statement to achieve the same effect as a command or request. 'It's getting very chilly', uttered by A in a context in which B is in a good position to close the window, will probably have the same effect on B as 'Will you close the window, please?' But, in Davidson's view, it cannot be said to *mean* 'Will you close the window, please?' It has literal truth conditions, so that it is true if and only if it is indeed getting very chilly. It could be truthfully uttered in all sorts of circumstances in which closing the window is not an option or not desired. Furthermore, grasping what it means as a statement is a precondition for B's acting on it *as if* requested: we can imagine B working it through: 'What is A saying? What does he want me to do about it?' The second step can only proceed if the first step has been successfully taken.

For Davidson, a metaphorical statement *means* something false or tautologous, but is *used* to direct attention towards similarities or differences. Max Black, responding to Davidson, accuses him of holding a 'comparison' view of metaphor, though this is not in our view the damning objection that Black takes it to be.[13] But if someone brought to Davidson an insight or thought they had had as a result of a metaphor which didn't lend itself to being characterized as comparison-based, he would not be particularly surprised: we do not confine ourselves to comparison when we are trying to work out why a literally peculiar thing has been said.

Theories of metaphor which speak of special metaphorical meanings, according to Davidson,

mistake their goal Where they think they provide a method for deciphering an encoded content, they actually tell us (or try to tell us) something about the *effects* metaphors have on us. The common error is to fasten on the contents of the thoughts a metaphor provokes and to read these contents into the metaphor itself. No doubt metaphors often make us notice aspects of things we did not notice before; no doubt they bring surprising analogies and similarities to our attention; they do provide a kind of lens or lattice, as Black says, through which we view the relevant phenomena. The issue does not lie here but in the question of how the metaphor is related to what it makes us see. (45)[14]

This relationship is not, Davidson insists, that of the communication of a finite cognitive content (and hence a finitely paraphraseable content):

[T]o suppose [a metaphor] can be effective only by conveying a coded message is like thinking a joke or a dream makes some statement which a clever interpreter can restate in plain prose. Joke or dream or metaphor can, like a picture or a bump on the head, make us appreciate some fact — but not by standing for, or expressing, the fact. (46)

To use a 'twice-true' metaphorical example from Ted Cohen[15] to which Davidson himself alludes: there is a great difference between how the (tautological) proposition 'No man is an island', corresponds to the single fact that no man is an island, and how *using* 'No man is an island' can cause the reader or hearer to reflect generally on human interconnectedness. 'If this is right', says Davidson, 'what we attempt in ''paraphrasing'' a metaphor cannot be to give its meaning, for that lies on the surface; rather we attempt to evoke what the metaphor brings to our attention'.(46)

Davidson's key evidence for this difference between meaning and evocation[16] is the difficulty of satisfactory paraphrase; his concluding remarks on this are worth giving at length:

[W]e imagine there is a content to be captured when all the while we are in fact focusing on what the metaphor makes us notice. If what the metaphor makes us notice were finite in scope and propositonal in nature, this would not in itself make trouble; we would simply project the content the metaphor brought to mind onto the metaphor. But in fact there is no limit to what a metaphor calls to our attention, and much of what we are caused to notice is not propositional in character. When we try to say what a metaphor 'means', we soon realize there is no end to what we want to mention. If someone draws his finger along a coastline on a map, or mentions the beauty and deftness of a line in a Picasso etching, how many things are drawn to your attention? You might list a great many, but you could not finish since the idea of finishing would have no clear application. How many facts or propositions are conveyed by a photograph? None, an infinity, or one great unstatable fact? Bad question. A picture is not worth a thousand words, or any other number. Words are the wrong currency to exchange for a picture.

It's not only that we can't provide an exhaustive catalogue of what has been attended to when we are led to see something in a new light; the difficulty is more fundamental. What we notice or see is not, in general, propositional in character. Of course it *may* be, and when it is, it usually may be stated in fairly plain words. But if I show you Wittgenstein's duck-rabbit, and I say, 'It's a duck', then with luck you see it as a duck; if I say, 'It's a rabbit', you see it as a rabbit. But no proposition expresses what I have led you to see. Perhaps you have come to realize that the drawing can be seen as a duck or as a rabbit. But one could come to know this without ever seeing the drawing as a duck or as a rabbit. Seeing as is not seeing that. Metaphor makes us see one thing as another by making some literal statement that inspires or prompts the insight. Since in most cases what the metaphor prompts or inspires is not entirely, or even at all, recognition of some truth or fact, the attempt to give literal expression to the content of the metaphor is simply misguided. (46-7)

It seems to us significant that while Davidson's strategy is to make it seem *generally* unmysterious that metaphors should not have special metaphorical meanings through his instancing of a variety of other phenomena which are equally non-propositional in character—jokes, dreams, pictures, bumps on the head[17]—he concludes his argument with a strong concentration on visual examples (maps, Picasso etchings, photographs, the Wittgenstein duck-rabbit drawing), and that this tendency to think of metaphor in primarily visual terms is also present in his approval of Black's representation of it as 'a kind of lens or lattice'.

What is special about metaphorical evocation? How it is that the poet can calculate these effects? (Calculation of effects is consistently assumed by Davidson; the unlimitedness of evocation is not to be confused with randomness.) Confusion is easy here because the notion of similarity is basic both to how literal meanings works and to what metaphorical evocation does, but it is put into play differently in the two cases. 'Ordinary similarity' which 'depends on groupings established by the ordinary meanings of words' (33-4), is what instances of the same class of objects or actions bear to one another: all the entities that can be literally and truthfully characterized as books are similar (in 'sharing the property of' bookhood). Now say we want to encourage Juliet to notice ways in which Paris is attractive and a Paris–Juliet match desirable. Lady Capulet's strategy is to present Paris *as* something else that is attractive—as it happens, a book. To say 'Paris is a book' is literally false, because the Paris–book similarity is non-ordinary: it would be a mistake to look for some super-class of objects including both real books and Paris and say that (i) 'book' has changed its meaning: it is for the nonce the signifier for a wider class, amongst which Paris is to be found; and (ii) since 'book' now means this wider class, the statement is true.

Beyond 'ordinary similarity' is what we might call 'trivial similarity.' *Simply* to transform 'Paris is a book' into 'Paris is like a book' achieves a change in literal truth-value but doesn't make the statement more (or less) usable. What renders the similarity expressed by literal 'like' trivial is the point frequently made by philosophers that 'everything is like everything, and in endless ways' (Davidson, 39). So while saying 'Paris is a book' is literally false, by virtue of the facts of ordinary similarity, saying 'Paris is like a book' is literally trivial, by virtue of the limitless nature of trivial similarity.

Metaphorical evocation, triggered by our failure to find any reason for the literal utterance of a falsity or a tautology, involves a search for *novel* similarity. (Though Davidson scrupulously points out that 'what we call the element of novelty or surprise in a metaphor is a built-in aesthetic feature we can experience again and again, like the surprise in Haydn's Symphony no. 94, or a familiar deceptive cadence' (38).) We know that, once we have classified an expression as figurative, the main maxim governing its use is that we are to search for 'unexpected or subtle parallels and analogies' (40) on the basis of that expression. And, as Simon Blackburn puts it in an account strongly influenced by Davidson:

> The metaphor is in effect an invitation to explore comparisons. But it is not associated with any belief or intention, let alone any set of rules, determining when the exploration is finished.[18]

There are rules for determining whether something is or is not a book—rules depending on, but at the same time sustaining, 'ordinary similarity' in what may be a circular, foundationless way. But there are no rules limiting the aspects of the world that our attention might be drawn to by being asked to search for surprising ways in which Paris and a book are analogous. This kind of novel similarity is distinguished from trivial similarity in so far as our thoughts are not random but are determined by the situation in which the analogy is used and the further verbal context in which it is embedded.

How would *visual* similarity operate across these categories? Where ordinary similarity is in question, this would depend on the nature of the class involved. There are surprisingly few objects which we group together *purely* because of how they look, though some degree of looking-alike often follows from or goes hand-in-hand with other similarities. On the other hand, it is very easy to think of classes which are based on wholly non-visual criteria (e.g. carcinogens, democracies, metaphors), or cases where a visually-based classification turns out to involve error (e.g. whales classified as fish). Trivial similarity is too broad to be visual; to determine that something is like something else visually, is to narrow the field of pertinent comparison sharply. Hence visual similarity is *available* as a point which novel similarity can make one notice. But nothing suggests that it is necessarily *the* point.

Nothing, that is, except for the confusion brought into the field by one further application of the protean notion of similarity, and one fact about human thought. (i)The final (fourth) and often crucial relationship involving similarity is iconic similarity—what a picture (or map or diagram) shares with what it is a picture of. This particular relationship between a representation and what it represents determines many of the everyday uses we make of the word 'like'. (ii) In thinking about something, we often can, and sometimes need to, form a mental picture or diagram of it. This image resembles its object, or a prototypical example of the class being thought of, iconically. The general importance of mental imagery in remembering and problem-solving, plus the ubiquity of pictorial representation in our culture, are probably sufficient together to account for the odd pull towards thinking of visual similarity as necessarily central to the comparisons metaphor invites us to explore.

This pull can be felt at work in Davidson's remarks on the difference between living and dead metaphor. Compare his remarks on the mouths of bottles—

when 'mouth' applied only metaphorically to bottles, the application

175

made the hearer *notice* a likeness between animal and bottle openings. (Consider Homer's reference to wounds as mouths.) Once one has the present use of the word, with literal application to bottles, there is nothing left to notice. There is no similarity to seek because it consists simply in being referred to by the same word. (37)

with those on the idiom—now, he believes, dead as a metaphor—'He was burned up':

> 'He was burned up' is genuinely ambiguous (since it may be true in one sense and false in another), but although the slangish idiom is no doubt the corpse of a metaphor, 'He was burned up' now suggests no more than that he was very angry. When the metaphor was active, we would have pictured fire in the eyes or smoke coming out of the ears. (38)

There is no suggestion that the bottle—mouth likeness when alive, was primarily or exclusively visual. But 'burned up' is assumed to have once evoked a fairly specific *picture*. Too specific, we may feel; the everyday metaphor whereby ANGER IS HOT can remain alive without our having to picture a person on fire. Consider the moment when Shakespeare's King John says to the King of France,

> France, I am burn'd up with inflaming wrath,
> A rage whose heat hath this condition,
> That nothing can allay, nothing but blood.
>   (3.1.340-2)

John does not intend his hearers to picture him on fire but King Philip perversely does this and proceeds to bring out the implications of the image in an adversarial way: 'Thy rage shall burn thee up, and thou shalt turn/ To ashes, ere our blood shall quench that fire' (3.1.344-5). King Philip here is not a better reader of the initial metaphor than King John, simply a hostile one.

In fact, it would be possible to follow both King John's threat and King Philip's retort on a purely conceptual level. It is what we *know* about fire, not what we *visually remember* of it, that is necessary if the lines are to be effectively usable. King John relies on two basic items of knowledge about fire: that it is dangerous and that pouring liquid over it can extinguish it. King Philip retorts on the basis of a third item of knowledge: that fire destroys its fuel, transforming it into ashes. These are not difficult facts to 'image', by producing mental pictures of prototype fires, prototype liquids thrown over them, and prototype heaps of ashes. But the longer one lingers over the images, the less productive the picturing exercise seems. Do we want to 'see' buckets of French blood thrown over King John, or his barely recognizable charred corpse? Did anyone indeed ever 'see' Davidson's angry man as the victim of combustion?

What Likeness Guarantees: Printing and Legitimacy

We have looked at some metaphors in which print or writing is used to evoke how visual signs in a person's face indicate or seem to indicate a more general condition (Morton is the bearer of bad news, Lucrece has been raped). Here are three comparable examples: in *Much Ado About Nothing* Leonato misreads Hero's appearance (presumably her blushes) as evidence of her sexual guilt: 'Could she here deny/ The story that is printed in her blood?' (4.1.121-2). Othello looks for similarly readable signs in Desdemona: 'Was this fair paper, this most goodly book,/ Made to write ''whore'' upon?' (*Othello,* 4.2.71-2). Here the face is not specified and Desdemona as a whole seems to be paper or book. Another instance where the body as a whole is readable occurs in *Measure for Measure* when Claudio acknowledges that Juliet is visibly pregnant by remarking, 'The stealth of our most mutual entertainment/ With character too gross is writ on Juliet' (1.2.154-5).

It is striking how regularly when a woman's face or person is in question, it is her sexual guilt or innocence that is to be read from it. The general tendency is for women to be seen as the books or papers which are to be read by men—having been written or printed upon by other men. (This notion of women, especially young girls and virgins, as 'blank pages' waiting to be inscribed by the male pen/penis is by no means exclusive to Shakespeare or to the Renaissance period, as Susan Gubar has demonstrated.[19])

When we move from the book as an end product to the method of its production, the actual process of copying or printing, the patriarchal aspect of the metaphorical field becomes even more marked: women are merely devices by which men make copies of themselves. Ideally, it is implied, their role should be as neutral as possible; the important thing is to produce a child which is an exact copy of the father. In *The Winter's Tale* Paulina claims that Hermione has fulfilled this requirement in giving birth to Perdita:

> Behold, my lords,
> Although the print be little, the whole matter
> And copy of the father — eye, nose, lip,
> The trick of's frown, the forehead, nay, the valley,
> The pretty dimples of his chin and cheek, his smiles,
> The very mould and frame of hand, nail, finger.
>
> (2.3.98-103)

She exaggerates somewhat in her insistence (can one really see a likeness in fingernails?) and it is curious how the gender of the possessive pronouns ('The pretty dimples of *his* chin') is dominated by the male father rather than the female child. Later in the same play Leontes intends a compliment to Florizel's mother (missing, presumed dead, like most mothers in Shakespeare) when he speaks in similar terms to him:

> Your mother was most true to wedlock, Prince,
> For she did print your royal father off,
> Conceiving you.
>
> (5.1.124-6)

In these passages, visual likeness is presented as vital: the child should be as like the father as one copy of a printed book is like another. Such resemblances can occur in real life, and it is not surprising that essential disanalogies between copy-likeness and kinship-likeness should be suppressed by the metaphor (little books do not 'grow up' and become big books!). But an important gap between visual resemblance and legitimacy has already been opened up in *The Winter's Tale* by the time Paulina tries to use the resemblance argument.

Visual resemblance is *not*, after all, a necessary and sufficient condition for legitimacy, which is a matter rather of fact, as determined by kinship and/or property relations: might not an illegitimate or unauthorized copy of a book be physically very like an authorized one (even before photocopying technology)? The human analogy here would be illegitimacy when it is the responsibility of the father: nothing guarantees that legitimate Edgar looks more like Gloucester than illegitimate Edmund. The crucial question, 'Is this an *authorized* copy?' in such cases is not addressed by the criterion of physical resemblance. On the other hand, it is common knowledge that legitimate offspring *need* not resemble the father, nor indeed either parent. This leaves only the case where the mother's fidelity is in question and a father–child resemblance does exist as one in which the latter fact is pertinent. This is of course the burden of Paulina's speech (although it later transpires at 5.1.225-8 that Perdita actually looks like Hermione).[20]

Leontes himself has raised questions about people's assertion of parent–child resemblance earlier in conversation with his young son Mamillius:

> What? hast smutch'd thy nose?
> They say it is a copy out of mine . . .
> . . .they say we are
> Almost as like as eggs; women say so —
> That will say anything . . .
> . . . Mine honest friend,
> Will you take eggs for money?
> (1.2.121-2, 129-31, 160-1)

In his jealousy, Leontes first acknowledges that the resemblance is generally recognized, then dismisses it as a trivial resemblance: egg-to-egg resemblance sounds like a strong claim, but it is only women who are making it—and anyway, are eggs true coin? (The associative process is of course set up as peculiar: 'He something seems unsettled', as Hermione says).

The similarity between sexual and literary rights of reproduction is made explicit in *The Taming of the Shrew* when Biondello uses the language of copyright in urging Lucentio to elope with Bianca: 'Take you assurance of her, *cum privilegio ad imprimendum solum*' (4.4.92-3). The Latin phrase, meaning 'with exclusive rights to print' was a standard one in the book trade and implies that by marrying Bianca Lucentio will establish his copyright in her body, gaining the sole right to print—copies of himself presumably. Bianca's subsidiary role in the business is emphasized ten lines later when Biondello refers to her as 'your appendix'.[21]

How genuinely open-ended is the metaphorical evocation process in cases such as those we have just cited? A difficulty that Davidson shares with Kittay and Lehrer is that his description of what happens in metaphorical use can seem to overstate the cognitive riches that a particular metaphor ought to provide. Leontes tells Florizel that his mother has printed his father off in the first two-and-a-half lines of a fifty-five line conversation in which printing is not alluded to again. Restoring it to its immediate context, we can see how 'print' operates as part of a series of devices for embodying and varying the idea of doubling:

> Your mother was most true to wedlock, Prince,
> For she did print your royal father off,
> Conceiving you. Were I but twenty-one,
> Your father's image is so hit in you
> (His very air) that I should call you brother,
> As I did him, and speak of something wildly
> By us perform'd before. Most dearly welcome!
> And your fair princess—goddess! O! alas,
> I lost a couple, that 'twixt heaven and earth
> Might thus have stood, begetting wonder, as
> You, gracious couple, do; and then I lost
> (All mine own folly) the society,
> Amity too, of your brave father, whom
> (Though bearing misery) I desire my life
> Once more to look on him.
>
> (5.1.124-38)

Florizel doubles Polixenes as print, as image; he and Perdita double Leontes' lost children (who 'might thus have stood'); Polixenes and Leontes were doubles ('brother', with reference back, for the audience, to the conversation idealizing this youthful friendship in 1.1); the present seems to double the past ('something . . . By us perform'd before'). The net result of all these likenesses is no doubt evocative in an open-ended way, but for this to occur the local 'print' metaphor needs to be touched quickly and then dropped—so quickly in fact that to give a literal paraphrase of it does not seem impossible or inappropriate. Doesn't Leontes simply *mean* 'You are just like your father'? Davidson would correctly reply that, while this may be what Leontes *uses* the words to mean, it is not what the words mean. The case is one in which Davidson's careful qualification applies: 'Of course, [what we notice or see]

180

may be [propositional in form], and when it is, it usually may be stated in fairly plain words'. (47)

Actually, Davidson's account is sufficiently nuanced to allow both for this sort of strictly limited evocation, whereby the literally false statement is understood as saying something which can easily be paraphrased, and for evocation as an open-ended invitation. When the reader, perhaps more readily than the hearer, pauses over a metaphor such as the one Leontes uses, relates it to other moments in this text and other texts, examines its ideological implications, and so forth, he or she makes a different use of the words from that which works best when hearing the whole speech in its immediate context. It is a helpful feature of Davidson's account that, since the products of the wider and narrower evocative processes are not meanings, we do not need to argue over whether the wider results are 'really' what Leontes means, or 'go beyond' what Leontes means, or whether the narrower result represents some impoverishment of meaning.

How Likeness is Achieved: The Press

While the conceptual question of legitimacy constitutes a major element in the SEX IS PRINTING metaphor, there is also a more physical link between the two activities. This centres on the word 'press' itself: in J.F. Ross's terminology (see previous chapter) 'press' differentiates from one context to another, taking on a printing sense, a sexual-activity sense, or one of many other senses.

Take for example Mistress Page in *The Merry Wives of Windsor* speaking scathingly of Falstaff's love-letters to herself and to Mistress Ford:

> I warrant he hath a thousand of these letters, writ with blank spaces for different names (sure, more!); and these are of the second edition. He will print them, out of doubt; for he cares not what he puts into the press, when he would put us two. I had rather be a giantess, and lie under Mount Pelion.

> 2.1.74-80

'Press' here is dominated first by 'print'. Falstaff has violated one of the conditions that is supposed to separate the hand-written from

the printed: his love-letters are form-letters. 'He will . . .' signals a
hyperbole expressed via the future tense, a not uncommon way of
varying simile. (Compare 'It is as if he had . . .') What the use of the
future tense adds to the simile is a suggestion that this would be a
logical extension or next step in his folly. But then the real next
steps contemplated by Falstaff are affairs with, if possible, both of
the Merry Wives. That this is similarly foolish ('careless'?) can be
nicely captured by allowing 'press' to differentiate retrospectively,
under the dominance of 'us two', so as to take on a sexual sense.
Then the idea of being pressed upon physically by the full weight of
Falstaff gets taken up in a further hyperbole as Mistress Page uses
another simile variant ('I had rather be' for 'It would be like'), a
Falstaff-as-mountain metaphor, an allusion to the proverbial piling
of Mount Pelion on Mount Ossa as a metaphor for excess, and a
hard-to-characterize associative move whereby, since according to
the logic of the figure she is identified with Mount Ossa, Mistress
Page would need, in order to sustain the likeness, to be a giantess.
At this point, the printing sense of 'the press' has yielded to a more
general sense (application of force) into which the context infuses
both a sexual meaning and a reminder of Falstaff's bulk.

Is this a fully-fledged example of a SEX IS PRINTING
metaphor? The passage is certainly a fine instance of the apparently
effortless, witty co-ordination of a number of distinguishable
figures and verbal operations. One of these is, it would appear, a
pun on 'press'. Davidson is keen to distinguish pun from
metaphor, since in a pun it does seem reasonable to hold that two
separate meanings of a word are involved. He uses Shakespeare to
exemplify this:

> When Shakespeare's Cressida is welcomed bawdily into the Grecian
> camp, Nestor says, 'Our general doth salute you with a kiss'. Here we
> are to take 'general' in two ways: once as applying to Agamemnon, who
> is the general; and once, since she is kissing everyone, as applying to no
> one in particular, but everyone in general. We really have a conjunction
> of two sentences: our general, Agamemnon, salutes you with a kiss; and
> everyone in general is saluting you with a kiss.
>
> This is a legitimate device, a pun, but it is not the same device as
> metaphor. For in metaphor there is no essential need of reiteration;
> whatever meanings we assign the words, they keep through every
> correct reading of the passage. (35)

How does 'press' differ from 'general'? Ross would describe the 'general' pun as involving merely equivocal senses of the word. The 'press' pun, however, both depends upon and reawakens the *analogy* between the senses of 'press' being played on. Shakespeare uses 'press' elsewhere in unambiguously sexual contexts, as when in *Venus and Adonis* he describes Venus (apparently Falstaffian in size in this poem, if in no other respect) overwhelming Adonis with her embrace: 'He with her plenty press'd, she faint with dearth,/ Their lips together glued, fall to the earth' (545-6). Here 'press'd' is literal, and has nothing to do with printing. And when Pandarus invites Troilus and Cressida to 'press . . . to death' the bed of their 'pretty encounters' (*Troilus and Cressida*, 3.2.208-9) he similarly uses a verb which conveys just what will literally be done to the bed (leaving aside the personification-plus-hyperbole of 'to death'[22]). Now, if Shakespeare had written 'for he cares not what he puts into the press, when he would press us two', the passage would have simply punned on the 'press' of printing (a noun) and the 'press' involved in intercourse (a verb). But as it stands, the latter clause is grammatically elliptical for 'when he would put us two into the press'. 'Press' in its second occurrence in the spelt-out version remains a noun, and 'into the press' as a whole phrase must be understood metaphorically. No doubt what is immediately evoked could be 'stated in fairly plain words' (in this case adding a euphemistic motive for the word-play) but keeping 'in the press' as a metaphor for sex does allow for further evocative reflections.[23]

Given our earlier discussion of legitimacy questions, incidentally, it is interesting to look at the sentence preceding the passage we have been commenting on. Mistress Page produces for Mistress Ford 'the twin-brother of thy letter; but let thine inherit first, for I protest mine never shall' (2.1.72-4). That which makes the letters like printed material, their over-similarity, also makes them like over-similar children whose rights of inheritance are thereby confused.

Coins and Wax

Coins, like books, are produced through the transfer by pressure of a pattern onto material previously blank. Another activity which could be similarly characterized is one common in Elizabethan times but almost lost in our own: the authentication of a document by attaching to it a piece of wax onto which some design, the property of the issuer, has been pressed. 'Seal' differentiates, in appropriate contexts, to mean both the design and the wax bearing the design. Also, given that the wax could serve the further function of securing the document against unauthorized examination, 'seal' comes to mean a method of keeping things closed, or the activity of securing them, as when we seal letters, or rooms.

In this section, we lay out some examples of coining and sealing metaphors as print-*like;* the immediate purpose of the exercise is to show how coining and sealing are also operative within what we have so far characterized as the SEX IS PRINTING metaphor, so that we see how Shakespeare exploits what all four activities have in common for figurative purposes. In the following section we shall use some of these materials in a different way, to see how well they are covered by one post-Davidson account of how metaphor functions.

Whereas the notion of the illegitimate printed book must have been of direct interest to a comparatively narrow group of Elizabethans concerned with publishing, the notion of the counterfeit coin would have been more generally accessible. So Angelo can make use of an UNLAWFUL SEX IS UNLAWFUL COINING metaphor when he rejects Isabella's plea for mercy for her brother who has made the unmarried Juliet pregnant:

> It were as good
> To pardon him that hath from nature stol'n
> A man already made, as to remit
> Their saucy sweetness that do coin heaven's image
> In stamps that are forbid. 'Tis all as easy
> Falsely to take away a life true made
> As to put metal in restrained means
> To make a false one.
> *(Measure for Measure, 2.4.42-9)*

Illegitimate children are still essentially seen as 'stolne and surreptitious copies',[24] but now as forged coins rather than as pirated texts. Moreover, the infringement of copyright is seen in this context as not just a crime against an individual (as in the case of an unauthorized copy of a book) or against the state (as in the case of a forged coin) but against 'heaven' in so far as human beings are supposed to be made in the image of God.

The word 'metal' is of interest here. Angelo has previously tried to refuse his appointment as the Duke's deputy, saying:

> Let there be some more test made of my mettle
> Before so noble and so great a figure
> Be stamp'd upon it.
>
> (1.1.48-50)

In the First Folio, the spelling is 'mettle' in both cases; indeed the *OED* begins its entry under 'mettle' by saying that it is 'originally the same word as *metal* of which *mettle* was a variant spelling, used indiscriminately in all senses'. The attempt to differentiate between concrete and non-concrete senses, using the spelling 'metal' for the former and 'mettle' for the latter, did not begin until the eighteenth century. So one's mettle, one's 'ardent or spirited temperament' (*OED*) can also be an impression-taking surface, a substance that a figure can be stamped upon. Coins are made of metal because metal, once cool again after the minting process, is durable enough to hold a shape.[25]

Later in her dialogue with Angelo in 2.4, Isabella surprisingly (and dangerously) agrees with him that women too are 'frail' in the sense of being vulnerable to sexual temptation:

> Ay, as the glasses where they view themselves,
> Which are as easy broke as they make forms.
> Women? Help heaven! men their creation mar
> By profiting by them. Nay, call us ten times frail,
> For we are soft as our complexions are,
> And credulous to false prints.
>
> (2.4.125-30)

The passage demonstrates how, if one wants to make a point about women's weakness, the print metaphor offers only too rich resources. Women are reflecting surfaces, breakable surfaces, soft surfaces. Metonymy—women are associated with mirrors because they use them frequently—and synecdoche—the complexion can stand in for the whole woman—slide into metaphor. The two metaphors are inconsistent at surface level (complexions neither reflect nor break), but can be felt to be coherent at a deeper level because both are grounded on women's capacity to produce copies, to 'make forms' or be printed upon as a result of the masculine 'stamp'. Clear as the general idea is, 'credulous' is odd. To be soft is to be too easily printed upon (or 'impressed'?), and that is like being too ready to believe something or someone (presumably, in this context, men's promises or men themselves). But this line of thought seems to make the 'print' the external stamp which causes the woman to be printed (i.e. the false man) rather than the result of the printing, the false (illegitimate) child, as the parallel with 'make forms' would suggest.

To say women are as soft as their complexions is actually not the best basis for sexist printing metaphors, since it is facial mobility rather than skin texture that sustains FACES ARE BOOKS metaphors, and no printing process uses for material on which to print any substance as soft as living skin. This is where wax has the advantage, as an impression-taking substance which has all the softness, malleability, inconstancy and so forth of patriarchy's Eternal Feminine. A good example of a straightforward simile along these lines can be found in Tourneur's *The Atheist's Tragedy* when Levidulcia, encouraging Fresco to be bold in his love-making, assures him

> Ladies are as courteous as yeoman's wives, and methinks they should be more gentle. Hot diet and soft ease makes 'em, like wax always kept warm, more easy to take impression.

> (2.5.20-3)

A different patriarchal point is made by Theseus at the beginning of *A Midsummer Night's Dream* when he tells Hermia that she is bound to obey her father:

> To you your father should be as a god;
> One that compos'd your beauties; yea, and one
> To whom you are but as a form in wax,
> By him imprinted, and within his power,
> To leave the figure, or disfigure it.[26]

> (1.1.47-51)

Hermia's status as female and as child gives her in law a *duty* to be malleable to the right men (her father, the man her father has chosen for her). However, her *nature* as female and as child makes her as susceptible ('credulous'?) to the wrong men as Levidulcia's ladies. This is Egeus' complaint: Lysander has

> stol'n the impression of her fantasy
> With bracelets of thy hair, rings, gawds, conceits,
> Knacks, trifles, nosegays, sweetmeats—messengers
> Of strong prevailment in unhardened youth.
> With cunning hast thou filch'd my daughter's heart,
> Turn'd her obedience (which is due to me)
> To stubborn harshness.
>
> (1.1.32-8)

At this point in our argument we should be sensitized to the implications of 'impression'; Hermia is presented as soft in the wrong way ('unhardened') in respect of Lysander's unauthorized courtship, and correspondingly hard in the wrong way ('harsh') towards her father. In this framework, women's weakness is both desired (in so far as it achieves their subordination) and feared (in so far as it makes them unreliable as property: cf. Egeus' 'last word' on the subject, 'And she is mine, and all my right of her/ I do estate unto Demetrius' (1.1.97-8)).[27]

A more cheerful use of the WOMEN ARE WAX metaphor occurs in *Venus and Adonis* when Venus exclaims after being kissed by Adonis:

> 'Pure lips, sweet seals in my soft lips imprinted,
> What bargains may I make, still to be sealing?
> To sell myself I can be well contented,
> So thou wilt buy, and pay, and use good dealing,
>   Which purchase if thou make, for fear of slips,
>   Set thy seal manual on my wax-red lips'.
>
> (511-16)

Kisses are frequently seen as the 'seals' of the 'bargain' of love in Shakespeare (see *The Taming of the Shrew*, 3.2.123; *The Two Gentlemen of Verona*, 2.2.7; and *Measure for Measure*, 4.1.5-6) and 'slips' could mean 'counterfeit money' (see *Romeo and Juliet*, 2.4.45-8). Without lingering over all the sell—seal wordplay here, we should point out the surprisingly asymmetrical view of kissing that is implied. How can Adonis' lips be the seals while Venus' lips are the receiving wax? Of course, lips are here meant euphemistically for other parts of the body. All these printing, pressing and stamping metaphors potentially rely on our grasping that what is really 'behind it all' is the male penis as what (im)presses and the female vagina as what receives the impression. Decorum no doubt blocks this from being directly evoked in many cases, but not here. (Nevertheless, the patriarchal assumptions that structure most of our examples may turn out to depend ultimately on a view of activity—passivity which cannot otherwise be 'grounded'.)

The WOMEN ARE WAX metaphor, like the others in this group, can serve to excuse women, though in a patronizing way: it is striking however how narratively irrelevant these excuses tend to be in Shakespeare. Possibly this is less true of Viola's reflection in *Twelfth Night* on how easily, disguised as a male, she has unintentionally won Olivia's heart:

> How easy is it for the proper-false
> In women's waxen hearts to set their forms!
> Alas, our frailty is the cause, not we,
> For such as we are made of, such we be.
> (2.2.29-32)

But even here, it is hard to feel that Viola herself is at all soft and passive like wax; much less so are Hermia or Venus—or Isabella, as Angelo immediately discovers when he proposes in the wake of her 'credulous to false prints' speech that she should 'Be that you are' (*Measure for Measure*, 2.4.134), i.e. frail, only to be rejected forcefully. Probably the most inexplicable occurrence of the motif is in *The Rape of Lucrece,* where the narrator takes it upon himself to excuse Lucrece:

> For men have marble, women waxen minds,
> And therefore are they form'd as marble will;
> The weak oppress'd, th'impression of strange kinds
> Is form'd in them by force, by fraud, or skill.
> Then call them not the authors of their ill,
> > No more than wax shall be accounted evil,
> > Wherein is stamp'd the semblance of a devil.
> > (1240-6)

The phrase 'by force' here is more to the point than the wax metaphor: the obvious reason why Lucrece cannot be called 'the author of [her own] ill' is that she has been forcibly raped, not because women are too weak to be held responsible for anything at all![28] The next stanza, incidentally, concludes with a FACES ARE BOOKS remark which asserts that the softness of women's faces makes them more readable:

> Though men can cover crimes with bold stern looks,
> Poor women's faces are their own faults' books.
>
> (1252-3)

On one occasion, however, Shakespeare presents a character who moves from using the metaphorical field we have been discussing in the usual misogynistic way to a novel and repentant development of it. In *Cymbeline,* Posthumus, like other Shakespearean heroes, angrily damns all women because he thinks he has reason to suspect the fidelity of one:

> Is there no way for men to be, but women
> Must be half-workers? We are all bastards,
> And that most venerable man which I
> Did call my father, was I know not where
> When I was stamp'd. Some coiner with his tools
> Made me a counterfeit.
>
> (2.5.1-6)

But later in the play, repenting of his order to Pisanio to kill Imogen on the strength of his suspicions, he offers the gods his own life by way of compensation for the murder:

>   take
> No stricter render of me than my all.
> I know you are more clement than vile men,
> Who of their broken debtors take a third,
> A sixth, a tenth, letting them thrive again
> On their abatement. That's not my desire.
> For Imogen's dear life take mine, and though
> 'Tis not so dear, yet 'tis a life; you coin'd it.
> 'Tween man and man they weigh not every stamp;
> Though light, take pieces for the figure's sake;
> You rather, mine being yours; and so, great pow'rs,
> If you will take this audit, take this life,
> And cancel these cold bonds.
>
> (5.4.16-28)

189

Like Angelo, Posthumus develops the coining metaphor in terms of men being made in the image of God (or, in this ostensibly pre-Christian setting, the gods): 'take pieces for the figure's sake;/ You rather, mine being yours.' The gods themselves are the only authorized coiners in this context. Whereas the phallic action of 'stamping' was central to his earlier speech, the financial side of coins comes to the fore in the later one. (Indeed, the whole play has a strongly mercantile strain, perhaps because of the influence of one of its sources, *Frederyke of Jennen,* which tells the wager story from a decidedly commercial viewpoint.) But when he describes the 'pieces' or coins of his own life as 'light' he is no longer devaluing himself on account of his supposed bastardy but merely asserting that Imogen's life is more valuable ('dear' in both senses) than his own.

This assertion is in fact remarkable both in its wider implications (Posthumus still believes Imogen to be guilty) and in the way it is expressed. The word 'light' was frequently used at this time to mean 'wanton' or 'promiscuous', but almost always with reference to women, as when Lucio in *Measure for Measure* comments cynically that 'women are light at midnight' (5.1.279-80), or when Portia in *The Merchant of Venice* more playfully says 'Let me give light, but let me not be light,/ For a light wife doth make a heavy husband' (5.1.129-30). Whores were proverbially said to be 'light' and were also frequently seen as counterfeit coins, as in the trial scene in Webster's *The White Devil* when Monticelso ends his 'character of a whore' with

> What's a whore?
> She's like the guilty counterfeited coin
> Which whosoe'er first stamps it brings in trouble
> All that receive it.

> (3.2.98-101)

Given this background, Posthumus' image of himself as a light coin is very unusual; it reminds us that he is asking to be punished for having acted on the assumption of Imogen's 'lightness'. Once the donor field of coinage is thought of not in terms of how coins are produced but of how they are exchanged, the motif of a male—female asymmetry gives way to one of reciprocity, or at least of inequality being a question of personal character rather than gender.

But overall we must see the printing metaphors as carrying a strong phallocentric bias. The only exception to the pattern whereby men do the printing or stamping and women are the paper or wax is to be found in the romantic convention whereby it can be claimed that a woman's image is imprinted on a man's heart. This is actually rare in Shakespeare and even when it does occur is expressed ambiguously, as when Boyet in *Love's Labour's Lost* tells the Princess of France how he knows that the King of Navarre is in love with her:

> Why, all his behaviors did make their retire
> To the court of his eye, peeping thorough desire:
> His heart like an agate with your print impressed,
> Proud with his form, in his eye pride expressed.
>
> (2.1.234-7)

Although the man's heart has received the woman's print it seems significant that it is not seen as something soft and malleable like wax, but as something hard, a precious stone (an agate) which has been carved—and which could in fact be used to make an impression on wax!

The Trouble with Experience

Stephen Davies, in 'Truth-Values and Metaphors',[29] takes a strongly Davidsonian line on the question of metaphorical meaning. Indeed, his discussion is virtually a restatement of Davidson's argument, here and there extended and buttressed against potential criticism. We shall not be concerned with these overt extensions. What interests us is that in just one respect Davies' straightforward exposition of Davidson adds a new conceptual element to Davidson's own formulations. That element is 'experience'.

Here are some examples of how 'experience' is introduced by Davies into the Davidson account. Introducing Davidson's article, Davies says, 'On his account . . . [m]etaphors literally direct our attention to an experience of similarity between the subjects of the metaphor' (292). Expanding Davidson's point about the gap between the paraphrase of a metaphor and the original, he writes:

191

The paraphrase describes the experiences to which the metaphor was (perhaps) intended to lead one, but the appreciation of the metaphor depends on one's *having* those experiences rather than upon one's *knowing* that those experiences are the experiences that one was intended to have. Metaphors seem to aim at conveying experiences rather than mere understanding. (294)

Davidson's crucial evocation-*versus*-meaning contrast is understood as involving the claim that 'metaphors aim at the evocation of experiences' (294). The point about the difference between literal propositional assertion and what metaphor does is expressed thus: 'The metaphor-maker aims not at asserting belief but at conveying an experience to his audience' (297). Later this is expressed as 'Metaphors express experiences rather than state beliefs'. (301). On the unlimitedness of what a metaphor can lead one to 'grasp', we are told:

Although this propositional content of the metaphor plays a part in controlling, as well as occasioning, this experience, neither it nor the utterer's intentions determine the scope of this experience. (298)

As to what happens when a metaphor dies, Davies holds that

As a dead metaphor, 'Cigarettes are coffin-nails' is understood as the assertion of a (necessarily trivial) truth rather than as an invitation to an experience of a relation between cigarettes and coffin-nails. (300-1)

The word 'experience' does not, as it happens, enter into the original Davidson argument at any point, so it is interesting to watch a restatement of that argument being so relentlessly invaded by it. What in the original line of thought could allow for this development?

The broad argument, it will be recalled, is that no special meaning is understood when a metaphor is appreciated. In putting it this way, we are using the verb 'to understand' more narrowly than it is used in everyday speech, restricting it to imply successful uptake on literal meaning. Then, to cover the total evocative content that a metaphor has for a reader or hearer, we shall need a different verb. This may seem pedantic, but the meaning–use distinction will be blurred if we speak of someone *understanding* from the statement 'Men have marble, women waxen minds' some such open-ended paraphrase as 'Women are more easily influenced than men, less firm in their resolves, less aggressive . . .' and so on. All, Davidson claims, that is *understood* is what the words *mean*—namely, that the minds of men are made of marble and those of women are made of wax. (The further *use* that is made of this statement, without which it would be so pointless to assert it, nevertheless depends on that literal understanding.) So, just as words other than 'mean' will be needed to stand for what metaphor does that goes beyond meaning ('evoke' turns out to be very useful), so words other than 'understand' and 'understanding' will be needed to indicate the process and upshot of successful metaphorical appreciation respectively.

Davidson's own article is very resourceful at finding a variety of ordinary expressions that can serve this purpose. Some examples: 'Metaphor does lead us to notice what might not otherwise be noticed' (41): 'metaphor provokes or invites a certain view of its subject' (45); 'Metaphor makes us see one thing as another' (47); 'The legitimate function of so-called paraphrase is to make the lazy or ignorant reader have a vision like that of the skilled critic' (47). All these ways of putting the matter imply alternatives to 'understanding': noticing, viewing in a certain way, seeing-as, having a vision. Getting, or seeing, the point of a metaphor should be added to the list.

We notice again that there is a pull towards the visual in these locutions. This need not be dangerous, in terms of our worries about 'imagery', so long as we are clear that no claims about mind's eye phenomena need be implied by the phrases. Compare the case of the indirect command, where the utterance 'It's getting very chilly' is used to request that the window be closed. A natural way of expressing this is to say that the hearer has heard the statement *as* a request, *as* equivalent to 'Please close the window'. But to talk about 'hearing as' need not imply that the auditory imagination of the hearer has been stimulated into 'hearing' a faint voice uttering the replacement sentence. The same goes for 'seeing as'; if, as Davidson points out, 'Seeing as is not seeing that', it also is not, or not necessarily, inner-eye seeing either.[30] However, a phrase like 'have a vision' does seem to bring us dangerously close to image language.

193

We can now return to Davies' phrasing. It seems that he has felt the need for a pair of words that can be consistently employed so as to be to metaphor-in-use what 'understand' and 'understanding' are to meaning. Further, he too exhibits some caution about the pull towards the visual in Davidson's article.[31] So a non-visual term for the beyond-literal-understanding uptake on metaphor is desired. Unfortunately, 'experience' (verb and noun) seems deeply problematic as a term to choose. Its unsuitability turns out to be instructive in the light of the difficulties surrounding the extension of 'imagery' beyond the visual to include the other senses.

Davies offers the following as a description of how 'My love is a rose' could be used metaphorically. (It should be said that the description is offered in the context of a larger argument.)

> If someone says to me 'My love is a rose' and if this is a live metaphor, in recognizing it as a metaphor I know that the metaphor-maker intends me to have the experience of his loved-one's being rose-like. The literal meaning of the words and the context in which the words are stated point my thoughts not only to these subjects, but also in a direction. For example, the word 'love' suggests that I should not dwell upon the stalky build and thorny temperament of the person referred to. I know, then, that I am intended to experience *something* about the rose-likeness of the utterer's loved one (and perhaps also I know that I am intended to acquire beliefs about the loved one as a result of this experience). But can I know enough about the metaphor-maker's intentions from his statements of the metaphor and from the context of this statement to know, for example, whether or not I have completed the intended experience? I think not. (295)

Surely 'to have an experience' here is being used in just the same ways as 'to have an image' might have been. 'Experience', in time-honoured empiricist fashion, is the sum total of what comes to one via the senses. Experiencing the rose-likeness then must mean not only 'seeing' it but 'touching', 'tasting', 'feeling' and 'hearing' it—with certain contextual constraints against 'touching' the thorns, and so forth. (The quotation marks around the sense-participles are supposed to put them into the realm of the imagination; presumably nobody would want to claim that a *full* experience is in question. Fully to experience a person as a rose would be to suffer a severe hallucination.)

But what happens to a Shakespearean metaphor when it is taken to 'aim at the evocation of experiences'? Let us look back at two of the examples considered in the preceding section. Men who father illegitimate children are said to 'coin heaven's image/ In stamps that are forbid'. To grasp the point of this involves thinking about the culprits' activities in terms of counterfeiters' activities, of the two outcomes (children and coins) as analogous, and of the reasons for the activities' being criminal being similar (just as the coiner issues an unauthorized image of the sovereign for private gain, so the adulterer produces an unauthorized image of God—if we are all so made—for private pleasure). But if one has never had the experience of producing counterfeit coinage, is one's grasp of the metaphor impaired? For that matter, Angelo is addressing Isabella, a woman who lacks experience not only within the donor field but (as a prospective nun) within the recipient field: does this mean that his words fall on deaf ears? Similarly, when Posthumus asks the gods to take his life in compensation for Imogen's, is it one's *experience* of giving and receiving change that is important to one's grasp of the speech? Davies would say so ('the appreciation of the metaphor depends on one's *having* those experiences rather than upon one's *knowing* that those experiences are the experiences that one was intended to have' (294)).

In the second case, there is some historical background to be filled in for the modern reader, for whom the notion of weighing coins is alien; one needs to know that there was a literal problem of 'light' coinage for the Elizabethans, with the edges of coins being clipped for the precious metal they contained, so that while in Elizabethan transactions not every 'stamp' would have been weighed, some would have been. We could say then that the Elizabethan experience of coining was different from ours, in a manner which the metaphor depends on. But does one need to *have* that experience, even imaginatively, to appreciate the point of the passage? It would seem more natural to say that one just needs to *know* the detail about coin-clipping for that part of the metaphor to work.[32] Indeed, in a dramatic context, to burden the hearer with a responsibility to experience each donor field imaginatively is wholly impracticable; one figure gives way to the next figure too quickly, all in the service of the macro-level representations of experience with which the audience-member is primarily concerned: the experience we care about in Posthumus' speech is his repentance, not some mental reconstruction of what it would be like to try to pay an Elizabethan or Jacobean tradesman with a clipped coin.

Davies might reply that we are misreading him, and that the experience he is referring to is purely and simply the experience of appreciating the similitude, rather than that of *having experiences* within the donor or recipient fields as such. 'Experience' could then virtually drop out of the account: it is just a nominative for one's reaction to (= experience of) the metaphor. Sometimes Davies' formulations can be so treated. For instance, to claim of metaphors that they 'direct our attention to an experience of a similarity between the subjects of the metaphor' (292) seems just to claim that they direct our attention to the similarity between the subjects of the metaphor. It is our contention, however, that it is the all-senses expanded version of imagery theory, plus perhaps in the background views about the (usually lyric) poem as a 'verbal icon'—somehow peculiarly equivalent to experience[33]—which have been balefully influential in literary studies, that are exerting enough pressure on Davies' thought to lead him to try to use 'experience' more substantially.

Under this pressure, metaphor really does get conceptually devalued. 'The metaphor', Davies writes, 'is the *expression,* rather than a description, of an experience' (297-8); and 'An expression of an experience is more like a sophisticated exclamation—such as 'How lovely'—than it is like a statement' (298). (If you confine your exemplification of metaphor to 'My love is a rose', of course, you may be unduly prone to seeing metaphor as exclamation.) If this, despite 'sophisticated', seems simplistic, the role of 'experience' in the metaphorical experience turns out a few lines later to be anything but simple:

> The appropriate response to a metaphor is the thought, entertained without belief, that the metaphor states a significant truth. This thought is entertained as a means to the evocation of an experience which reveals the point at which the utterance of the metaphor aimed (or might have aimed). (298)

Surely here 'experience' is presented as something separate from, and necessary to, one's getting the point. For Davidson, the interpreter of a metaphor does two things: understands the metaphorical sentence, and grasps the point of its use. Davies spins this out into four stages: we understand the words in order to entertain them without belief in order to evoke an experience in order to get the point. And it is stage three, the experience, which is being expressed. Furthermore, it transpires that the metaphor-maker is *essentially* concerned with experience:

> The fact that metaphor-makers do not usually go on to paraphrase their live metaphors suggests that they are more directly concerned with evoking experiences than with imparting beliefs. (288-9)

One might think that metaphor-makers refrain from paraphrase because they are confident that their point will get across. But then this whole line of thought looks very shaky when matched against any of our examples. To say of Angelo and Posthumus that they are evoking experiences, expressing them, or exclaiming about them radically understates both the cognitive interest of the likenesses their speeches invite us to explore and the importance of the perfectly straightforward belief-statements that are central to, if not exhaustive of, the material evoked by their metaphors. Angelo really should be heard as stating that there is a significant similarity between murder and fathering illegitimate children, just as Posthumus is praying seriously and thoughtfully in a way which involves interesting beliefs about human worth.

Davies' unfortunate manner of expounding Davidson at this point brings out an element in the Davidson account which does invite misunderstanding or misuse. Davidson doesn't want the whole 'point' of a metaphor to be able to be given in a single sentence with a truth value or in a finite set of sentences with truth-values, because then the metaphor really would mean that sentence or super-sentence; full paraphrase would be possible. So he argues both that there is (or need be) no finite list of things a metaphor leads one to notice, and that some of these things are non-propositional in form; he privileges the visual realm as one in which we are accustomed to non-propositional noticing. Now it is not inconsistent with these accounts to say that *some* things a metaphor leads one to notice are propositional in form, or to say that certain propositions are virtually required to be understood by the metaphor if it is to do its work. (Whatever else we think as a result of Angelo's speech, we had better think, 'This man is claiming that there is a significant similarity between murder and fathering illegitimate children'.) But nothing in Davidson's presentation stresses the importance of what we might call core-propositions; the drift is always towards emphasizing that these core-propositions are not capable of simply replacing the metaphor without loss. What Davies has done is to move further,[34] via the confusing doctrine of 'experience', in the direction of denying any importance to the core-propositions at all; and to do so is to make *dramatic* nonsense of speeches which are both strongly figurative and useful for conveying facts, beliefs and arguments.[35]

A final reason for challenging Davies' use of 'experience' is its potential for confusion with the use of the term in Lakoff and Johnson, which we do find illuminating. Lakoff and Johnson discuss, speculatively, the grounding of everyday metaphors in experience. For instance, why is it generally the case that HAPPINESS IS UP, apparently cross-culturally? (Consider the expressions to cheer up, to raise someone's spirits, to be on top of the world/over the moon/in the clouds. Or, conversely, to be in low spirits, to be feeling down, etc.) Perhaps this is based in our experience of our own bodies whereby to be 'up' (standing or sitting) goes with activity and consciousness, while to be 'down' (in a horizontal position) is associated with illness, sleep or death.[36]

The SEX IS PRINTING metaphor, as we have already suggested, seems to work phallocentrically by grounding itself in one particular experience of heterosexual sex, whereby the active penis, moving in the passive vagina, leaves its mark, ultimately, in the form of a baby. No doubt in a ribald context, as in our *Merry Wives* and *Venus and Adonis* examples, this experience, or experiential gestalt, is part of what is directly evoked by the printing figure. (This is also the case with the first Posthumus example, where disgust at the experience is involved.) But we would want to say that Angelo's remarks, and even Theseus' remarks, may be grounded similarly—that is to say that the belief-system they belong to appeals to that particular experience of sexuality even as it circularly valorizes that experience as *the* proper and central sexual experience—without implying that in these particular passages Angelo or Theseus wish to bring the experience before their hearer's minds (or that Shakespeare wishes to bring the experience before our minds) via their metaphors.

Sexism in Metaphor, Sexism in the Text

To find questions of gender, sexuality, reproduction and property so centrally raised by Shakespeare's printing metaphors may be unexpected but is certainly topical, given the recent explosion of work on gender-discriminatory ideologies inspired by the women's movement. Readers will have gathered that we are not ourselves very enthusiastic about the women-as-wax-or-paper 'picture'; it seems to us to conceal important aspects of women's activity, both as sexual partners and as mothers, in a way which leaves the ownership of both women and children 'naturally' in the hands of men. If we think for a moment about biological facts, it seems to say the least curious to embrace a set of metaphors which imply that men, not women, are the ones who do the real 'shaping' in the process of birth.[37]

However, the degree of sexism of the Shakespearean text clearly cannot be directly read off from micro-level analysis of these metaphors. The intrinsic bias of a metaphor may be overridden if it is placed in the mouth of a character to whom things are going to happen and who will be broadly evaluated by the audience on that basis. For Isabella to speak of women's frailty in the particular context of trying to get a pardon for her brother, or for Viola to speak in the same vein in a context in which the difficulties she faces make it understandable that she should temporarily feel a little frail herself—these are different things from having an authorial voice stating as a general principle, 'Women are frail'. A debate about the overall degree of phallocentrism of *Measure for Measure* would have to take into account larger issues, such as the final assessment to be made of the play's central but ambiguous male character, the Duke.

Shakespeare cannot be expected to have stood somehow outside the broad belief systems of his time. Amongst these were patriarchal assumptions—not of course quite the same patriarchal assumptions as those which sustain sexism today. In general, there is a strong tendency in the plays for belief-systems to be challenged, suspended or ironized in the course of the action (rather more than at the conclusion of the action). This reflects (i) the intrinsic instability or internal stresses which all ideologies exhibit; (ii) a positive Renaissance willingness to accept that exploring or playing with these difficulties is a positive or educative activity;[38] and (iii) a temperamental affinity for this sort of operation as a part of play-writing on the part of Shakespeare himself.

It is not then contradictory to hold that patriarchal assumptions can be both challenged within the plays at the macro-level and found broadly to structure them (or, if you prefer, vice versa). Similarly, at the micro-level, patriarchal assumptions structure many of the metaphors which Shakespeare has as it were to hand, ready to be worked up for specific purposes. So, in the course of elaborating and 'decorating' Angelo's argument about the equivalence of murder and illegitimate begetting, the SEX IS COINING metaphor, with its active male–passive female assumption, gets taken up and explored. If it would be wrong to say that the assumption is thereby endorsed (since in the dramatic context the argument *may* turn out to be as unreliable as its proponent), it would be equally wrong to see the assumption as necessarily challenged. Isabella and the audience are busy enough trying to work out what if anything is wrong with Angelo's argument as a whole without challenging the patriarchal assumptions built into the metaphor through which the argument is unfolded. (For that matter, Isabella and most of any given audience probably share those assumptions. This is the problem!) But *sometimes* a micro-level problematizing of assumptions is achieved which is equivalent to, and generally linked to, the macro-level questioning occasioned by characters and events. This is what we see happening with Posthumus. One coin metaphor seems to be challenged by a very different one which, in shifting from the production of coins to their exchange, 'finds' equality.

More usually, however, it is the self-limiting or self-problematizing nature of an analogy which plays at the micro-level the assumption-challenging role. Our ultimate reservation about Davidson—or, more exactly, about how his arguments might be incautiously paraphrased or extended—centres on how 'getting the point' or 'seeing the vision' evoked by a metaphor can come to sound like a unitary and *unchallengeable* experience. Once you have *seen women as wax,* that would seem to be that, if what has happened is fundamentally non-propositional. How could such a 'vision' be denied, if nothing is being asserted? An account of metaphor which, on the other hand, gives full weight to the propositional content of what a metaphor evokes will be better able to describe how the evoked propositions may in turn be in tension with one another, may indeed upon examination self-destruct, as examined ideology tends to do. It will also be able to allow for the possibility of criticism from an external position, the reaction to l.1240 of *The Rape of Lucrece* ('For men have marble, women waxen minds') which is simply to say, 'No'.

Notes

1. Donald Davidson, 'What Metaphors Mean', *Critical Inquiry* 5 (1978), 31-47. Our page references are to this original publication. The article has been frequently reprinted, for example in the collections edited by Mark Johnson and Sheldon Sacks (see Introduction, n. 10, p.12 above) and in Davidson's own collection, *Inquiries into Truth and Interpretation* (Clarendon Press, Oxford, 1984), pp.245-64.

    Davidson's formidable philosophical reputation rests on the gap between a logic-oriented and a linguistics-oriented philosophy of language; he has argued strongly for 'the idea of assigning meanings to sentences of natural languages by associating the sentences with truth-theoretically interpreted formulas of a logical system' (as William Lycan puts it in *Logical Form in Natural Language,* (The MIT Press, Cambridge, Mass., 1984), p.8; 'truth-theoretically interpreted formulas' here invokes earlier work in pure logic by Alfred Tarski). Some sense of Davidson's overall programme may be obtained from the other essays in his *Inquiries,* from Lycan's excellent exposition, and from other recent treatments of the current philosophical scene such as Blackburn's (see below, n. 18); but we believe the essay on metaphor to be sufficiently free-standing to be illuminating for readers—like ourselves—who lack the background in formal logic that is really required to engage fully with the broader Davidsonian position.
2. The point that metaphorical 'imagery' is not necessarily or primarily visual is made by I.A. Richards both in *Principles of Literary Criticism* (Kegan Paul, London, 1925), p.119 and in *The Philosophy of Rhetoric* (Oxford University Press, New York and London, 1936), p.98. It is also made by John Middleton Murry in 'Metaphor', *Countries of the Mind* (Oxford University Press, Oxford, 1931), pp.1-16, by René Wellek and Austin Warren in *Theory of Literature* (Jonathan Cape, London, 1949), pp.166-8, and by Paul Ricoeur in *The Rule of Metaphor,* trans. Robert Czerny (Routledge and Kegan Paul, London, 1978), pp.207-15.
3. Wellek and Warren discuss these variations in *Theory of Literature,* pp.166-7.
4. In modern usage, consider 'You can read him like a book', 'I never got beyond page two with her', 'He's an open book'. 'You can't tell a book by its cover'. Life itself can also be seen as a book, as in 'That chapter of my life is now closed'.

5. In finding non-Shakespearean examples, we have made use of Louis Charles Stagg, *Index to the Figurative Language of the Tragedies of Shakespeare's Chief Seventeenth-Century Contemporaries* (Memphis University Press, Memphis, 1977. Reprinted by Garland, New York and London, 1984). References are to the following editions: *The Plays of George Chapman,* ed. T.M. Parrott (George Routledge, London, 1910); Thomas Heywood, *A Woman Killed with Kindness,* ed. R.W. Van Fossen (Methuen, London, 1961); *The Plays of John Marston,* ed. J. Harvey Wood (Oliver Boyd, Edinburgh and London, 1938); Cyril Tourneur, *The Atheist's Tragedy,* ed. Irving Ribner (Methuen, London, 1964); John Webster, *The Duchess of Malfi* and *The White Devil,* ed. John Russell Brown (Methuen, London, 1964 and 1960).

6. In this period, the index would generally be placed at the front of the book rather than at the back; see our discussion of an 'index' metaphor in *Troilus and Cressida,* p.30-1 above.

7. 'Book and volume' is another example of hendiadys in *Hamlet;* see pp.100-1 above, and footnote 19, p.128.

8. This self-reflexity is taken up in the Dolphin's response to the King's request to 'Look in the Lady's face':

> I do, my lord, and in her eye I find
> A wonder, or a wondrous miracle,
> The shadow of myself form'd in her eye,
> Which being but the shadow of your son,
> Becomes a sun and makes your son a shadow.
> I do protest I never loved myself
> Till now infixed I beheld myself
> Drawn in the flattering table of her eye.
>   (2.1.496-503)

Some of this reads like a first draft for the mirror sequence in *Richard II* (4.1) which begins with Richard sending for a mirror in response to Northumberland's insistence that he should read over the list of his own faults: 'I'll read enough,/ When I do see the very book indeed/ Where all my sins are writ, and that's myself' (273-5).

9. See our discussion of this synecdoche above, p.109.

10. Compare our discussion of Gertrude's request to Hamlet to 'let thine eye look like a friend on Denmark', pp.99-100 above. This oscillation effect, whereby a word can have both 'subjective' and 'objective' meanings, is particularly common in Shakespeare in relation to eyes and the act of seeing: 'sightless', for example, can mean both blind ('sightless eyes' in Sonnet 43.12) and invisible ('sightless couriers of the air' in *Macbeth,* 1.7.23)—as well as just ugly ('sightless stains' in *King John,* 3.1.45) and 'to hoodwink' can mean to cover the eyes ('We'll have no Cupid hoodwink'd with a scarf', *Romeo and Juliet,* 1.4.4) or to cover an object from sight ('the prize I'll bring thee to/ Shall hoodwink this mischance', *Tempest,* 4.1.205-6).

11. Some editors add that 'cover' here may imply a pun on the legal expression *femme couvert,* meaning married woman.

12. While speech acts with this sort of indirect ('illocutionary' in J.L. Austin's terminology) force can be usefully compared with metaphor to bring Davidson's argument into focus, the two phenomena are in some respects quite unalike; for the differences, see Lycan (cited in n. 1 above), pp.172-5. Davidson need not be read as offering a fully-fledged 'speech act theory of metaphor', only as claiming that speech act theory illuminates a gap between meaning and use which theorists of metaphor would do well to ponder.

13. Max Black, 'How Metaphors Work: A Reply to Donald Davidson', in Sheldon Sacks (ed.), *On Metaphor* (University of Chicago Press, Chicago, 1979), pp.181-92. The 'comparison' view implies that metaphor in eliminating such overt comparative lexical items as 'like' and 'as', is fundamentally no different from simile which includes them. We have been assuming throughout this book that to distinguish between metaphor and simile (especially in Shakespearean usage) would be artificial. As Winifred Nowottny puts it (*The Language Poets Use,* Athlone Press, London, 1962, p.51), 'not infrequently it will be found that in poetry an analogy is expressed first as a simile and then as a metaphor, so there can hardly be much difference between the two, with respect to their truth-claims or imaginative depth. One might reflect on Cleopatra's description of Antony: ''his delights/ Were dolphin-like; they show'd his back above/ The element they liv'd in'' (*Antony and Cleopatra,* 5.2.88-90)'. Regarding Davidson's position here, we agree with Stephen Davies (see below, n. 29) when he writes (p.293), 'In fact rather than effecting a reduction of metaphor to the level of simile, he is suggesting an upgrading of simile to the level of metaphor' since for him, as for others (including Black!) 'the problems posed by metaphors are also posed by similes, so that an account of the one in terms of the other contributes nothing to the solution of the difficulties raised by either'.

14. Davidson is here referring to Max Black's earlier essay, 'Metaphor', *Proceedings of the Aristotelian Society,* N.S. 55 (1954-55), 273-94. This essay is also reprinted in the collection edited by Mark Johnson (see Introduction, n. 10, p.12 above).

15. Ted Cohen, 'Figurative Speech and Figurative Acts', *Journal of Philosophy* 72 (1975), 669-84. See also our discussion of the phenomenon in relation to some examples from *King Lear* above, pp.66 and n. 23, p.86.

16. The term 'evocation' brings out the striking similarities between Davidson's position and that taken by Dan Sperber in *Rethinking Symbolism* (Cambridge University Press, Cambridge, 1975). Sperber, an anthropologist reflecting on Lévi-Strauss's work in the light of cognitive psychology, has similar problems with the notion that cultural symbolism can be a matter of meaning. ('A representation is symbolic precisely to the extent that it is not entirely explicable, that is to say, expressible by semantic means' (113)). Rather, he postulates a separate cognitive mechanism, the symbolic mechanism, which works on all those inputs—including the figurative—that cannot be instantly handled cognitively in propositional form. Such puzzling inputs require a search through long-term memory and possibly a reassessment of the classificational principles ordering that memory; this process he speaks of as 'evocation'. As with Davidson, some of the results of evocation will be

propositional in form while others will not be, remaining as potential inputs for further rounds of symbolic processing.

17. Davidson has a footnote to this passage making it clear that he views '*any* use of language' (our italics) as similarly opening up processes of noticing to which 'there is no clear end'. So all of language-in-use floats semi-free from the propositional meanings it nonetheless depends on.

18. Simon Blackburn, *Spreading the Word* (Clarendon Press, Oxford, 1984), p.174.

19. Susan Gubar, ' "The Blank Page" ' and the Issues of Female Creativity', *Critical Inquiry* 8 (1981), 243-63. Reprinted in Elizabeth Abel (ed.), *Writing and Sexual Difference* (Harvester Press, Brighton, 1982), pp.73-93.

20. Paulina in fact goes on to pray that the baby has not also inherited her father's jealousy 'lest she suspect, as he does,/ Her children not her husband's!' (2.3.107-8). The absurdity of this underlines the asymmetry of the sexes in this respect: women are usually in a much better position than men to *know* the provenance of their children.

21. Shakespeare's apparent interest in copyright metaphors and his knowledge of the relevant terminology might seem odd given his own publishing record which, compared with that of Ben Jonson, for example, does not look like that of a man determined to establish his authorial rights. Some of his printing metaphors do cluster around the period 1593-94 when he seems to have been personally involved in seeing *Venus and Adonis* and *The Rape of Lucrece* through the press (see the Riverside editor's note on the text of *Venus and Adonis,* pp.1718-9)—perhaps his only direct experience of publishing his work—but this does not account for all of them. On Shakespeare's experience of copyright problems, see A.W. Pollard, *Shakespeare's Fight with the Pirates* (Cambridge University Press, Cambridge, 1937). And, for a claim that Shakespeare *was* concerned about copyright and even added an extended copyright allegory to the revised text of *Hamlet,* see D.S. Savage, *Hamlet and the Pirates* (Eyre and Spottiswoode, London, 1950).

22. Actually, two senses of 'press' are being punned on here. The personified bed, who can be pressed to death, is presumably, as editors point out, seen as being like an accused person who remains silent in court (refuses to plead) and is sentenced to the particular death which consists of 'pressing to death with weights' (Riverside). The evocation opened up by the metaphorical half of the pun is truly open-ended, because it is not at all clear just what propositions one is to entertain on the basis of the similitude 'A bed on which a couple making love is like someone dying of *peine fort et dur'*. Once one goes beyond Pandarus' own ground for the comparison, silence—and going beyond it is invited by the gathering darkness of the play—the evocative field of the metaphor is powerful but indeterminate.

23. 'Press' as a verb, needless to say, used to be literally what was involved in the printing process. With today's photographic methods of printing, this is no longer the case; compare 'to dial' as now used of push-button telephones. One aspect of the sex-printing likeness thus begins to fail for us.

24. This phrase comes of course from Heminge and Condell's prefatory address 'To the great Variety of Readers' in the First Folio. It seems appropriate that, when Shakespeare's plays were eventually published in this volume, his

colleagues and editors reversed the PEOPLE ARE BOOKS metaphor by seeing the plays as 'Orphanes' and themselves as 'Guardians' (in the 'Epistle Dedicatorie') and by going on to describe previous unauthorized editions as 'diverse stolne, and surreptitious copies, maimed, and deformed by the frauds and stealthes of injurious imposters, that exposd them'. They promised that 'those, are now offer'd to your view cur'd, and perfect of their limbes'.

25. A related metaphor that Shakespeare frequently uses could be expressed as THE MIND IS A MINT (or FORGE); consider the King's description of Don Armado in *Love's Labour's Lost* as one 'That hath a mint of phrases in his brain' (1.1.165) or Nestor's view of Thersites in *Troilus and Cressida* as 'A slave whose gall coins slanders like a mint' (1.3.193). Similarly, Imogen in *Cymbeline* has 'a mother hourly coining plots' (2.1.59) and the Chorus in *Henry V* refers to 'the quick forge and working-house of thought' (5, prologue 23).

26. Both 'compose' and 'form' (which also comes up in the *Measure for Measure* passage) were used as technical terms in printing in this period (the *OED* gives 'form(e)' in this sense (= a body of type) from 1481 and 'to compose' (= to set up type) from 1637 but 'compositor' (= a typesetter) from 1569). We have not however found any examples of Shakespeare exploiting these senses.

27. This bald assertion of parental power is of course conventional at the beginning of a comedy. Equally conventional is the overthrow of such power, though it is significant that a woman's freedom in this respect is limited to replacing a father with a husband.

28. Oddly, in *Twelfth Night,* it seems that Olivia's personal seal depicts the figure of Lucrece: Malvolio, opening the love-letter forged by Maria, comments 'By your leave, wax. Soft! And the impressure her Lucrece with which she uses to seal'. Inside, he finds a further reference to the story: 'I may command where I adore,/ But silence, like a Lucrece knife,/ With bloodless stroke my heart doth gore;/ M.O.A.I. doth sway my life' (2.5.91-3, 104-7). Just before remarking upon the design of the seal, Malvolio has identified his lady's 'hand' (handwriting) by the shape of certain letters, the choice of which is clearly (but puzzlingly) sexual: 'These be her very c's, her u's, and her t's, and thus makes she her great P's' (2.5.86-8). Letters, 'impressure', sex and the Lucrece motif are clustered together in a comic context here, several years after the composition of the tragic poem.

29. *The Journal of Aesthetics and Art Criticism* 42 (1984), 291-302.

30. A determination to assimilate seeing-as, and specifically Wittgenstein's treatment of seeing-as, to 'having images' of an inner-eye sort is a feature of Marcus B. Hester's *The Meaning of Poetic Metaphor* (Mouton, The Hague, 1967). This sensitive and enthusiastic attempt to bring together philosophy and literary theory seems today weakest on the literary-theory side; Hester relies on positions taken by the American New Critics (Warren, Wellek, Brooks, Wimsatt, Wheelwright) which have not worn well, especially on just this question of imagery. However, his study deserves more detailed comment than we can give it here. In particular, many of his conclusions would read very like Davidson's if expressed without using the word 'meaning'. For example: '[T]here are no definitive criteria, as Wittgenstein understands them, for metaphorical meaning. There is no definitive source of appeal which

can tell in what relevant sense time is like a beggar or nerves sit like tombs. The experience-act of seeing as is irreducible to any . . . specific set of procedural rules . . Metaphorical meaning is always open-ended' (216).

31. Three passages display these reservations. Where Davidson writes 'Words are the wrong currency to exchange for a picture', Davies, expressing a worry about the point, substitutes 'experience' for 'picture'. ('Davidson is wrong in suggesting that words are the wrong currency for an account of the experience; it is assertions, not words *per se*, which are inadequate here' (298).) On the question of how far metaphor-makers intend their audience to acquire new beliefs, albeit indirectly, he writes: 'One makes metaphors in preference to assertions not because metaphors lead to the acquisition of beliefs more successfully than do assertions, but rather because one is concerned to get the audience to ''see'' something and not merely to know something' (299). The quotation marks around 'see' suggest caution. Finally, criticizing Davidson's inner-eye discussion of 'He was burned up', Davies holds that 'it is doubtful . . . that the live metaphor would have evoked quite such a vivid picture' (300).

32. Similarly, Isabella need have neither counterfeiting nor sexual experience and yet *know* the (fairly minimal) amount about each which she needs in order to grasp Angelo's comparison.

33. Hester's *The Meaning of Poetic Metaphor* (see n. 30 above) is a good source of references to arguments for this odd position. See particularly p.97, where Suzanne Langer and Paul Valéry are brought in to bolster the New Critics team (in this case Wimsatt and Wheelwright) in arguing for poem-as-experience. The position seems to waver between taking reading a poem to be an experience (of course it is: how could it fail to be?) and taking the poem to have 'the appearance of experienced life', to be some sort of stand-in for (other) experience. The latter view is the one that seems bizarre. 'In reading a poem one has the illusion that he is directly experiencing life' says Hester in summarizing Langer's views. This sounds like a higher-brow version of believing in the reality of the characters in *Coronation Street*. How could a poem equal lived experience in this way? Why would one want it to?

34. While Davies does not deny that 'possibly metaphors are sometimes used indirectly to impart beliefs', and claims that 'such a view is compatible' with his account of metaphor, he is strongly averse to it nonetheless: 'I see no reason to assume that such a consideration could account for the appeal and prevalence of metaphor'(299).

35. A corrective reading of Davidson in this regard is provided by Blackburn who emphasizes that, although evocation and an open-ended exploration of likeness are basic to metaphor, still 'the only way that a metaphor can provide a gain in understanding is by provoking a quest which may end up in our grasping some new strict and literal truths' (*Spreading the Word*, p.175).

36. See *Metaphors We Live By*, pp.14-21.

37. It could well be argued that the CREATION IS BIRTH/IDEAS ARE BABIES group of metaphors helps to strengthen men's claim to be the 'real' creators, since most of those doing the conceptualizing tend to be male.

38. Such a willingness is posited and explored by Joel B. Altman in *The Tudor Play of Mind* (University of California Press, Berkeley and London, 1978).

Afterword

Readers with a literary background might have expected that a major problem with our strategy for this book would turn out to be the chasm that would open between the theoretical approaches drawn from linguistics and philosophy on the one hand and the Shakespearean examples on the other. Since the theorists tend to be largely, if not exclusively, interested in everyday metaphors as they appear in twentieth-century colloquial prose, it might have been predicted that Shakespeare would be located somewhere entirely off their maps for at least three reasons: he is a writer from a much earlier period, he is a poet, and he is a 'genius'. Moreover, linguists and philosophers tend to study metaphors because they are mundane, literary critics tends to study them because they are exotic, elaborate, archaic or idiosyncratic.

As it worked out, however, we have found ourselves constantly emphasizing the continuity between the metaphors of contemporary everyday language and those of Shakespearean drama. It has not proved to be a particularly strenuous or ingenious task to discuss the time metaphors of *Troilus and Cressida* in the light of Lakoff and Johnson's *Metaphors We Live By,* or to discuss Shakespeare's printing metaphors in relation to Davidson's 'What Metaphors Mean'. This in itself has taught us something we ought perhaps to have already known about Shakespearean metaphor—that it is rooted firmly in patterns of everyday thought and speech which have not changed very much between his time and ours.

We have then, by a different route, confirmed a perception that Shakespeare's metaphors are not especially 'far-fetched' but are often very mundane in their derivation at least: the human body, its

207

actions and its relationship to its environment has often dominated this book as the vehicle or donor field for many metaphors. We have also had frequent occasion to note the prevalence of the commonplace, the proverbial, even the cliché in Shakespearean metaphor. This is not of course to deny that Shakespeare's metaphors can be extraordinarily dense and difficult, but to some extent we have been arguing that despite their density and difficulty they remain accessible and 'alive' because of their associations with everyday speech. They are still comprehensible in the theatre and they are amenable to analysis in the same way that ordinary metaphors are. Some of the most complex ones—for example, the spatial time metaphors in *Troilus*—can be seen as having been 'worked up' from a basis in everyday language (which, in turn, begins to seem that much more rich and strange).

Why should any of this be surprising? Why should we have supposed Shakespeare to be so remote and intangible, so beyond the grasp of linguistic and philosophical theory? This is partly a product of disciplinary specialization on both sides. Most of our theorists are very shy about tackling literary examples, modestly assuming they are the province of literary specialists. The literary critics on the other hand are still haunted by a Romantic view of poetry which emphasizes and values what is special and distinctive in the language of a particular writer rather than what is shared and familiar: the term 'conventional' as applied to either thought or expression is assumed by most students of literature to be one of abuse. 'Imagery' itself as a critical movement had close associations with the assumptions of the Imagist poets who valued isolated metaphors (especially visual ones) for their own sake as flashes of inspiration or creative genius. Donne was duly reinstated but Shakespeare remained a problem. Since it could not be claimed that many of Shakespeare's images were in fact very novel or distinctive, the 'image-cluster' approach allowed critics to privilege combinations of metaphors which could be said to be special or authorial: fawning dogs are a commonplace metaphor for flattering people and melting sweets are not exactly a novel metaphor for the favours of such people, but together the 'cluster' is distinctively Shakespearean.

Literary critics always want to 'do something more ' with metaphor. If it is not striking or remarkable for its own sake they want to fit it into a larger view of either the text or the author. Is it part of a thematic pattern? Does it distinguish one character from another? Does it tell us anything about the author's experiences or opinions? Does it relate to contemporary social or political assumptions? We would say that Shakespearean metaphor *can* do most of these things with the exception of characterization: it does not seem to us that Shakespeare uses metaphors to distinguish one character from another, though he certainly does use other aspects of their speech in this way, notably vocabulary and syntax.

This is apparently a controversial point: when we have given papers on metaphor at conferences there has always been at least one questioner who has wanted to argue that Shakespeare *does* use metaphor to distinguish one character from another, and this also seems to be a popular initial assumption amongst students. We should pause to clarify the nature of our scepticism in this area, though the question is complex and we have not seen our project as involving us in addressing it fully.

It is true that on occasion a character will be given particular metaphors or a particular range of metaphors chosen in the light of his or her nature and circumstances: Othello, for example, employs a number of animal metaphors to express his sexual disgust at the point where he has been convinced that Desdemona has been unfaithful to him. It is also true that some characters use a wider range of metaphors than others: Hamlet probably draws on a wider range than anyone else in Elsinore. But might not these phenomena best be seen as *following from* decisions at the action-character level rather than as *establishing* that level? Iago, at the action-character level, deliberately sets out to change Othello's way of thinking about Desdemona and sexual relations in general in a coarsening, reductive way. What Iago says, and what Othello says under his influence, will naturally not be difficult to distinguish from what, say, Romeo says about love: Romeo is saying something in such different circumstances and is such a different kind of man.[1] All three characters may use heightened, figurative speech, and their differences will be reflected in their heightened speech—but not, we would argue, in *how each character's speech is heightened.* In fact, several characters besides Othello use animal metaphors to express sexual disgust—Leontes, Posthumus and Lear, for example—but this is not because they are similar characters, rather that they express similar thoughts through similar metaphors.

Likewise, as we have noted above (pp.41-3), most of the major characters in *Troilus and Cressida* talk about time, and in doing so they draw on a fund of personifications, proverbs, metaphors and other figurative expressions that is common to them all. This does not mean that Troilus *as a character* is similar to Ulysses, or to Agamemnon. Nor does it mean that they are mere ciphers, indistinguishable from each other. As we said before, their individuality is not undermined by this any more than, in real life, we feel our individualities to be undermined by the fact that we share many common conceptual schemes and common conceptual metaphors with other people, including people very different from ourselves. One thing we should at this point say in favour of the 'imagery' approach is that it helps to break down notions of the relations between character and metaphor: if images of disease dominate *2 Henry IV* or images of light and darkness dominate *Macbeth*, the implication is that a particular range of metaphors is *specific to the play as a whole*, not to the language of any particular character. Nameless soldiers or servants are as likely to contribute to such a dominant pattern as kings or heroes.

As for the question of a character's metaphorical range, this is not something that we have been concerned to measure, but we would approach it with some caution. May it not be that range is simply related to the length of a character's part? May not Hamlet have the widest range because he speaks the most lines rather than because he is the most intense or imaginative character? We have noticed that Claudius has some very interesting metaphors derived from painting and from skin, but we would not like to have to prove that these differentiate his *character* from that of Hamlet—by being more crude, more immoral, less imaginative, and so on. We would however expect Claudius to share with Hamlet and the other upper-class characters a competence and fluency in the use of metaphor which, like their competence and fluency in the use of language generally, differentiates them *as a class* from the lower orders, who are often depicted by Shakespeare as being comic precisely because they attempt to use a level of figurative language which is beyond their control—and implicitly beyond their social station.

We would not want to be too dogmatic on this question, but at the same time the notion that a character could or should be differentiated from others by his or her use of metaphors has increasingly come to seem odd to us. A cinematographic analogy may help: it would be possible to distinguish point-of-view shots for a given character in some visual manner (black and white *versus* colour, a narrowed rather than a wide screen, consistently softer focus, non-standard camera angles or length of shot); but to do so would be apt to seem mannered. Similarly, a character is not likely to be characterized by being the only person on stage to speak in fourteeners.

The few characters who *are* individuated by their mode of speech in the plays are usually comic characters who make mistakes (Dogberry), cultivate excess in obvious ways (Holofernes, Pistol), or employ an idiosyncratic accent or style (Fluellen, the Nurse in *Romeo and Juliet*). In every case the individuation is done primarily through vocabulary and syntax rather than through metaphor. Perhaps one day someone will be able to demonstrate that different characters in Shakespeare deploy metaphor in different ways, but we do not think it has been satisfactorily done as yet, despite the popularity of the broad assumption. Meanwhile our point remains that Shakespearean metaphors can be studied, and are worth studying, without necessarily being taken up into such a demonstration.

Similarly, metaphor *can* be closely associated with a thematic pattern—the time metaphors in *Troilus* are a case in point—or it can be part of a general 'background': the animals in *Lear* and the body parts in *Hamlet* are not so much 'themes' in this sense as crucial elements in the world of the play as a whole. We feel it ought to be possible to talk about them without feeling obliged to inflate their ultimate significance. Similarly, metaphors *can* tell us something about Shakespeare's attitudes in the context of his time, though, as we have discovered in our survey of printing metaphors, what they tell us should not be read off too simply: the *use* by specific fictional characters in specific situations of specific metaphors does not necessarily constitute an authorial endorsement of those metaphors.

At the same time that we have been arguing that Shakespearean metaphor is more securely grounded in the everyday and the commonplace than some schools of criticism would assume, we have frequently acknowledged that considerable technical expertise is involved. Shakespeare not only received a serious rhetorical training himself but wrote for an audience which would have been far more conscious of the exploitation of rhetorical devices as a prominent part of literary composition that we are today. Yet here again the gap is not as wide as it might seem: despite the generally low status accorded to Elizabethan rhetoricians today, we have found that the formulations of writers like Peacham and Hoskins, though naively expressed, are in fact quite subtle, and remarkably consistent with those of modern theorists.

Readers who come to us from a philosophical or linguistic background may well feel that we have failed to bring out fundamental incompatibilities amongst the approaches we have discussed. Where an approach has seemed to us to illuminate our texts we have endeavoured to display the effects of that illumination; only when shadows seem to be cast have we turned mildly polemical. We are not too apologetic about this. The complexity and diversity of metaphorical phenomena make it likely that what appear to be very different theories will eventually turn out to capture parts of the truth. However, we should outline briefly some of the difficulties that would be encountered by anyone who sought to reconcile the theories we have used.

One could see the business of any study of metaphor as being to find the best restrospective description of how a metaphor has worked (what it has 'meant'). 'Retrospective' here is necessary because of the strength of Davidson's arguments against there being any prospective calculus or algorithm for 'computing' in advance all that a metaphor will eventually convey. Davidson holds too, as we have seen, that in many (not all) cases even a retrospective description cannot be complete—after a certain amount of paraphrasing the voice will trail off into an indefinite 'and . . . and . . .'.[2] Now this may be so while at the same time retrospective accounts of the 'paraphrasable core', so to speak, follow roughly similar lines from case to case. It is not as if common features do not link our strategies for coping with metaphor as a linguistic genre.

In their different ways, Group μ and Kittay and Lehrer can be seen as offering descriptions of how things stand *broadly* (before the 'and . . . and . . .') once metaphors have worked. Their descriptions differ in abstractedness—that is, in how far they *further* constrict the paraphraseable core for their own theoretical purposes. Group μ constrict the core radically: we are left with whatever in the paraphrase can be expressed as 'this for that',[3] and an account, in terms of genus—species and part—whole relationships, of how the this and the that are conceptually related.

But to the degree that finite paraphrase of a metaphor is possible, is it not true that a 'this for that' element in the paraphrase can be determined? If so, Group μ have a perfectly respectable object to address themselves to. Kittay and Lehrer-type semantic fields offer a way of setting the this (vehicle, donor field) and the that (tenor, recipient field) in a much richer network of relationships, both positive (the syntagmatic, as they put it: elements which 'go together' in a particular scenario) and negative (the aspect of their work which responds to the Saussurean legacy, a view of language as a system of differences: the paradigmatic). Again it is difficult to see how, retrospectively, the paraphraseable core of a metaphor would not yield to description along these lines. It is only when the approach is used prospectively, as predictive of what sorts of comparative work the listener or reader will want to do, independently of context—the prediction is that the comparative exploration should be maximal and in a broad sense serious—that we feel it falters. (This should remind us that, while Davidson's account stresses how unpredictably much a metaphor can convey, his arguments would do as well if directed towards how unpredictably *little* the donor field may actually be called upon to contribute.)

If Kittay and Lehrer differ from Group μ principally in terms of the specific semantic and real-world relationships that they focus on in the paraphrase, Lakoff and Johnson are united with Ross in concentrating primarily on phenomena in ordinary language which seem not to require any paraphrase or interpretation at all. Their central concerns are metaphors we scarcely notice, analogies that allow words to differentiate imperceptibly; it is only as a spin-off from these topics that they spend some time considering elaborated metaphors and properly metaphorical analogies respectively. We are not at all sure how each would react to the other's framework. Ross would handle via (non-metaphorical) analogy a number of phenomena which for Lakoff and Johnson are cases of everyday metaphor. Yet their books share a delight in demonstrating the flexible, non-regimented aspects of ordinary language which seems to us to put them fundamentally 'on the same side'. One might provisionally characterize their divergence as reflecting a more paradigmatic difference-based orientation on Ross's part (a strong whiff of Saussure via John Lyons) and a more syntagmatic, experiential-gestalt orientation on the part of Lakoff and Johnson (influenced by recent artificial intelligence work). Both, interestingly, are led to conclude their books by challenging the picture of literal language which they ascribe to the dominant forces in contemporary analytic philosophy—such as Davidson! (Of the two, Ross's challenge may be the more radical, despite Lakoff and Johnson's more breezily polemical style.)

We have not felt the need to resolve questions which we find fascinating but from which we recognize ourselves to be at a certain disciplinary distance. In the end, this is a study in literary criticism—more so, perhaps than we might have wished. Where this becomes most apparent is in our use of 'examples'. There is something paradoxical about how one finds oneself discussing texts in literary criticism. In linguistics, or philosophy of language, it is not part of the enterprise to 'get more out of' the text than first meets the eye. When, to take a classic instance, Chomsky used the two readings of 'They are flying planes' ('They are planes that fly' *versus* 'They— the pilots— are engaged in flying planes') to argue for different underlying syntactic structures for the 'same' sentence, he was not seeking to enrich a reading (either reading) of the sentence: it is only after you have fully grasped each of the readings (an easy task) that the theoretical point can be seen. The literary critic, however, tends to take up an example with intent to wring more out of it; the rhetoric of presentation may be retrospective ('This is what it means'), but the discipline gravitates towards producing new readings ('Now—and not before—we can see that what is going on is . . .'), in what is actually an active, interventionist process. This is not the place to explore the overall strengths and weaknesses of this orientation. But we must admit that our matching of passages to theorists has generally been done in the hope of getting the Shakespearean text to 'yield more secrets'—though, thanks to a currently familiar theoretical move, we would want to claim that these secrets are nothing more than a making explicit of what the spectator or reader experiences pre-reflectively. Of course, theoretical argument in linguistics and philosophy is advanced by just the opposite procedure: rather than matching a theorist with a congenial example, one looks for the hardest case for the theory to handle, the potentially lethal counter-example.

Yet to proceed in a confirmatory rather than a disconfirmatory mode, that is to accept provisionally a particular theoretical approach in order to see how far it deepens our experience of a complex text—constitutes in its way no less demanding a test of theory. To a superficially cogent and attractive but in fact inadequate theory, the text can simply fail to respond. Our view, which we hope at this point our readers share, is that the approaches we have explored have passed this test.[4] This suggests that, despite their genuine difficulties and incompatibilities, they all participate in a newly emerging understanding of metaphor more adequate than any which has yet been available to students of literature.

Notes

1. Similarly, thinking now not of metaphor but of verbal matter generally: Lear has a tendency to reflect on the ingratitude of daughters, while Hamlet has a tendency to reflect on the inconstancy of women. These facts follow from the actions in which they are involved; it would seem odd to claim that Shakespeare characterizes Lear by giving him daughter-ingratitude speeches while characterizing Hamlet by giving him female-inconstancy speeches.

2. A natural way to read Davidson would be to take him as contrasting metaphorical language with literal language in terms of prospective computability and retrospective completeness of accounting: literal language would be that which a rule system could completely describe prospectively, and which did no more and no other than it was expected to restrospectively. One could then quarrel with him about whether literal language is 'closed' in this way. However, his account of the openness of metaphorical language does not collapse if a less algorithmic account of literal language should eventually be wanted. All it depends upon is agreement that metaphorical language is open-ended *in a recognizably different way* from how literal language is. And this seems to be true.

3. The spirited attacks by Paul Ricoeur on 'one word in place of another' accounts of metaphor in *The Rule of Metaphor* (see especially the discussion culminating on p.132) seem less pertinent if one takes that formula to describe one component—rather than the whole—of a typical metaphorical paraphrase.

4. Of the many approaches we have not explored on this occasion the ones that will occur at once to many readers interested in current literary theory are those associated with the names of C.S. Peirce, Roman Jakobson, Jacques Lacan and Jacques Derrida. We would hope this may be seen as deferral rather than rejection. (The appropriately sensitized reader may well find traces of the latter two thinkers in particular informing stretches of the discussion in a ghostly fashion, especially in Chapters 3 and 5). Another deferred topic is the contribution that recent experimental psychology has made to the understanding of how we 'process' metaphors.

Bibliography of Works Cited

Abend, Murray, ' "Ingratitude" and the "Monster" Image', *Notes and Queries* 194 (1949), 535-6.

Altman, Joel B., *The Tudor Play of Mind*, University of California Press, Berkeley and London, 1978.

Anson, John, '*Julius Caesar:* The Politics of the Hardened Heart', *Shakespeare Studies 2* (1966), 11-33.

Armstrong, Edward A., *Shakespeare's Imagination*, Lindsay Drummond, London, 1946.

Baldwin, T.W., *William Shakespere's Petty School*, University of Illinois Press, Urbana, Illinois, 1943.

Baldwin, T.W., *William Shakespere's Small Latine and Lesse Greeke*, University of Illinois Press, Urbana, Illinois, 1944.

Bayley, John, *The Uses of Division*, Chatto and Windus, London, 1976.

Beck, Brenda, 'Root Metaphor Patterns', *Récherches Sémiotiques/ Semiotic Inquiry 2* (1982), 86-97.

Berry, Francis, *Poets' Grammar*, Routledge and Kegan Paul, London, 1958.

Berry, Ralph, *The Shakespeare Metaphor*, Macmillan, London, 1978.

Black, Max, 'Metaphor', *Proceedings of the Aristotelian Society*, N.S. 55 (1954-55), 273-94. Reprinted in Mark Johnson (ed.), *Philosophical Perspectives on Metaphor*, University of Minnesota Press, Minneapolis, 1981, pp.63-82.
(1954-55), pp. 273-94. Reprinted in Mark Johnson (ed.), *Philosophical Perspectives on Metaphor*, University of Minnesota Press, Minneapolis, 1981, pp.63-82.

Blackburn, Simon, *Spreading the Word*, Clarendon Press, Oxford, 1984.

Blount, Thomas, *Academy of Eloquence*, 1654, Scolar Press Facsimile, Menston, Yorkshire, 1971.

Booth, Stephen (ed.), *Shakespeare's Sonnets*, Yale University Press, New Haven and London, 1977.

Bradley, A.C., *Shakespearean Tragedy*, Macmillan, London, 1904.

Brooke-Rose, Christine, *A Grammar of Metaphor,* Secker and Warburg, London, 1958.

Cercignani, Fausto, *Shakespeare's Works and Elizabethan Pronunciation,* Clarendon Press, Oxford, 1981.

Ching, Marvin K.L., Haley, Michael C. and Lunsford, Ronald F. (eds.), *Linguistic Perspectives on Literature,* Routledge and Kegan Paul, London, 1980.

Clayton, Thomas, 'The Quibbling Polonii and the Pious Bonds: the Rhetoric of *Hamlet* I.iii', *Shakespeare Studies* 2 (1966), 59-64.

Clemen, Wolfgang, *The Development of Shakespeare's Imagery,* Methuen, London, 1951.

Cohen, Ted, 'Figurative Speech and Figurative Acts', *Journal of Philosophy* 72 (1975), 669-84.

Danby, John F., *Shakespeare's Doctrine of Nature: A Study of 'King Lear',* Faber, London, 1949.

Daniel, P.A., 'Time Analysis of Shakespeare's Plays', *New Shakespere Society Transactions* (1877-79), 117-346.

Davidson, Donald, *Inquiries into Truth and Interpretation,* Clarendon Press, Oxford, 1984.

Davidson, Donald, 'What Metaphors Mean', *Critical Inquiry* 5 (1978), 31-47. Also in Mark Johnson (ed.), *Philosophical Perspectives on Metaphor,* University of Minnesota Press, Minneapolis, 1981, pp.200-20; in Sheldon Sacks (ed.), *On Metaphor,* University of Chicago Press, Chicago and London, 1979, pp.29-45; and in Donald Davidson, *Inquiries into Truth and Interpretation,* Clarendon Press, Oxford, 1984, pp.245-64.

Davies, Stephen, 'Truth-values and Metaphors', *The Journal of Aesthetics and Art Criticism* 42 (1984), 291-302.

Donaldson, E. Talbot, *The Swan at the Well: Shakespeare Reading Chaucer,* Yale University Press, New Haven and London, 1985.

Donawerth, Jane, *Shakespeare and the Sixteenth Century Study of Language,* University of Illinois Press, Urbana, Illinois, 1984.

Eco, Umberto, *Semiotics and the Philosophy of Language,* Macmillan, London, 1984.

Edwards, Philip (ed.), *Hamlet,* The New Cambridge Shakespeare, Cambridge University Press, Cambridge, 1985.

Elam, Keir, *Shakespeare's Universe of Discourse,* Cambridge University Press, Cambridge, 1984.

Empson, William, *Seven Types of Ambiguity,* Chatto and Windus, London, 1930.

Empson, William, *The Structure of Complex Words,* Chatto and Windus, London, 1951.

Evans, G. Blakemore (ed.), *The Riverside Shakespeare,* Houghton Mifflin, Boston, 1974.

Fillmore, Charles, 'The Case for Case', in E. Bach and R. Harms (eds.), *Universals of Linguistic Theory,* Holt, Rinehart and Winston, New York, 1968.

Fly, Richard D., 'Cassandra and the Language of Prophecy in *Troilus and Cressida',* Shakespeare Quarterly 26 (1975), 157-71.

Foakes, R.A., 'Suggestions for a New Approach to Shakespeare's Imagery', *Shakespeare Survey* 5 (1952), 81-92.

Fowler, Alastair, *Conceitful Thought,* Edinburgh University Press, Edinburgh, 1975.

Furness, H.H. (ed.), *Hamlet,* The Variorum Shakespeare, Lippincott, London and Philadelphia, 1877.

Gale, Richard M., *The Language of Time,* Routledge and Kegan Paul, London, 1968.

Goodman, Nelson, *Languages of Art,* Oxford University Press, London, 1969.

Grice, H.P., 'Logic and Conversation', in Peter Cole and Jerry L. Morgan (eds.), *Syntax and Semantics 3: Speech Acts,* Academic Press, New York, 1975, pp.41-58.

Grimaud, Michel, 'Mindful and Mindfree Rhetorics: Method and Metatheory in Discourse Analysis', *Semiotica* 45 (1983), 115-79.

Group μ, *Rhétorique de la poésie,* Editions Complexe, Brussels, 1977.

Group μ, *Rhétorique générale,* Larousse, Paris, 1970. Translated by Paul B. Burrell and Edgar M. Slotkin as *A General Rhetoric,* Johns Hopkins University Press, Baltimore and London, 1981.

Gubar, Susan, ' "The Blank Page" and the Issues of Female Creativity', *Critical Inquiry* 8 (1981), 243-63. Reprinted in Elizabeth Abel (ed.), *Writing and Sexual Difference,* Harvester, Brighton, 1982, pp.73-93.

Guern, Michel Le, *Sémantique de la métaphore et de la métonymie,* Larousse, Paris, 1973.

Hale, David G., *'Coriolanus:* The Death of a Political Metaphor', *Shakespeare Quarterly* 22 (1971), 198-202.

Hale, David G., *The Body Politic: A Political Metaphor in Renaissance English Literature,* Mouton, The Hague, 1971.

Halio, Jay L., 'The Metaphor of Conception and Elizabethan Theories of the Imagination', *Neophilologus* 50 (1966), 454-61.

Hammond, Gerald, *The Reader and Shakespeare's Young Man Sonnets,* Macmillan, London and Basingstoke, 1981.

Hankins, John Erskine, *Shakespeare's Derived Imagery,* University of Kansas Press, Lawrence, Kansas, 1953.

Henry, Albert, *Métonymie et métaphore,* Klincksieck, Paris, 1971.

Hester, Marcus B., *The Meaning of Poetic Metaphor,* Mouton, The Hague, 1967.

Honeck, Richard P. and Hoffman, Robert R. (eds.), *Cognition and Figurative Language,* Erlbaum, Hillsdale, New Jersey, 1980.

Hoskins, John, *Directions for Speech and Style c.*1599, ed. Hoyt N. Hudson, Princeton University Press, 1935.

Hulme, Hilda M., *Explorations in Shakespeare's Language*, Longmans, London, 1962.

Ingram, W.G. and Redpath, Theodore (eds.), *Shakespeare's Sonnets*, Hodder and Stoughton, London, 1964.

Inwagen, Peter van (ed.), *Time and Cause*, Reidel, Dordrecht, 1980.

Jakobson, Roman, 'Two Aspects of Language and Two Types of Aphasic Disturbances' in Roman Jakobson and Morris Halle, *Fundamentals of Language*, Mouton, The Hague, 1956, pp.53-82. Also in Jakobson's *Selected Writings*, vol. II, Mouton, The Hague, 1971.

Jenkins, Harold (ed.), *Hamlet*, The New Arden Shakespeare, Methuen, London, 1982.

Johnson, Mark (ed.), *Philosophical Perspectives on Metaphor*, University of Minnesota Press, Minneapolis, 1981.

Jones, Emrys, 'The Sense of Occasion: Some Shakespearean Night Sequences', in Kenneth Muir, Jay L. Halio and D.J. Palmer (eds.), *Shakespeare, Man of the Theater*, Associated University Presses, London, 1983.

Joseph, Sister Miriam, *Shakespeare's Use of the Arts of Language*, Columbia University Press, New York, 1947.

Katz, Jerrold J., *Semantic Theory*, Harper and Row, New York, 1972.

Kauffman, R.J., 'Ceremonies for Chaos: the Status of *Troilus and Cressida*', *English Literary History* 32 (1965), 139-57.

Kirkman, J., 'Animal Nature *versus* Human Nature in *King Lear*', *New Shakespere Society Transactions* (1877-79), 385-405.

Kittay, Eva, *The Cognitive Force of Metaphor: A Theory of Metaphoric Meaning*, Ph.D. dissertation, City University of New York, 1978.

Kittay, Eva, and Lehrer, Adrienne, 'Semantic Fields and the Structure of Metaphor', *Studies in Language* 5 (1981), 31-63.

Kökeritz, Helge, *Shakespeare's Pronunciation*, Yale University Press, New Haven, Connecticut, 1953.

Lakoff, George and Johnson, Mark, *Metaphors We Live By*, University of Chicago Press, Chicago and London, 1980.

Leech, Geoffrey, *Semantics*, Penguin, Harmondsworth, 1974.

Levin, Richard, *The Multiple Plot in English Renaissance Drama*, University of Chicago Press, Chicago, 1971.

Levin, Samuel R., *The Semantics of Metaphor*, Johns Hopkins University Press, Baltimore, 1977.

Lewis, Anthony J., 'The Dog, Lion and Wolf in Shakespeare's Descriptions of Night', *Modern Language Review* 66 (1971), 1-10.

Lycan, William, *Logical Form in Natural Language*, MIT Press, Cambridge, Mass. 1984.

Maclean, Hugh, 'Time and Horsemanship in Shakespeare's Histories', *University of Toronto Quarterly* 35 (1965-66), 229-45.

Mahood, M.M., *Shakespeare's Wordplay,* Methuen, London, 1957.

McAlindon, T., 'Language, Style and Meaning in *Troilus and Cressida',* *PMLA* 84 (1969), 29-43.

Martin, J. and Harré, R., 'Metaphor in Science', in David S. Miall (ed.), *Metaphor: Problems and Perspectives,* Harvester, Brighton, 1982, pp.89-105.

Mellor, D.H., *Real Time,* Cambridge University Press, Cambridge, 1981.

Metz, Christian, 'Metaphor/Metonymy, or the Imaginary Referent', in *Psychoanalysis and Cinema: The Imaginary Signifier,* Macmillan, London, 1982.

Meyer, Bernard, 'Synecdoches du genre?', *Poétique* 57 (1984), 37-52.

Miall, David S. (ed.), *Metaphor: Problems and Perspectives,* Harvester, Brighton, 1982.

Muir, Kenneth, 'Shakespeare's Imagery—Then and Now', *Shakespeare Survey* 18 (1965), 46-57.

Muir, Kenneth, Halio, Jay L., and Palmer, D.J. (eds.), *Shakespeare, Man of the Theater,* Associated University Presses, London, 1983.

Muir, Kenneth (ed.), *King Lear,* The New Arden Shakespeare, Methuen, London, 1952.

Muir, Kenneth (ed.), *Troilus and Cressida,* The Oxford Shakespeare, Clarendon Press, Oxford, 1982.

Murry, John Middleton, *Countries of the Mind,* Oxford University Press, Oxford, 1931.

Nowottny, Winifred, *The Language Poets Use,* Athlone Press, London, 1962.

Ortony, Andrew (ed.), *Metaphor and Thought,* Cambridge University Press, Cambridge, 1979.

Ortony, Andrew, 'The Role of Similarity in Similes and Metaphors', in Andrew Ortony (ed.), *Metaphor and Thought,* Cambridge University Press, Cambridge, 1979, pp.186-201.

Palmer, Kenneth (ed.), *Troilus and Cressida,* The New Arden Shakespeare, Methuen, London, 1982.

Panofsky, Erwin, *Studies in Iconology,* Oxford University Press, New York, 1939.

Parker, Patricia, 'The Metaphorical Plot', in David S. Miall (ed.), *Metaphor: Problems and Perspectives,* Harvester, Brighton, 1982, pp.133-57.

Peacham, Henry, *The Garden of Eloquence,* 1577, Scolar Press Facsimile, Menston, Yorkshire, 1971.

Pollard. A.W., *Shakespeare's Fight with the Pirates,* Cambridge University Press, Cambridge, 1937.

Pollio, Howard R. *et al.,* 'Need Metaphoric Comprehension Take Longer

Than Literal Comprehension?', *Journal of Psycholinguistic Research* 13 (1984), 195-214.

Puttenham, George, *The Arte of English Poesy,* 1589, Arber's English reprints, Constable, London, 1895.

Quinones, Ricardo J., *The Renaissance Discovery of Time,* Harvard University Press, Cambridge, Mass., 1972.

Reddy, Michael J., 'A Semantic Approach to Metaphor', in Marvin K.L. Ching, Michael C. Haley and Ronald F. Lunsford (eds.), *Linguistic Perspectives on Literature,* Routledge and Kegan Paul, London, 1980, pp.63-75.

Rice, Donald and Schofer, Peter, *Rhetorical Poetics,* University of Wisconsin Press, Madison, 1983.

Richards, I.A., *The Philosophy of Rhetoric,* Oxford University Press, New York and London, 1936.

Richards, I.A., *Principles of Literary Criticism,* Kegan Paul, London, 1925.

Ricoeur, Paul, *The Rule of Metaphor,* Routledge and Kegan Paul, London, 1978.

Ross, J.F., *Portraying Analogy,* Cambridge University Press, Cambridge, 1981.

Ruwet, Nicolas, 'Synecdocques et métonymies', *Poétique* 23, (1975).

Sacks, Elizabeth, *Shakespeare's Images of Pregnancy,* Macmillan, London, 1980.

Sacks, Sheldon (ed.), *On Metaphor,* University of Chicago Press, Chicago and London, 1979.

Sato, Nabuo, 'Synecdoque, un trope suspect', *Revue d'Esthetique* 1-2 (1979), 116-27.

Savage, D.S., *Hamlet and the Pirates,* Eyre and Spottiswoode, London, 1950.

Schmidt, Michael, 'Cannibalism in *King Lear',* *Notes and Queries* 216 (1971), 148-9.

Shapiro, Michael and Marianne, *Hierarchy and the Structure of Tropes,* Indiana University Press, Bloomington, Indiana, 1976.

Smart, J.J.C., 'Time and Becoming', in Peter van Inwagen (ed.), *Time and Cause,* Reidel, Dordrecht, 1980, pp.3-15.

Spencer, T.J.B. (ed.), *Hamlet,* The Penguin Shakespeare, Penguin, Harmondsworth, 1980.

Spencer, Theodore, *Shakespeare and the Nature of Man,* Macmillan, London, 1942.

Sperber, Dan, *Rethinking Symbolism,* Cambridge University Press, Cambridge, 1975.

Spurgeon, Caroline F.E., *Shakespeare's Imagery and What It Tells Us,* Cambridge University Press, Cambridge, 1935.

Stagg, Louis Charles, *Index to the Figurative Language of the Tragedies of*

Shakespeare's Chief Seventeenth-Century Contemporaries, Memphis University Press, Memphis, 1977, reprinted by Garland, New York and London, 1984.

Stern, Josef, 'Metaphor and Grammatical Deviance', *Noûs* 17 (1983), 577-99.

Strawson, P.F., *Introduction to Logical Theory,* Methuen, London, 1952.

Stříbrný, Zdeněk, 'Time in *Troilus and Cressida'*, *Shakespeare Jahrbuch* 112 (Weimar, 1976), 105-21.

Suppes, Patrick, *Introduction to Logic,* Van Nostrand, New York, 1957.

Taylor, Gary and Warren, Michael (eds.), *The Division of the Kingdoms: Shakespeare's Two Versions of 'King Lear',* Clarendon Press, Oxford, 1983.

Taylor, Richard, *Metaphysics,* Prentice-Hall, Englewood Cliffs, New Jersey, 1963.

Taylor, Richard, 'Moving about in Time', *Philosophical Quarterly* 9 (1959), 289-301.

Thompson, Ann, 'Philomel in *Titus Andronicus* and *Cymbeline'*, *Shakespeare Survey* 31 (1978), 23-32.

Thompson, Ann, *Shakespeare's Chaucer,* Liverpool University Press, Liverpool, 1978.

Thompson, Ann, 'Who Sees Double in the Double Plot?', in D.J. Palmer (ed.), *Shakespearian Tragedy,* Stratford-upon-Avon Studies, vol. 20, Edward Arnold, London, 1984.

Tilley, M.P., *A Dictionary of the Proverbs in England in the Sixteenth and Seventeenth Centuries,* University of Michigan Press, Ann Arbor, Michigan, 1950.

Trousdale, Marion, *Shakespeare and the Rhetoricians,* Scolar Press, London, 1982.

Ullmann, Stephen, *Style in the French Novel,* Cambridge University Press, Cambridge, 1957.

Walker, Alice (ed.), *Troilus and Cressida,* The New Shakespeare, Cambridge University Press, Cambridge, 1957.

Weimann, Robert, 'Shakespeare and the Study of Metaphor', *New Literary History* 6 (1974), 149-67.

Wellek, René and Warren, Austin, *Theory of Literature,* Jonathan Cape, London, 1949.

Wells, Stanley, *Re-editing Shakespeare for the Modern Reader,* Clarendon Press, Oxford, 1984.

Wells, Stanley and Taylor, Gary, *Modernizing Shakespeare's Spelling and Three Studies in the Text of 'Henry V',* Clarendon Press, Oxford, 1979.

Wilson, John Dover (ed.), *The Sonnets,* The New Shakespeare, Cambridge University Press, Cambridge, 1966.

Wright, George T., 'Hendiadys and *Hamlet'*, *PMLA* 96 (1981), 168-93.

Index

223

Index

227